AN ANALYSIS OF THE

USE OF ENGLISH COLLOCATIONS BY

FRENCH AND JAPANESE LEARNERS

AN ANALYSIS OF THE KNOWLEDGE AND USE OF ENGLISH COLLOCATIONS BY FRENCH AND JAPANESE LEARNERS

Shino KUROSAKI

DISSERTATION.COM

Boca Raton

An Analysis of the Knowledge and Use of English Collocations
by French and Japanese Learners

Dissertation.com

Boca Raton, Florida

USA • 2013

ISBN-10: 1-61233-417-2
ISBN-13: 978-1-61233-417-2

Cover image by Galdzer/Bigstock.com

ABSTRACT

While it has been recognized that the use of collocations is significant for L2 learners, much research has not been carried out on the knowledge and use of learner's collocations. The present study investigated differences on the knowledge and use of collocations between French and Japanese learners with regard to: 1) L1 influence; and 2) combinability and transparency influence.

The test materials included four categories of the lexical collocations: 1) verb + noun; 2) delexicalised verb + noun; 3) adjective + noun; and 4) adverb + adjective. The two types of tasks, Multiple Choice Question Tasks and Translation Tasks, were performed, and the learner corpora were also investigated in order to examine whether the learners from different L1 backgrounds demonstrate different results.

Since both French and English belong to Indo-European background languages, they share a number of cognate words. Thus, originally it was expected that L1 influence of the French learners would be higher in all of the four lexical collocations than that of Japanese learners, who have non-Indo-European backgrounds. Though L1 influence by both French and Japanese learners was demonstrated, the Japanese learners showed a greater L1 influence in the [adjective + noun] category than the French learners. The investigation also found that L1 influence does not necessarily result in accuracy of the collocations.

With regard to the combinability and transparency influence, the results of the two types of tasks followed the previous remark made by Kellerman (1978) who argues that L2 learners are unable to transfer words with figurative meaning. However, some contrasted results were also identified in learner corpus investigation. Thus the combinability and transparency influence were not necessarily identified.

The results of the present study have a potential to improve teaching/learning of collocations through recognizing the learners' tendencies of learning collocations.

CONTENTS

LIST OF TABLES

LIST OF FIGURES

GLOSSARY OF TERMS AND ABBREVIATIONS

BNC	British National Corpus
CEFR	Common European Framework of Reference
Collocation	A type of two- to three- word combination in a certain grammatical pattern, such as "verb+noun", which occurs frequently.
EAP	English for Academic Purposes
EFL	English as a Foreign Language
ESL	English as a Second Language
Formulaic Sequences	A sequence of words which is prefabricated, which contains from a few word sequences to a longer ones.
HKUST	Hong Kong University of Science and Technology
ICLE	International Corpus of Learner English
MCQ	Multiple Choice Questions
NNS	Non Native Speaker
NP	Noun Phrase
NS	Native Speakers
RC	Restricted Collocation
SLA	Second Language Acquisition
SPSS	Statistical Package for Social Science
ULIP	University of London Institute in Paris

ACKNOWLEDGMENTS

Firstly, I would like to thank my supervisor, Dr. Noriko Iwasaki, for her precious guidance, substantial suggestions and constant encouragement. Noriko has been an invaluable mentor especially in the last years of my study. Her careful and thoughtful feedback has made a huge contribution to the quality and presentation of my work. She has not only supported my work in the middle of the course but also given me constant encouragement.

I am grateful to my former supervisors, Dr. David Horner and Mr. Dennis Davy, for giving me the opportunity to study for a PhD. This thesis would not have been possible without their helpful guidance.

I would like to show my gratitude to the late Dr. Johannes Eckerth who gave me constructive suggestions and warm encouragement.

I owe my deepest gratitude to Professor Andrew Hussey, Director of Institute in Paris, University of London, and Dr. Louise Lyle, who gave constant and long-term support for my work.

My thanks go to the students who answered to the tasks and the teachers who cooperated with the tasks for my work both in France and in Japan.

I am grateful to Professor Ginette Roy at University of Paris X, who helped me to translate the tasks into French and gave me warm encouragement. I would like to thank her for her generous help and kindness during my stay in Paris.

Finally, I would like to thank my parents and my daughter, Shoko, for their continuous support and encouragement. I am especially grateful to my husband, Fumio, for sharing with me all the worries and anxieties that a PhD brings.

Chapter 1

INTRODUCTION

1.1 Background to the Study

Over the past three decades, more and more researchers (Krashen & Scarcella 1978; Nattinger & DeCarrico 1992; Schmitt & Carter 2004; Wray 2002; Read & Nation 2004) have focused on the importance of multiword unit of language such as formulaic sequences, idioms, and collocations in L2 learning. Multiword unit have been considered as widespread formula by L2 learners (e.g. Fillmore 1976), and its importance that they are stored and processed holistically has been discussed (e.g. Wray 2002). The empirical research has been carried out, for example, on the processing of multiword unit. Jiang & Nekrasova (2007) found that formulaic sequences are processed more quickly and more accurately than non-formulaic sequences. In recent research on written language, researchers use terms such as clusters, chunks or bundles to refer to formulaic sequences common in written texts. One of types of formulaic sequences, "lexical bundles", which are one type of "multiword units that occur most commonly in a given register" (Biber & Barbieri 2007) have recently been studied, because they are important building blocks of discourse in spoken and written registers and prevalent in university classroom teaching. They found that lexical bundles are more prevalent in non-academic university registers than in the instructional registers and more common in written course management than in spoken university registers. The studies on the use of formulaic language in speech were carried out (De Cock *et al.* 1998; Adolphs and

Durow 2004; Shin & Nation 2008) as well as those in writing (Granger 1998; Nesselhauf 2005; Webb & Kagimoto 2009). With regard to the written language, according to one of the previous studies (Hyland 2008), the frequent formulaic sequences used in the creation of academic discourse differ between disciplines.

The studies on another types of formulaic sequences, collocations, have been performed (e.g.: Nesselhauf 2003, 2004; Read 2000; Schmitt and Carter 2004; Wray 2002) and the empirical research has consequently been carried out with their implications for the classroom teaching of lexis[1]. With regard to collocations in L2 learning, the use and learning of collocations seems important, for example, for the construct of an advanced L2 user who will be able to use English at an academic setting. In order to become a fluent bilingual, the use of collocations is crucial because of their pervasiveness in the L2 language.

The past research has been implemented mainly through the analysis of the types of collocations by using either written or spoken corpora so far. For example, Nation (2001) who drew up a table for listing the most frequent two- to five-word collocations occurring in the Brown Corpus demonstrated that the number of collocations occurring fifty times or more in the million word corpus is found much more in the two adjacent items than three- to five- adjacent items. From a teaching point of view, he argued that frequent collocations deserve attention in the classroom if their frequency is equal to or higher than other high-frequency words. Kilgarrif (1997) studied the frequencies of some multiword items (two- to three-words) in the British National Corpus (BNC) and found that the most frequent items marked as collocations in the BNC are counted as many as 2000.

Moreover, research into the relationships between collocations and the problems of learners of ESL (English as a Second Language) / EFL (English as a Foreign Language) were performed (e.g. Bahns 1993; Bahns & Eldaw 1993;

---

[1] For example, Lewis (2002) indicates some tips for teaching collocations for L2 learners.

Biskup 1992; Chi, *et al.* 1994; Durrant & Schmitt 2009; Farghal & Obiedat 1995; Miyakoshi 2009; Yamashita & Jiang 2010). Among them, Nesselhauf (2005) who investigated a learner written corpus of advanced German learners of English focused on the deviations in the use of collocations including verbs. She analysed various types of deviational use in collocations and discussed the use of L2 elements, L1 influence and intralinguistic factors such as the degree of combinability restriction of a collocation. Out of more than 2,000 verb-noun collocations, a quarter was found to be wrong, a third deviant. Deviation was found not only in the verbs but also in other elements of the collocations (nouns, determiners, etc.) and in the use of collocations as wholes. She argued that there are two important factors affecting the German learners' collocations: 1) congruence between their L1 equivalents in collocations and the L2; 2) the degree of restriction of a collocation, i.e. whether a verb in a collocation is restricted to a few numbers of nouns or not. The German learners were more susceptible to deviation in the collocations which were not congruent to their L1 and less restricted in combinability.

On the other hand, the types and subjects of previous studies on L2 learners' use of collocations have been limited. Previous studies discuss two types of characteristics which define collocations, i.e. combinability and transparency, one of which has been included in the empirical study but another one, transparency, has been neglected. Also, while the studies on collocations including verbs and nouns have been the main focus of the previous studies, there were not many studies on collocations consisting of other elements, such as adjective and adverbs. The subjects who have been studied previously were mainly L2 learners with Indo-European L1 backgrounds and the studies on L2 learners with non-Indo-European backgrounds have been scarce. Moreover, the learner data previously have been mainly either translation or the use of learner corpus. The study using multiple types of tasks given to learners of different L1 backgrounds on the several groups of collocations has never been performed.

Thus, the present study classified collocations based on two characteristics, combinability and transparency, in combination. The target collocations include four types of collocations, such as [verb + noun], [delexicalised verb + noun], [adjective + noun] and [adverb + adjective], which are examined with regard to the French and Japanese learners who have different L1 backgrounds.

1.2 Aims of the Study

Based on the above-mentioned backgrounds, the research in this thesis therefore analyses collocations by means of the following classifications.

Firstly, a new framework in defining collocations is provided, based on combinability and transparency of words. Then, the present study tries to classify collocations based on the two categories, combinability and transparency of words, which have often been partially discussed (See for example, Howarth 1996) but have not actually put into practice in the experimental study of collocations.

Combinability refers to the restrictedness with different words in a collocation. For example, in a collocation "make/take a decision", "make" and "take" are both combined with "a decision", and there are two possibilities of verbs to combine with a noun, "a decision". Thus, it is not restricted in the possibility of combining with different words, which are shown as [- Restricted Combinability]. When the word in a collocation has only one possibility in combining with other words, it is referred to as [+ Restricted Combinability].

Transparency can be expressed as figurativeness of the words in a collocation. It means whether the elements of the combination and the combination itself have a literal or a non-literal meaning. [+ Transparency] means the collocation has a literal meaning, while [-Transparency] refers that the collocation has a non-literal meaning. Despite the ambiguity of deciding: 1) the differences between [+Restricted Combinability] and [-Restricted Combinability]; 2) the differences between [+Transparency] and [-Transparency], the present study attempts to provide an original framework in classifying collocations in order to bring out new findings of L2 learners' knowledge and use of collocations.

Secondly, the present study examines the knowledge and use of English collocations of different L1 backgrounds, i.e. French and Japanese learners. Among the previous studies of L2 learners' knowledge of collocations, past research has not been carried out as to compare two groups of learners with different L1 backgrounds. The present study chooses French and Japanese L2 learners to investigate how the knowledge and use of collocations are demonstrated by learners of different L1 backgrounds. Their L1s are not only different but also belong to different typological language groups: French as one of the Indo-European background languages and Japanese as one of the non-Indo- European languages.

Based on the above, the aim of the study is to investigate the differences of L1 inferences and the combinability and transparency influence of collocations between the L2 learners from different L1 backgrounds. The research questions in the present study are:

1) How different is the French and Japanese learners' L1 influence in their responses to the tasks in the present study?

2) How different are the French and Japanese learners' responses to the tasks in the present study depending on the two combinations of combinability and semantic transparency of collocations, i.e. [+Restricted Combinability, +Transparency] and [-Restricted Combinability, -Transparency]?

1.3 Outline of the Study

As shown in Figure 1.1, the present study is composed of nine chapters.

Following this introduction in Chapter 1, Chapter 2 provides a thorough overview of how to define collocation, an area where many previous vague definitions have made the concept elusive. In order to discuss the scope of collocation in the present study, two major approaches to collocation, i.e. frequency-based and phraseological approach are reviewed. The two important characteristics to define collocation are discussed based on the previous studies on them: combinability and transparency. Despite the fuzzy characteristics inherent in collocations, the present study makes an operational classification based on the features of combinability and transparency, as well as classifying collocations into lexical combinations, such as [verb + noun], [delexicalised verb + noun], [adjective + noun] and [adverb + adjective].

Chapter 3 critically reviews previous studies on collocations from the viewpoint of Second Language Acquisition. Firstly, the 'usage-based approach' in cognitive linguistics is presented in relation to learning collocations. Then, syntactic and morphological differences and commonalities between French/Japanese and English languages are presented. Moreover, the previous research on the learners' knowledge and use of collocations using corpora and other instruments by French and Japanese learners in addition to other various L1 backgrounds are presented in order to clarify what the present study aims to investigate.

Chapter 4 includes the research questions, selection of target collocations, pilot studies and the explanation of the different types of tasks the present study adopts. Firstly, the two research questions are presented to examine the following issues: 1) the French and Japanese learners' L1 influence in their recognition and production of collocations; and 2) the recognition and production of collocations depending on the combinability and semantic transparency of collocations. Then the procedures for selecting the target collocations are presented. The target collocations selected with the use of several dictionaries and British National Corpus are provided to the native speakers of English in the form of questionnaires in Pilot Study 1. Based on the results of Pilot Study 1, the new list of collocations was made and provided in the form of questionnaires in order to fine-tune. The final list of collocations selected for French and Japanese learners was then used in Multiple Choice Question (MCQ)

Tasks, Translation Tasks and learner corpora investigation. The explanation of these two types of tasks and learner corpora investigation is also presented.

Chapter 5 reports the results of the learners' knowledge of collocations obtained from MCQ Tasks, one of the three types of tasks the present study designed. The collocations selected based on the pilot studies are provided to the French and Japanese learners in the form of MCQ Tasks. This type of tasks is designed to investigate the two research questions presented in Chapter 4. In MCQ Tasks, both French and Japanese learners showed L1 influence in all of the four lexical collocations. The L1 influence was determined to be likely when the learners chose the words equivalent to their L1s in MCQ Tasks. The French learners showed a slightly greater L1 influence than the Japanese learners in the [verb + noun] and [delexicalised verb + noun] lexical categories. With regard to the [adjective + noun] category, the Japanese learners showed a slightly greater L1 influence. Regarding combinability and transparency influence, the significant differences between the responses of French and Japanese learners were found in the [+ ResComb, +Transp] and [- ResComb, - Transp] groups of collocations.

Chapter 6 shows the results of the learners' knowledge and use of collocations obtained from Translation Tasks. The collocations used in MCQ Tasks are also adopted in Translation Tasks. The results showed that though the L1 influence was found in both the French and Japanese learners, the French learners showed a slightly greater L1 influence than the Japanese learners with regard to the [verb + noun] and [delexicalised verb + noun] categories of collocations. This result is common to the one found in the MCQ Tasks in Chapter 5. Both the French and Japanese learners showed L1 influence in the "adjective + noun" category. In terms of the influence of combinability and transparency of collocations, the results showed that the Japanese learners have a tendency to answer more correctly to the collocations with [+ResComb, +Transp] than to those with [-ResComb, -Transp].

Chapter 7 investigates French and Japanese learners' learner corpora. Each of the French and Japanese L2 learner corpora is composed of their written essays in English. This third type of data was analysed to reveal their use of English collocation in totally free production. The collocations selected for the above two tasks are examined in each corpus in order to study whether the number of occurrences of collocations in respective learner corpus is different. The present study also studied whether French and Japanese learners show different/similar tendencies in their use of collocations. Though the number of occurrences of the target collocations was small, the learner corpora investigation found that both the French and Japanese learners are likely to show frequent use of the collocations which have the equivalent meaning and same syntax (word order) to their L1s. Regarding the influence of the combinability and transparency of collocations, the number of the relevant occurrences in the corpora showed that both French and Japanese learners have a tendency to produce more [-ResComb, -Transp] collocations than [+ResComb, +Transp] collocations in. These results did not necessarily follow the previous remark made by Kellerman (1978).

Chapter 8 firstly presents the summary of findings. These findings are indicated in terms of the two research questions about the learners' knowledge and use of English collocations by both French and Japanese learners. Based on the findings in the present study, some implications for teaching collocations are also suggested. The discussion also leads to offer some suggestions for further research followed by the final remarks.

As the final chapter of the present study, Chapter 9 states the limitations of the study. Although the present study investigates the knowledge and use of collocations of L2 learners from different L1 backgrounds, other important factors such as the socio-linguistic, psycho-social and socio-cultural dimensions need to be considered in the future study. The discussion suggests the future directions of the study of collocations.

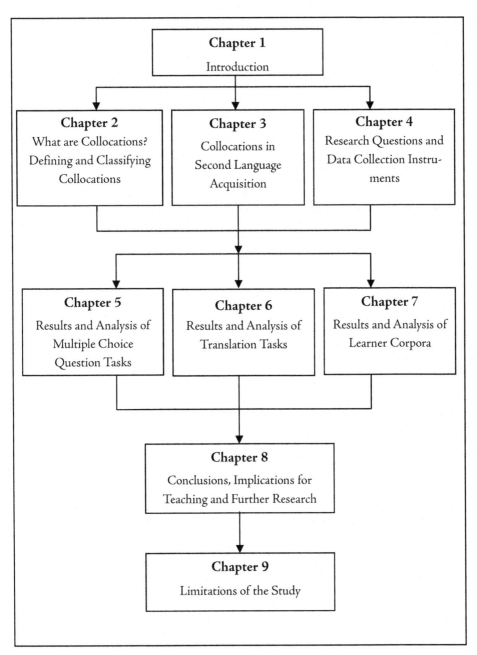

Figure 1.1 Thesis Structure

Chapter 2

WHAT ARE COLLOCATIONS?
DEFINING AND CLASSIFYING COLLOCATIONS

2.1 Introduction

A number of previous studies have discussed collocations and its significance in language learning with their teaching implications. In this chapter, firstly, various definitions of collocations will be discussed. Secondly, the characteristics of collocations will be described including the two main features that determine the types of collocations: combinability and transparency. Thirdly, the criteria for classifying collocation in the present study are discussed.

2.2 Definitions and Characteristics of Collocations

2.2.1 Scope of Collocations

In order to understand the nature of collocation, previous analyses have been carried out by a variety of researchers who used different scopes of defining collocations. A pioneering classification of English word-combination was made by Palmer (1933), who collected examples from dictionaries. He indicated that 'a collocation is a succession of two or more words that must be learnt as an integral whole and not pieced together from its component parts'(*ibid.*:1). Durrant & Schmitt (2010) indicate that Palmer's definition of collocations is pedagogically-oriented.

Based on his definition, 5749 collocations were collected from Saito's (1915) *Idiomological English-Japanese Dictionary* and appendices to various dictionaries, grammars, books of quotations, and other source texts. What is notable about his study is that he carried out this study for the benefit of teachers of English who have an 'impression that it is not so much the words of English nor the grammar of English that make English difficult, but that vague and undefined obstacle to progress in the learning of English consists for the most part in the existence of so many odd comings-together-of-words (*ibid.*:13)'. Although categorising 5749 collocations into several groups of collocations, such as 'verb + noun', 'adjective + noun', etc., was pioneering, his collection of collocations is based on arbitrary selection from dictionaries. He indicated the importance of 'recognition-knowledge' of collocations in order to use 'production-knowledge'; the learners need to be familiar with the collocations by reading and/or listening because they are not able to piece these collocations together from their component parts (*ibid.*: 14). While Palmer did not consider the frequency of collocations, Firth (1957) brought the frequency-based approach into the area of lexical studies, defining collocations as 'actual words in habitual company' (*ibid.*:4).

More recently, Nation (2001:329-332) addresses ten scales for setting up criteria for classifying word sequences as collocations. These ten scales indicate what is involved in learning collocations and they have been identified by a variety of researchers (*ibid.*). Although it is not clear how he measures these ten scales to classify items as collocations, the ten scales are:

1) Frequency of co-occurrence (Kjellmer 1982);

2) Adjacency (Renouf and Sinclair 1991);

3) Grammatically connected (Kennedy 1998);

4) Grammatically structured (Kjellmer 1982);

5) Grammatical uniqueness;

6) Grammatical fossilisation;

7) Collocational specialisation (Aisenstadt 1981);

8) Lexical fossilisation (Sinclair 1987);

9) Semantic opaqueness; and

10) Uniqueness of meaning.

While the term 'scale' usually implies the degree, no explicit criteria for a word sequence to be considered as a collocation is indicated. For example, as one of the ten 'scales' of collocations, "frequency of co-occurrence" is discussed as an important criterion, which has been studied particularly in the form of computer-based frequency studies of corpora. It is mentioned that the frequency of co-occurrence is a very important criterion from teaching point of view. Kjellmer (1982) counted the number of the frequent occurrences of the adjacent two-word sequences in Brown Corpus, such as "of the", "although he", and "but too". "Adjacency" indicates whether collocations occur next to each other as in "left handed", or separated by variable words or phrases as in "little did X realise". For a word sequence to be considered as a collocation, they need to be "grammatically structured". For example, "although he", "of the", "but too" are found in Brown Corpus (Kjellmer 1982:25), but they do not make up a collocation that takes account of the major divisions that are meaningful for learners. The difference between "3) grammatically connected" and "4) grammatically structured" is that the former includes cases such as "of the" and "although he", which are not considered to make up a collocation that takes account of the major divisions for analysing a clause. Thus, the latter one, "grammatically structured", involves cases which are not only connected but rather loosely-/well-structured (Nation 2001:330).

In addition, various researchers have discussed the concepts, such as 'formulaic sequences', which include collocations (Schmitt & Carter 2004; Read and Nation 2004). Among them, Schmitt & Carter (2004) extensively worked on 'formulaic sequences' and Wray (2002) introduced a key term, 'formulaicity', to embrace many types of terminologies related to collocations. 'Formulaic sequence' indicates 'a sequence, continuous or discontinuous, of words or other elements, which is, or appears to be prefabricated: that is, stored and retrieved whole from memory at the time of use, rather than being subject to generation or analysis by the language grammar' (Wray 2002:9). Thus, according to her definition, collocations are included in the 'formulaic sequence'.

Cowie (1981) distinguishes the word combinations from 'free collocations', 'figurative idioms', and 'pure idioms' as follows:

1) Free combinations (e.g. *drink tea*):
   - the restriction on substitution can be specified on semantic grounds.
   - all elements of the word combination are used in a literal sense.
2) Restricted collocations (e.g. *perform a task*):
   - some substitution is possible, but there are arbitrary limitations on substitution.
   - at least one element has a non-literal meaning, and at least one element is used in its literal sense; the whole combination is transparent.
3) Figurative idioms (e.g. *do a U-turn*, in the sense of completely change one's policy or behaviour):
   - substitution of the elements is seldom possible.
   - the combination has figurative meaning, but preserves a current literal interpretation.
4) Pure idioms (e.g. *blow the gaff*):
   - substitution of the elements is impossible.
   - the combination has a figurative meaning and does not preserve a current literal interpretation.

Cowie (1981) emphasises that the boundary of these types of combinations is not clear-cut but these types should be seen as forming a continuum. Although his categorization is comprehensive to understand the characteristics of free combinations, figurative/pure idioms and restricted collocations, within the framework of 'restricted collocations', it is considered that several types of collocations can be categorized based on different lexical combinations. The categorisation of collocations in the present study is based on the combinability and transparency, which Cowie introduced. While Cowie takes various word combinations, such as idioms and free combinations, into account, the present study deals with collocations.

Nesselhauf (2005) categorised the definition of collocations into two major types of approach: 1) the 'frequency-based approach' and 2) the 'phraseological approach'. In the former approach, the 'frequency-based approach', a collocation is regarded as the adjacent co-occurrence of words at a certain distance, which occur more frequent than could be expected if words combined randomly in a language. The latter one, the 'phraseological approach', addresses that a collocation is a type of word combination, as one that is fixed to some degree which contains major constituents in a clause. These two approaches are different in that the 'phraseological approach' requires that the elements of collocations should be syntactically related but the 'frequency-based approach' does not. Wolter and Gyllstad (2011:5) discuss that both frequency and semantics are important aspects which are related to both approaches. The present study adopts the perspective by Wolter and Gyllstad (2011) in that both approaches are not mutually exclusive. The following sections discuss these approaches in greater detail.

2.2.1.1 Frequency-based Approach

The frequency-based approach supports the idea that collocation is considered basically as 'the co-occurrence of words…, and a distinction is usually made between co-occurrences that are frequent … and those that are not' (Nesselhauf 2005:11). There are two major pioneering researchers who adopted the frequency-based approach: Firth (1957) and Sinclair (1991). 'Frequency' refers to how often a whole collocation is used, for example, in a corpus.

Firth (1957) is considered to be one of the pioneers of the frequency-based approach and the linguist who brought this approach into the area of lexical studies (Carter & McCarthy 1988:32). He defines collocations as 'actual words in habitual company' (Firth 1957:4), with a view to the important role of collocations in linguistic research in addition to those of phonetics, phonology and grammar. However, his definition remains ambiguous.

  Sinclair (1991:170) adheres to the Firth's definition of collocation as 'the occurrence of two or more words within a short space of each other in a text'. He sees collocations in a framework of 'node' and 'collocates' constituting a 'span', a view supported by Stubbs (2001), who defines collocation as 'frequent co-occurrence' (*ibid*.:29). A 'node' is the pivotal word which can be a core word, and 'collocates' are words which co-occur with a node in a corpus. Collocations are thus a certain span of words that consists of nodes and collocates to the left and right. It is generally considered that significant collocates are found within a span of 4:4, which means that they can be found in the span of four words before and after the node (Jones and Sinclair 1974). With the objective to provide evidences of collocations in corpus data in his study, in a COBUILD (1995) data, Stubbs (2001:29) selected "seeks" as a node, and found that it occurs 7847 times in a corpus of 200 million words[1], and the ten words which most frequently co-occur with it are: female 1113, black 972, male 785, attractive 619, similar 568, guy 499, lady 493, man 425, caring 401 and professional 389 (Stubbs 2001: 29). His definition is therefore a statistical one. Despite the fact that a text-type he chooses is more restricted than much language use, Stubbs (2001) argues that the co-occurrence relations between words often are strong and suggests that 'collocation is a relation between words in a linear string: a node predicts that a preceding or following word also occurs' (Stubbs 2001: 19).

---

[1] This corpus is *Collins COBUILD English Collocations* on CD-ROM which consists of general English from 70% British, 25% American and 5% other native varieties. About 65 percent of the text samples are from the mass media, written and spoken.

The most recent study on collocations using the frequency-based approach is that of Shin and Nation (2008) whose focus was on the most frequent collocations in spoken English. The objective of their study was to present a list of the highest frequency collocations of spoken English. When using the ten million word spoken section of the British National Corpus (BNC) as the data source to investigate the frequent collocations, they used a definition of collocation as a structure of two parts: pivot words (or nodes) which are the focal words in the collocation and its collocate(s), the word or words accompanying the pivot word. The total number of collocations they found is 5894, the top ten of which include "you know", "I think", "a bit", "thank you" and "in fact". They exclude those that are not grammatically structured. The distinctive difference between the study by Shin and Nation (2008) and the study by Stubbs (2001) is that Shin and Nation exclusively focused on spoken corpus, thus the most frequent collocations in the speech, such as "you know", "I think", were discovered.

As Nation (2001:335) points out, frequency needs to be considered with the types of collocations, i.e. whether they are unanalysed and/or whether the words are necessarily adjacent. The present study selects frequent collocations which occur in BNC as stimuli to investigate how L2 learners use collocations which are frequently used by L1 speakers with the focus on L1 influence on their recognition and production of collocations. The collocations with more than 50 hits in BNC are selected as the stimuli in the present study. Most of the collocations in the present study had more than 50 hits but a few of them are less than 50 hits. The analysis and investigation of collocations involving verbs, nouns, adjectives and adverbs are carried out.

2.2.1.2 Phraseological Approach

This approach views a collocation as an abstract unit of language and its instantiations in texts (*ibid.*:25) in a certain grammatical pattern. The term 'phraseology' can be traced back to Russian phraseological theory, which developed from the late 1940s to the 1960s (Cowie 1998). Followers of this approach include Cowie (1981), who defined collocations by distinguishing them from two other types of word combinations: free combinations and idioms (Cowie 1981; 1994). He suggests that collocations are found in the 'fuzzy' area on a continuum between free combinations and idioms. Cowie (1981) distinguishes 'free combinations' from 'restricted collocations' according to two criteria: 1) combinability; and 2) transparency.

Based on Cowie's (1981) discussion, combinability refers to whether and to what degree paradigmatic substitution of the elements in the combination is restricted, and transparency refers to whether the elements of the combination and the combination itself have a literal or a non-literal meaning (Nesselhauf 2005:14). For example, the verb "keep" in a collocation "keep a diary" can also be combinable with "write"[2]. The verb "keep" in this example, is not used with a transparent meaning, because the primary sense of "keep" is "to stay in a particular space, condition, or position, or to make someone or something do this" (*Longman Dictionary of Contemporary English* 2003) rather than "to regularly record written information somewhere" (*ibid.*). "Keep" in this collocation is therefore not transparent, whereas it is in the collocation "keep still".

The present study adopts both approaches since both frequency and phraseological viewpoint of collocations are important in order to investigate how L2 learners use the frequent collocations. Thus in the present study, a collocation is defined as: a type of word combination in a certain grammatical pattern, and they refer to an abstract unit of language that occur frequently. Collocations are characterized by two criteria: 1) combinability of words within a collocation; and 2) semantic transparency of word in a collocation. In the next section, these criteria are explained.

---

[2] Some native speakers of English answer that they use "write" as a verb to be combined with "a diary" in the pilot study, which will be mentioned in Chapter 4.

2.2.2 Characteristics of Collocations

2.2.2.1 Combinability

The present study considers the combinability of nodes in collocations by choosing the nodes in each lexical category of collocations. The classification of collocations established by Aisenstadt (1979, 1981) is based on the combinability of the elements within a collocation. For example, in a collocation "make/take a decision", one element of a collocation is considered to be restricted in its combinability. The verbs are said to 'have a rather wide and vague meaning and collocate with many different nouns' (Aisenstadt 1981:57), while the noun is restricted in its combinability, but is not always limited to only one verb (Aisenstadt 1981:56). As explained in Section 2.2.1.1, the 'nodes' and 'collocates' are important terms to define collocations. The previous studies, such as Stubbs (2001), selected verbs as the 'node' of a collocation in a corpus since the objective of their studies was to find the frequency of verbs which occur in collocations. However, one of the objectives of the present study is to find appropriate collocations which have the possibility of combining with a few words to express a specific meaning. Thus, in the case of a collocation, "make/take a decision", "make/take" are the 'collocates' and "a decision" is the 'node' which is pivotal. Therefore, in this collocation, there are two possibilities of collocates, "make" and "take", to combine with the noun, "a decision". The present study focuses on the combinability of the 'nodes' of collocation, since the possibilities of combinability in a collocation are more limited than those of the 'collocates'. Thus, this collocation involves the 'collocates' that are able to combine with more than one element and it is not restricted in the possibility of combining with different words. In the case of "common sense", in the 'adjective + noun' collocations, "sense" is the 'node' and "common" is the 'collocates' which co-occur with "sense" more frequently than other adjectives. In the case of "deeply involved" in the 'adverb + adjective' collocations, "involved" is the 'node' and "deeply" is the 'collocate'.

A more comprehensive and detailed classification based on combinability was attempted by Howarth (1996). His classification is carried out with regards to the verb-noun collocations in addition to whether one or both elements of a collocation is/are restricted as regards to combinability. The explanations and examples are explicitly listed with regard to verb and noun combinations only, as shown below (Howarth 1996:102). The objective of his study is to find whether there is any direct correlation between the type of verb in the combination and its level of restrictedness. The collocations Howarth deal with are not necessarily the same collocations but the synonymous ones, such as in "adopt a proposal" and "adopt a suggestion". In the present study, the target collocations are synonymous ones and the combinability of nodes is considered not only with regards to 'verb + noun' collocations but also to 'delexicalised verb + noun', 'adjective + noun' and 'adverb + adjective' collocations. In the following categories by Howarth (1996), either verb or noun is pivotal.

1) Freedom of substitution in the noun: some restriction on the choice of verb: an open set of nouns a small number of synonymous verbs.
e.g. adopt/accept/agree/ etc. to a proposal/suggestion/recommendation

2) Some substitution in both elements: a small range of nouns can be used with the verb. There are a small number of synonymous verbs.
e.g. introduce/table/bring forward a bill/an amendment

3) Some substitution in the verb: complete restriction on the choice of the noun: no other noun can be used with the verb in that sense there are a small number of synonymous verbs.
e.g. pay/take heed

4) Complete restriction on the choice of the verb: some substitution of the noun: a small range of nouns can be used with the verb in that sense there are no synonymous verbs.

e.g. give the appearance/impression

5) Complete restriction on the choice of both elements: no other noun can be used with the verb in the given sense there are no synonymous verbs.

e.g. curry favour

It is clear that Howarth (1996) considered combinability as a significant factor which characterizes collocations. In the present study, whether a collocation is [+/- Restricted Combinability] regarded as an important criterion. When one of the two elements of a collocation is restricted only to the other lexical element in a collocation, it is considered as [+Restricted Combinability] ([+ResComb]), whereas if it is not restricted but can be combined with more than one word, it is considered as [-Restricted Combinability] ([-ResComb]). Unlike Stubb (2001), since the present study examines the combinability of the nouns, in the case of [verb + noun] collocations, nouns are determined to be pivotal and verbs are collocates which are more restricted or less restricted in combinability to the noun in a collocation.

2.2.2.2 Transparency

In addition to the combinability of words, the other criterion essential in classifying collocations is the transparency. These two criteria, i.e. combinability and transparency, though correlating to some degree, do not regularly coincide (Nesselhauf 2005). Transparency is generally deemed to mean whether the elements of the combination and the combination itself have a literal or a non-literal meaning (Nesselhauf 2005). When a collocate of a collocation is 'literal', the collocation is [+Transparency], and when a collocate is 'non-literal' it is regarded as [-Transparency]. This criterion has often been used differently

41

to distinguish between collocations and idioms. For example, some scholars use only the criterion of combinability to distinguish collocations from free combinations, and others find both the criterion of combinability and that of transparency necessary to distinguish between collocations and idioms (Aisenstadt 1979; 1981).

Secondly, within the framework of transparency, two features can be identified at each extreme: + or - transparency. Although the distinction between + and − transparency is not dichotomous, for the research objective of the present study, the transparency is represented as either [+Transparency] or [-Transparency]. In collocations whose meanings are transparent, the literal and primary meaning of the word is used in combination with other words. Thus, in the set of "ask a question" in the 'verb + noun' collocations, for example, the literal meaning of the verb "ask" is used to mean "to speak or write to someone in order to get an answer, information, or a solution" as can be seen in the *Longman Contemporary Dictionary* as the very first meaning of the word. In terms of collocations whose meanings are not literal, the figurative sense of the word can be identified rather than its literal sense in combination with other words. Thus, in a set of "meet someone's needs", the literal meaning of the verb "meet" is not used but the figurative meaning of "meet" is used. According to the *Longman Contemporary Dictionary*, this "meet" means "to do something that someone wants, needs, or expects you to do or be as good as they need, expect, etc." and this description can be seen as the eighth category of meaning in the dictionary. In the case of "poor health" in the 'adjective + noun' collocations, "poor" primarily means "to have very little money", thus it is considered to be [−Transparency] which has figurative sense. In the case of "bitterly cold", "bitterly" primarily means "to be in a way that produces or shows feelings of great sadness or anger", thus it is categorised as [−Transparency].

Nesselhauf's (2005) gives three groups of collocations (only given for 'verb + noun' combinations) to demonstrate the non-coincidence of combinability and transparency. Unlike Howarth (1996), the collocations included in the following groups are non-synonymous. The groups are divided as follows:

· **Group A**: it involves those combinations in which a collocate is considered literally, but which are nevertheless restricted in their combinability. An example of such a combination is "commit a crime". In this collocation, "crime" is considered as pivotal and is restricted in its combinability, and both "commit" and "crime" are considered to have literal meanings, which are explained in dictionaries as their primary senses.

· **Group C**: it contains combinations in which a collocate in a collocation is used in a non-literal or figurative sense, but a great degree of combinability is possible. An example of such combinations is "take steps". This combination allows combinability of three or more verbs as in "envisage steps" or "consider steps" or "make steps".

· **Group D**: according to Nesselhauf (2005), this group includes those combinations in which a collocate is used in a non-literal sense from the transparency point of view, but in which the elements are arbitrarily restricted as regards their combinability. Examples of this type of combination are those with the verb "face" in its non-literal or figurative meaning of "to have to deal with a particular situation", such as "face a financial crisis", "face a task", "face a period of unemployment", "face her anger". Based on the objective of her study is to examine the frequent collocations including "face", in these combinations, "face" is a 'node' and is used in a figurative sense, i.e. [-Transparency], and it is combinable with a variety of nouns, which can be represented as [-Restricted Combinability]. When the collocations in focus are not synonymous to each other, according to Nesselhauf (2005), the verb "face" is limited with the objects which refer to some kind of difficult or unpleasant situation. Thus, in this case, Nesselhauf (2005) focuses on neither "a financial crisis" nor "a task" but on the verb "face" which collocates with the words describing difficult situations.

Since Nesselhauf's (2005) takes only combinability into account to define collocations, she did not make distinction between groups A and D. However, the present study takes both combinability and transparency into account, and decide the collocations whether they are [+ /- Restricted Combinability] and [+ /- Transparency]. Thus, a list of all the possible combinations of the criteria shows three groups of collocations:

Group A: [+ Restricted Combinability] / [+ Transparency] (literal in meaning)
Group C: [- Restricted Combinability] / [- Transparency] (figurative in meaning)
Group D: [+ Restricted Combinability] / [- Transparency] (figurative in meaning)

[+ Restricted Combinability] means that the node can be combined with one or two possible words, while [- Restricted Combinability] means that the node can be combined with three or more possible words. [+ Transparency] means that a collocate (e.g. a verb in a [verb + noun] collocation) in a collocation is literal, thus if the collocate has a literal meaning, it is classified as [+Transp] even if a node (e.g. a noun in a [verb + noun] collocation) has a figurative meaning. [- Transparency] means that a collocate (e.g. a verb in a [verb + noun] collocation) in a collocation is non-literal or figurative, thus if a collocate (e.g. a verb in a [verb + noun] collocation) has a non-literal meaning, it is classified as [-Transp] even if a node (e.g. a noun in a [verb + noun] collocation) has literal meaning.

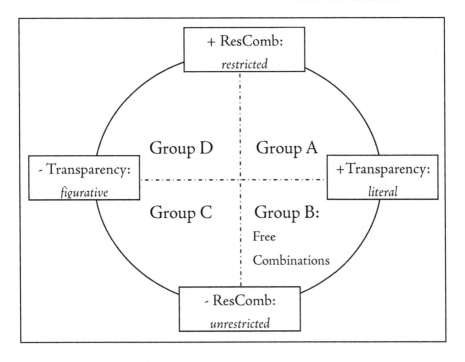

Figure 2.1: Three Possible Combinations of Collocation Criteria

Among the four groups of possible combinations, Nesselhauf (2005) excludes Group B which is [-Restricted Combinability] and [+ Transparency] (literal in meaning) because Group B is not collocations but free combinations. Since it is easier to define combinability than transparency (*ibid*: 27), she applies only combinability criterion to define collocations. Nevertheless, it is also true that the transparency criterion plays a crucial role in defining collocations in spite of the inherent difficulty in measuring it.

The present study involves whether or not one of the elements, i.e. a collocate, in collocations are transparent in addition to the combinability of one of the two elements in a collocation, i.e. a node, to categorize collocations. Unlike Nesselhauf (2005), the transparency should be considered as one criterion to characterize collocations, and the present study tries to include transparency as one of the two criteria to categorize collocations.

In the present study, collocations are further classified by considering grammatical categories of words and the perspectives of combinability and transparency.

2.3 Collocations in the Present Study

2.3.1 Lexical and Grammatical Collocations

In addition to the two criteria of combinability and transparency outlined above, the present study applies the classification according to the grammatical pattern in which the collocation is realised. Benson, Benson and Ilson (1985, 1997) divide collocations into two types in their 90,000-entry dictionary of collocations – one of the largest so far because of the large number of entries and of words that collocate to the entries[3]. The two types of collocations are: lexical collocations and grammatical collocations.

The lexical collocations consist of two open-class words, for example, "adopt a policy" and "an aquiline nose". Unlike Nesselhauf (2005), in lexical collocations a distinction is often drawn between the 'node' (the noun in the case of a [V + N] or [Adj. + N] collocation) and the 'collocate' or 'collocator' (the verb in the case of [V + N] and the adjective in the case of [Adj. + N]). Benson, Benson and Ilson (1985)'s second category consists of a combination of 'noun/verb/adjective + a closed-class word'. In this combination, in most cases a closed-class word is a preposition such as in "different from", "an argument about". These two types of collocations according to word-class seem to be easily recognizable to language learners. Additionally, as Fontenelle (1998) has pointed out, there are other categories 'frequently found in combination with one another' (*ibid.*:192) such as 'adjectives and nouns ([Adj. + N])', 'adverbs and verbs ([Adv + V])', or even 'nouns and nouns ([N + N])'.

---

[3] Although the *Oxford Dictionary of Collocations* (2005) is also the most recent dictionary of collocations, it does not give any categorisation of collocations in lexical or grammatical terms, as Benson, Benson and Ilson (1985) have done.

Among various groups of collocations, the present study particularly focuses on four combinations in lexical collocations as shown in Table 2.1. The first and second categories, the 'verb + noun' and 'delexicalised verb + noun' collocations, have been discussed by several researchers as not only the most difficult for the learners (Biskup 1992) but also the core patterns of elements which are frequent (Howarth 1996:120) and constitute speech. Altenberg (1993:227) claims that 'they tend to form the communicative core utterances where the most important information is placed'. The third category, the 'adjective + noun' collocations, has hardly been studied at all. Siyanova and Schmitt (2008) studied the 'adjective + noun' collocations, such as "social services", and discovered that only about half of the collocations, including inappropriate combinations of words, produced by Russian learners of English in their essays were appropriate. With regards to these learners' recognition about the frequency of the collocations and their speed of processing collocations, they are poorer than those of native speakers. It was found that only about half of the collocations produced in their essays by the Russian learners frequently appeared in the British National Corpus (BNC). These findings suggest that L2 learners have problems not only with their knowledge of 'verb + noun' collocations, which are commonly studied by researchers (e.g. Nesselhauf 2005; Bahns & Eldaw 1993), but also with that of 'adjective+noun' collocations. Thus, 'adjective + noun' collocations are investigated in the present study. The last category, the 'adverb + adjective' collocations, has been studied only rarely. Granger (1998), for example, investigated native and non-native knowledge of 'adverb (i.e.'-ly') + adjective' collocations based on the essays of French learners of English and native speakers. She concludes that French learners had a poorer sense of salience for collocations and underused native-like collocations and used atypical word combinations instead. It is useful to investigate whether French learners of English show such poor salience for collocations in comparison with Japanese learners, because the knowledge of 'adverb + adjective' collocations have been considered to be very difficult for learners to acquire (Granger 1998).

Table 2.1 Four Combinations of Lexical Collocations

Category	Types of Lexical Collocations	Example
1	Verb + Noun: [V+N]	*cross the border*
2	Delexicalised Verb + Noun: [del.V+N]	*do me a favour*
3	Adjective + Noun: [Adj.+N]	*large population*
4	Adverb + Adjective: [Adv.+Adj.]	*bitterly cold*

2.3.2 Target Collocations in the Present Study

Types of collocations in the present study are classified with reference to two parameters; combinability and transparency, for the four lexical collocations; [V+N], [del.V+N], [Adj.+N], and [Adv.+Adj.]. Although, in total, sixteen groups based on [+/- Restricted Combinability] and [+/- Transparency] with four lexical combinations are possible, the present study focuses on eight target groups of collocations which have distinct characteristics as shown in Table 2.2. The two groups of combinability and transparency, i.e. [+Restricted Combinability, +Transparency] and [-Restricted Combinability, -Transparency] groups, will be investigated. Based on Cowie's (1981) discussion that he distinguished collocations from free combinations and idioms according to combinability and transparency, [+Restricted Combinability, -Transparency] group of collocations have a characteristic of so called 'idioms'. Thus, the present study does not deal with this group of collocations.

Table 2.2 Eight Target Groups of Collocations in the Present Study

Category	Types of Collocations	[+/- Restricted Combinability] , [+/- Transparency]
1	Verb + Noun: [V+N]	[+Restricted Combinability, +Transparency]
		[-Restricted Combinability, -Transparency]
2	Delexicalised Verb + Noun: [Del.V+N]	[+Restricted Combinability, +Transparency]
		[-Restricted Combinability, -Transparency]
3	Adjective + Noun: [Adj.+N]	[+Restricted Combinability, +Transparency]
		[-Restricted Combinability, -Transparency]
4	Adverb + Adjective: [Adv.+Adj.]	[+Restricted Combinability, +Transparency]
		[-Restricted Combinability, -Transparency]

2.4 Summary

In this chapter, the scope of collocation was explored based on previous research related in particular to frequency-based and phraseological approaches. The frequency-based approach, espoused by Firth (1957) and his successors, viewed a collocation as a certain span of words that consists of nodes and collocates to the left and right (Sinclair 1991). In contrast, the phraseological approach was popularized by Cowie (1981, 1994) and Howarth (1996), who defined collocations as belonging to the fuzzy area on a continuum between free combinations and idioms. It was explained that the present study would be based on the phraseological approach bearing the frequency approach in mind to collocations in order to examine learners' use of collocations.

Moreover, previous research on the two major criteria of combinability and transparency for characterising collocation was presented. [+/-Restricted Combinability] indicates whether the words (node) can co-occur with a word or three or more words (collocates). [+/-Transparency] refers whether one of the elements of a combination have literal or non-literal meanings (Nesselhauf 2005). The justification for applying these two criteria in classifying collocations in the present study was also provided.

In addition to the two criteria, [+/- Restricted Combinability] and [+/- Transparency], the target types of collocations based on the grammatical pattern of the collocations are introduced; lexical and grammatical collocations. Lexical collocations include the open-class words while grammatical collocations involve closed-class ones. Then, the four major lexical groups of collocations on which the present study focuses were presented: 'verb + noun', 'delexicalised verb + noun', 'adjective + noun' and 'adverb + adjective' collocations.

Each of the lexical categories can consist of three types of combinability and transparency groups: [+Restricted Combinability, +Transparency], [-Restricted Combinability, -Transparency], and [+Restricted Combinability, -Transparency]. Among them, the present study investigates the two categories, [+Restricted Combinability, +Transparency] and [-Restricted Combinability, -Transparency].

Chapter 3

COLLOCATIONS IN
SECOND LANGUAGE ACQUISITION

3.1 Introduction

The previous chapter presented the two major approaches - the frequency-based and the phraseological - to define collocation so as to present the scope of discussion in the present study. In the phraseological approach, two indispensable features of collocation were identified: combinability and transparency. These are crucial properties in characterising collocation that they have been repeatedly discussed in previous studies (See Section 2.2.2). Despite the significance of these two features in defining collocations, however, the investigation of L2 learners' collocational knowledge and use from the viewpoints of combinability and transparency has not been carried out. Thus, the present study chose target collocations in terms of combinability and transparency to investigate L2 learners' collocational knowledge and use. These two criteria are applied, along with the lexical categories – [V+N], [del.V+N], [Adj.+N] and [Adv.+Adj.]. Another important feature of the present study is to examine L1 influence by comparing two learner groups whose L1s are typologically different. They are French and Japanese speakers, whose languages are typologically vastly different; one in an Indo-European group and the other in a non-Indo-European group.

The influence of L1 in L2 learning has been controversial since the decline of Contrastive Analysis in the 1970s. Although L2 learners do not always choose collocation only with the mediation of their L1s, some studies have indicated that L1 influence is one of the factors that have some possibilities to affect the knowledge of collocations by L2 learners (Nesselhauf 2003, 2005; Yamashita & Jiang 2010; Wolter & Gyllstad 2011). Thus, the L1 influence is dealt with in the present study.

This chapter reviews the previous research into collocations in language learning and discuss how the present study can contribute to this area of research. Firstly, one of the roles of prefabs and their relevance to collocations are presented. Secondly, the usage-based approach to language learning is presented and how lexical processing is dealt with in this field of study is discussed. Thirdly, previous research on the use of collocations by adult L2 English learners, including L1 French and L1 Japanese learners, is presented. Lastly, the recent corpus-based studies on collocations are discussed since various researches on lexis have been carried out with the use of corpus.

3.2 Collocations in Language Learning

3.2.1 Studies on Prefabs and their Relevance to Collocations

Since collocations have usually been discussed in relation to other lexical units, such as prefabs typically, it is necessary to discuss the studies on prefabs including collocations. Prefabs and/or formulaic language, of which more than fifty types are considered to exist (Wray 2002), have become a major focus of interest. Prefabs/prefabricated language are considered to be unanalyzed chunks of language used in certain predictable social contexts (Nattinger & DeCarrico 1992: xv). Bolinger (1975:96) had already pointed out that, for example, English, among many other languages, provides us with an incredibly large number of prefabs[1]. Moreover, Pawley and Syder (1983:208) argue that

---

[1] It is considered that prefabs are abundant in any language, but in the present study English is the main focus since the present study examines the learners' knowledge of collocations in English.

'memorized sentences and phrases are the normal building blocks of fluent spoken discourse, and at the same time, . . . they provide models for the creation of many (partly) new sequences that are memorable and in their turn enter the stock of familiar usages'. They pointed out the importance of collocations and other similar units of language and claimed that 'by far the largest part of the English speaker's lexicon consists of complex lexical items' (*ibid.*:215). They also mention that the number of memorized complete clauses and sentences known to the mature English speaker is probably many thousands (*ibid.*:25). What they call 'memorized complete clauses and sentences' include collocations of grammatical patterns such as [V+N].

According to the previous studies, one of the advantages of using prefabs and/or collocations is to save processing time and effort, and to promote fluency. As indicated by Peters (1983:3): '[A prefab] saves processing time and effort, allowing the speaker to focus attention elsewhere'. This view is supported by Nation (2001) who claims that the advantage of 'chunking' is to reduce processing time. The various types of prefabricated patterns - including collocations – constitute a single category amongst the four different types of 'chunks' (Ellis: 2001), which can be seen as units with several words stored together in long-term memory. Ellis (2001) indicates that chunking occurs at various levels, such as letters, morphemes, words and collocations. He sees the learning of collocation as one level of chunking, which is the long-term storing of associative connections. Since it is not necessary to spend time paying attention to each word but it is enough to process several words at a time as a unit, prefabricated patterns play a role in saving time for the comprehension or production of speech. In addition, Jiang and Nekrasova (2007) indicate that both L1 and L2 speakers respond to the formulaic sequences significantly faster and with fewer errors than they did to non-formulaic sequences. They conducted grammaticality judgement tests, which consist of formulaic and non-formulaic phrases, to English as a second language speakers and L1 English speakers.

Thus, learning formulaic sequences have been found to be efficient for L2 learners.

3.2.2 Memory-based and Usage-based Approaches

From the viewpoint of the cognitive approach to language learning, the role of large chunks of memorized language is vital, including collocations (Skehan: 1998). Compared with the 'rule-based approach' to language acquisition, a much more 'memory-based' (*ibid.*) one needs to be focused on (Skehan 1998:29). The 'rule-based approach' to language represents the idea that 'rules have primary importance and language is produced by "filling out" these rules with lexical exponents since the priority is to construct sentences which conform to the grammar (rule system) of the language in question' (*ibid.*). However, he indicates some drawbacks to this approach: 'it requires a considerable degree of on-line computation during language production' (*ibid.*). Thus, instead of the rule-based approach, he favours a memory-based approach to language. Skehan (1998) indicates that this has been argued by Bolinger (1975) who asserted that language use is based on lexical elements of varying sizes to a much greater extent than used to be thought:

> Bolinger proposed…that much of language use is, in fact, repetitive, and not particularly creative. While not denying the potential for creativity and novelty, he suggested that most of the speech we produce is likely to have been produced before, probably by the speaker. We do not typically, he argued, deal in originality: much interaction is of a spectacularly non-creative type, being more concerned with mundane and fairly predictable matters. (Skehan 1998: 32)

Not rejecting the role of a rule-based approach to language, but highlighting the significant role of memorized language, he adds that 'there are limits to the newness of the language and to the propositions that we can cope with' to 'facilitate conversational development, and also make things less threatening'

(Skehan 1998: 34). This seems to support the idea that the role of collocations is crucial for learners in that collocational competence makes L2 learners more fluent in their L2. The collocational competence refers to the putative fluency across the linguistic board in various registers in collocation knowledge and use.

Moreover, usage-based approach is discussed as one of the central principles of cognitive linguistics (Zeschel 2008) and has been originally developed as an area of studies in L1 acquisition (Langacker 1987; Goldberg 1995; Bybee 1985; Tomasello 2003). Usage-based approach sees that the essence of language is its symbolic dimension (Tomasello 2003). When human beings use symbols to communicate with one another, patterns of use emerge and become consolidated into grammatical constructions by the use of the language. They conceive language as meaningful linguistic symbols and as patterns in which meaningful linguistic symbols are used in communication. In Chomskyan generative grammar[2], according to Tomasello (2003), natural languages are characterized in terms of a set of abstract rules or 'core' grammar and a lexicon or linguistic 'periphery'. The core and periphery dichotomy led to the dual process approach to language acquisition. In the dual process approach to language acquisition, whereas children acquire elements of the linguistic periphery using "normal" learning processes, which is carried out in an inductive way, the linguistic core, universal grammar, cannot be so learned; it is an innate property of the human mind (Tomasello 2003:5). In contrast, in the usage-based approach, competence with a natural language consists of the mastery of all its items and structures. Thus, fluent speakers of English control not only highly abstract syntactic constructions, such as past tense and the passive construction, but also expressions based on individual words and phrases including greetings, idioms and collocations (Tomasello 2003:6).

---

[2] Tomasello (2003) refers to Chomsky's theory of universal grammar which he asserted is a "formal" theory and an innate property of the human mind.

In addition, they argued that L1 language acquisition is achieved from item-based constructions to abstract constructions rather than vice versa. Several studies in children's L1 acquisition (e.g. Tomasello 1992) indicate that the initial stages of children's linguistic competence is characterized not as 'a grammar' but as an inventory of relatively isolated, item-based constructions. It is argued that children can build up the concept or rule of a language from their item-based constructions using their general skills of intention-reading of the speakers and pattern-finding (Tomasello 2003:143). This approach explains that children understand the communicative functions of utterances that embody various syntactic constructions by reading the intentions of the speaker.

In relation to collocations, the usage-based approach seems useful since it considers the significance of usage of language. Memorizing the collocations cannot lead to the mastery of collocations but the frequent use of collocations in communication is necessary. Wulff (2008:17) states that "usage-based models particularly emphasize that categorization is based on inductive learning processes, that is, 'the mental grammar of the speaker [...] is formed by the abstraction of symbolic units from situated instances of language use'". Learning collocations can be a part of this inductive process of learning since collocations are themselves specific linguistic symbols of units.

In the next section, the differences between the two languages, French and Japanese, are discussed, which is followed by the review of previous research on L2 collocations.

3.3 Previous Research on the Use of Collocations by L2 Learners

3.3.1 Syntactic, Lexical and Morphological Differences and Commonalities between French/Japanese and English

One of the hypotheses is that the syntactic differences and commonalities between French and English, and between Japanese and English are one of the background factors which can affect the participants' responses in the tasks in the present study. Based on the study of typological universals initiated by Greenberg (1974), the cross-linguistic comparison of a wide range of languages drawn from different language families was carried out in order to discover the features they have in common (Ellis:1994). He classified languages according to their ordering of subject, verb and object in sentences. The languages in the world are divided at least into two large groups:

1) Subject + Verb + Object
   (e.g. English, French, 39% of the world's languages)
2) Subject + Object + Verb
   (e.g. Japanese, Korean, 44% of the world's languages)

Though most of their basic order patterns of languages, including English and French, can be classified into SVO group (Tsunoda 1991),[3] in some limited cases English and French have SOV patterns such as in using pronouns. In French, for example, the SVO pattern in a sentence,

Je lis un livre,

changes into the SOV pattern when using pronouns;

Je	le	lis.
Subject	*Object*	*Verb.*
I	it	read.

---

[3] Tsunoda (1991) suggests that French has SOV patterns with previous objects but major patterns can be classified into SVO group.

In Japanese, despite the position of an object in a sentence, the SOV pattern rarely changes:

Watashi	wa	honn	wo	yomu.
Subject	*Case Particle*	*Object*	*Objective Case Particle*	*Verb*
I		a book		read.

In other words, English and French belong to one group and Japanese to the other, but sometimes French and Japanese belong to one group and English to the other. One of the hypotheses is that the SOV pattern in French and Japanese can be one factor affecting the L2 learners' access in collocations because English [verb + noun] collocations do not change into SOV patterns. The word order matters when L2 learners translate L1 sentences into L2 word by word, but it does not necessarily matter when they translate L1 sentences as wholes. The word order of their L1 equivalents may cause some problems in their accurate production of collocations into English.

Moreover, the order of "adjective + noun" collocations is not identical between French and English. In French, in principle, the adjectives usually come after the nouns, such as in "les élections présidentiells". However, the short adjectives, such as *bon, mauvais, beau, joli*, which describe the characteristics and forms of referents of nouns, usually come before the nouns. There are some adjectives which change its meanings depending on whether they come before or after nouns, such as in "un grand homme (a great man)" and "un homme grand (a tall man)". It is possible that these aspects of different order of "adjective + noun" between French and English may cause difficulty due to L1 interference on their L2 knowledge and use of English collocations.

In addition to the syntactic commonalities between French and English, it is crucial to discuss the lexical discrepancies and commonalities between French and English in terms of their cognates which are closely related to collocations. Even for the learners at the beginning stage the existence of cognates in a target language makes reading comprehension more accessible (Holmes & Ramos 1993). The important roles of cognates in L2 vocabulary acquisition are recognized when the learners' L1 and L2 belong to the same language family (Holmes and Ramos, 1993; Kroll, 1993; De Groot, 1993; Meara, 1993). French and English share a number of cognate words since they are the branches of the Indo-European language family: French belongs to Romance language family and English belongs to Germanic language family. For example, a study claimed that French and English share 6,500 homophonic cognates, and 17,000 'parographs', i.e. which are cognate but not identically written (Séguin and Tréville 1992, as cited in Meara 1993). Some examples of homophonic cognates are 'fin ('end' in French), 'pain ('bread' in French), and 'champ ('field' in French). 'Parographs' are found, for example, in 'carotte' in French and 'carrot' in English. There are also words called 'false friends' which have similar forms in L1 and L2, but different meanings. For example, English "magazine" and French "magasin (shop)" share similar forms but do not have the same meaning. Thus, it is assumed that learners are likely to misrecognize the meaning of the cognates which have orthographic similarity.

On the other hand, Japanese is a non-Indo-European language which has some cognates. It includes loanwords such as "teeburu (table)", "lettasu (lettuce)", "kyabetsu (cabbage)", "furaipan (frying pan)" and many others, with English. Daulton (1998) points out that Japanese has a large number of English loanwords (up to 38% of the 2000 most frequent words of English) and they can help the learning of English. Though the use of cognate words is said to be restricted to certain domains or registers in the case of Romance words in English which tend to be low frequency items used in formal situations (Meara 1993:285), there are some loanwords from English in French, such as "tennis", "planning", "bar" and "crash". In either case, the fact that cognate words exist in the learners' L1 is considered to affect their knowledge and use of L2 English collocations.

With respect to the influence of cognates in L2 learning, it is claimed that the learning stage of the L2 learner is important. The L2 learner at a beginning stage has a tendency to generalize equivalences and to use the principle of making equivalences with L2 and their L1 in comprehension and production (Schmitt and McCarthy 1997). Establishing equivalences between words in their L1 and L2 helps learners in the phase of recognition of words by oversimplifying. When learners are at more advanced level, they hesitate to use cognates for which phonetic or graphic resemblance with L1 equivalents is limited. However, the studies on French intermediate learners' L2 knowledge and use of collocations in relation to their cognates have scarcely been carried out. Thus, the present study can contribute to the discussion on intermediate L2 learners' learning of collocations.

Furthermore, with respect to the morphological aspects of French and Japanese languages, the distinction between singular and plural forms of countable nouns in the L1s may affect the use of learners' English collocations. While French distinguishes singular and plural forms of countable nouns, such as in "journal" and "journaux", for example, Japanese does not. When English and French countable and mass noun distinctions are the same, it is probable that the French learners do not necessarily make errors related to making distinction between the singular or plural nouns, but the Japanese learners do. In the present study, the influence of such singular-plural distinction is expected to be found since the participants are required to fill in the blanks for certain collocations.

3.3.2 Research on French Learners of English

De Cock *et al.* (1998) investigated the nature of French learners' English collocational knowledge as compared to L1 speakers of English using two comparable corpora: a 62,975-word corpus of 25 informal interviews with advanced French mother tongue EFL learners, and an 80,448-word corpus of 24 informal interviews with L1 speakers of British English collected at the University of Lancaster. The proportion of males to females is the same in both corpora: 6 males and 19 females. The age of the students interviewed for the corpora are between 19 and 25. Using programs to analyse the corpora (Tuples and Combinator) –De Cock *et al.* (1998) examined on the basis of recurrent word combinations, i.e. 'any continuous string of words occurring more than once in identical from' (Altenberg 1993) from two-word to five-word recurrent combinations. By counting both L1 and L2 speaker speech, De Cock *et al.* concluded that advanced L2 learners use more prefabs than L1 speakers in some cases, which suggested their use of the idiom principle[4]. The idiom principle claims that in many cases 'semi-preconstructed phrases' are used, where a phrase will be selected rather than a series of discrete words. However, the chunks L2 learners use: 1) are not necessarily the same as those used by L1 speakers; 2) are not used with the same frequency; 3) have different syntactic uses, and fulfil different pragmatic functions. (*ibid.*:78)

Unlike the spoken data which De Cock *et al.* (1998) collected, Granger (1998) investigated the writing skills of French learners. Hers was also a comparative study of L1 and L2 written English. For the learner corpus, she used a subcorpus of advanced French-speaking learners consisting of 251,318 words: 164,190-word corpus of untimed argumentative essays, 24,174-word corpus of timed argumentative essays and 62,954-word corpus of timed literature exam papers. The L1 speaker corpus she used is made up of three parts: 89,525 words of the Louvain essay corpus, 50,202 words of International Corpus of English and 94,787 words of the Lancaster-Oslo-Bergen corpus. The male to female proportion and age of the participants are not indicated. She distinguishes 'collocation,' such as *"commit suicide"* and *"sound asleep"*, from 'formulae', such as *"be that as it may"* or *"it seems (to me) (that) X"*. 'Collocation' is defined as 'the linguistic phenomenon whereby a given vocabulary item prefers the company of another item rather than its "synonyms" because of constraints which are not on the level of syntax or conceptual meaning but on that of usage' (Roey

---

[4] Sinclair (1991) suggests that when co-structuring meaning we operate under two principles: the idiom principle and the open-choice principle. The open-choice principle, on the other hand, asserts that free choice of individual lexical items will be carried out grammatically.

1990:46); 'formulae' are defined as having 'a pragmatic rather than a syntactic function" and include "fixed expressions" (e.g. good morning, how are you?) that function in discourse as greetings, apologies, etc., and more or less frozen patterns used to regulate conversation (e.g. come again? you were saying?)' (Granger 1998: 154). She focused in particular on the collocational category of intensifying adverbs such as amplifiers ending in –ly and functioning as modifiers. For example,

1) although this feeling is *perfectly* natural.

2) Themes in *Les Mouches* which are very *closely* linked with …

3) A young man who is *deeply* in love.   (Granger 1998: 147)

Using the text-retrieval software TACT, she examined all the words ending in –ly that were automatically retrieved from the two corpora, the L1 and L2 corpora. These retrieved words were then 'manually sorted according to pre-defined semantic and syntactic criteria' (*ibid.*:147), to yield the finding that learners use fewer prefabs than their L1-speaker counterparts and that the collocations used by the learners are for the most part congruent with their L1, French.

As far as amplifiers used by French L2 learners are concerned, Granger's study showed less frequent use of prefabs by L2 learners. This result is different from De Cock *et al.*'s finding that L2 learners use more prefabs than L1 speakers in some cases. While both De Cock's and Granger's studies adopted frequency-based approach, their results are not necessarily consistent. The difference between the types of corpus may lead to the contradictory results between them: De Cock used the corpora consisting of spoken data, while Granger adopted the corpora made up of written data. Also, the type of prefabs that De Cock investigates and the collocations Granger examines are different with each other in that the former involves two to five word recurrent word combinations while the latter limits the types of collocations to the lexical collocations such as *"commit suicide"*.

3.3.3 Research on Japanese Learners of English

As far as the research on Japanese L2 learners' knowledge and use of collocations are concerned, several studies have been carried out.

Sugiura (2002) investigated the collocational knowledge of Japanese learners using a corpus of his own students. He collected his students' written data by using an essay assignment, amounting to 80,000 words in total. The participants are first and second year university students. L1 speakers of English were asked to check and paraphrase the learners' essays when they found expressions which were not accurate or natural. The two corpora, the original learners' essay data and the paraphrased learners' essays by L1 speakers of English, were analyzed for comparison of the quantity and the characteristic differences in the use of fixed expressions. Here, what is defined as 'fixed expressions' is not clear since he states that 'the present study used the broader definition of collocation or "fixed expression"' (Sugiura 2002: 317) and does not necessarily distinguish between 'fixed expressions' and 'collocation'. The results show that learners have less collocational knowledge in written English than L1 speakers and that learners used limited expressions. Even though the present study collected a certain amount of learners' written data to make a corpus, his study does not focus on the collocations as defined in the present study but rather on the prefabs or fixed expressions used by learners. Thus, more systematic analysis of the Japanese L2 learners' knowledge and use of collocations is necessary. In addition, methodologically, he collected essays written by learners without any of the other kinds of elicitation tasks that the present study will use, and therefore, his analysis does not appropriately account for Japanese learners' collocational proficiency.

In terms of L1 influence on the acquisition of collocations, Murao (2004) carried out a study involving 50 sentences with [verb + noun] collocations. The

33 participants were third and fourth year English major students at Japanese universities. These participants were judged according to their TOEIC scores: their scores were between 600 and 850. The collocations she dealt with were primarily the [verb + noun] collocations and acceptability judgement test was adopted. Acceptability judgments are carried out to determine the seriousness of an error learners make. Acceptability judgments are considered to be a rather vague criterion, since they involve judgments of the seriousness of an error (Ellis 1994:66). Also, the judgments vary according to the sociolinguistic backgrounds of the person who judges the linguistic items. Murao (2004) hypothesized that learners may depend on their L1 knowledge because they are familiar with L2 high-frequency verbs and regard them as having equivalents in their L1. For example, learners are expected to regard "*take* communication with a foreigner" as correct because they use "komyunikeshon wo toru" in Japanese and the equivalent verb to "toru" is "take" in English. The Japanese learners were required to judge whether each collocation in 50 English sentences was acceptable or not without any contexts or translations. L1 transfer was found even among advanced learners and that language transfer in the domain of lexical collocation remains constant at any level of proficiency. Because the collocation list is not presented and the distinction between [verb+noun] and [delexicalized verb+ noun] collocations did not seem to be made, it is difficult to draw ultimate conclusions.

With regard to L1 influence on the acquisition of collocations, L1 congruency effect was found by Yamashita & Jiang (2010). It was shown that both L1 congruency and L2 exposure affect the acquisition of L2 collocations and that once stored in memory, L2 collocations are processed independently of L1. They adopted a phrase-acceptability judgment task to compare EFL Japanese learners of lower-proficiency group, ESL Japanese learners of higher-proficiency group and L1 speakers. The materials consisted of 24 congruent collocations, such as "heavy stone", 24 incongruent collocations, such as "kill time", and 48 implausible word combinations. The 24 congruent collocations they investigated consist of 7 'verb + noun', 2 'delexicalised verb + noun', and 15 'adjective + noun' collocations. The 24 incongruent collocations they selected consist of 5 'verb + noun', 3 'delexicalised verb + noun' and 16 'adjective + noun' collocations. The congruent collocations share identical lexical elements between two languages, and the incongruent collocations involve different words. For example, both English and Japanese have the identical collocation of "hot tea", which is congruent, while "strong tea" in English is called *koi ocha* "dark tea" in Japanese, thus it is incongruent. Both EFL and ESL learners made more errors with incongruent collocations than congruent collocations. The Japanese learners tend to make more errors in incongruent collocations than in congruent collocations. However, Yamashita and Jiang (2010) studied a small number of collocations for each of the 'verb + noun' and 'delexicalised verb + noun' collocations. Thus, more collocations of each category need to be studied for a comprehensive understanding of L2 learning collocations. Also, the effect of congruency of collocations not only by Japanese L2 learners but also learners from different L1 backgrounds needs to be further explored from the pedagogical point of view.

Moreover, in relation to the L1 equivalents to collocations, Nakata (2007) compared the effect of two different task types, meaning-focused and form-focused tasks, for acquiring collocations in order to find whether congruent and non-congruent collocations benefit differently from the two types of tasks. The 16 target collocations of only [verb + noun] collocations consisting of congruent and non-congruent collocations were provided to the 28 Japanese first-year university students. The congruent collocations, such as "do business", "get certificate" and "take pulse", and the non-congruent collocations included "do survey", "give blow", and "pay visit". Pre-test and Post-test were carried out to measure the learners' development after the meaning-focused and form-focused tasks. He concluded that the form-focused activities led to higher score than meaning-focused tasks especially for the non-congruent collocations. Since his study focused on the effect of tasks type, whether congruent collocations are acquired easily than non-congruent collocations was not verified but he discussed that non-congruent collocations are difficult for learners than those which are congruent between L1 and L2.

In addition to L1 influence, there are other various attributes that affect learners' difficulties with collocations. Miyakoshi (2009) investigated "verb + noun" collocations, such as "take notes" and "place an order", in fill-in-the-blank tests with 66 Japanese graduate and undergraduate students at the University of Hawaii at Mānoa, and students studying English in an intensive English program. Half of them were intermediate, and the other half were advanced. She provided the learners with pre-test and instruction, involving an introduction to collocations and a discussion of common mistakes with collocations, the study categorized eleven error types, such as inappropriate paraphrases, interference of their L1, use of words other than verbs. Among them, paraphrases and misuse of verbs including L1 interference were the strongest indicators of difficulty of collocations for the learners. The study not only found the interference of the L1 which many previous studies already pointed out but also other factors affecting the difficulty of collocations the Japanese learners face with. In the present study, especially in translation tasks, the results are categorized into several error types in order to discuss whether there is any difference by the French and Japanese learners.

3.3.4 Research on Learners with Other L1 Backgrounds

Since the early 90s, several studies on the use of English collocations by L2 learners of English from a variety of different L1 backgrounds appeared. The data elicitation methods selected in these studies varied from translation tasks, to gap-fill tasks, multiple choice tasks, and essays. Translation tasks were one of the major methods favoured in the early studies. For example, to investigate the main causes of observed collocational errors and determining the role of the L1, Biskup (1992) provided two groups of participants, Polish and German university students of English, with a translation task, focusing only on the lexical collocations, which are the combinations of open class words such as verbs and nouns and adjectives, as defined by Benson, Benson and Ilson (1997: xxiv). The task required the students to translate the Polish and German collocations into English equivalent collocations respectively, and their answers were later assessed by L1 speakers of English on a 4-point scale from "unacceptable" to "full equivalent". His study indicates that there were differences between the errors made by Polish and German learners because of the influence by their L1s. While the errors Polish learners made were either loan translations or extensions of L2 meaning on the basis of the L1 word, the errors German learners made resulted from assumed formal similarity. For example, for a target collocation, "to run a bookshop", Polish learners answered "to lead/drive/introduce/hold a bookshop" and German learners answered "to lead/manage/keep a bookshop". The language forms of German and English are similar such as in "sing" in English and "singen" in German and "break" in English and "breken" in German. Although Biskup (1992) seems to have collected a large number of collocations, the list of collocations was not presented and the types of lexical collocations were not explicitly described either. Also, since his study was carried out by one type of task, a translation task, another task type may be beneficial to confirm these results.

Another study using translation task was carried out by Bahns (1993). Bahns (1993) conducted a contrastive analysis of [verb + noun] (as in "withdraw an offer") and [noun + verb] (as in "blizzards rage") collocations. He showed that there is direct translational equivalence for a large number for English [verb + noun] collocations in their German [noun + verb] counterparts. Providing the participants (German English learners) with 30 German [noun + verb] collocations in a translation task in which there were 15 items with direct English translational equivalence, he concluded that the German learners of English had no difficulty in producing the English collocations of the 15 items he studied. They only had to translate both constituents in a rather straightforward way (ibid.: 60). In terms of German [noun + verb] collocations for which there is no direct translation equivalence in English (15 items), 'the probability of committing collocational errors rises enormously', while the errors in [verb + noun] were not found. Although he emphasizes, in teaching, the necessity of distinguishing those collocations which the learners already know because of their particular L1 background from those which are language-specific, the variety of collocations is not sufficient to draw the conclusion that the learners depend on their L1 for the production of collocations.

Moreover, the previous studies mentioned above used translation tasks which may not really reflect the learners' actual free production of lexical collocations, since it has been recognized that learners react in different ways in different tasks (Ellis: 1994; Källkvist: 1999; Larsen-Freeman & Long: 1991:32). A greater variety of tasks is therefore necessary as Ellis (1994: 675) suggests that 'to demonstrate consistency, it is necessary to show that the data are not just a reflection of the instrument used to collect them. This can be achieved by comparing the results obtained from one set of data with those obtained from another'. To confirm the objectivity of the effects of collocations by L2 learners, adopting different types of tasks is necessary.

In addition to translation tasks, Bahns and Eldaw (1993) adopted cloze task and investigated learners' knowledge of collocations in terms of the same 15 'verb + noun' collocations, such as "keep a diary" and "attend lectures", for the advanced German learners of English. Measures for determining the participants as advanced were not mentioned. The two kinds of tests were: 1) a translation task in which the selected collocations were provided in German and the learners are required to translate them into English; 2) a cloze task where learners were asked to fill in the missing verbal collocate to the given noun node. They compared the results of these tasks to examine whether the freedom of production in translation task would allow the participants to produce correct English. The answers in both tasks were evaluated by L1 English speakers as acceptable or unacceptable. Their study showed that the participants were more successful in the translation task, where it is possible to paraphrase the target collocations into other expressions, than in the cloze task, where it was not possible to paraphrase. The target collocations in their study were only collocations including verbs. Thus it is not clear whether their conclusions are applicable only to the collocations including verbs or they can be applied to the collocations involving other collocations including adjectives, adverbs, and so on. Also, it is not obvious whether this outcome is peculiar to German L2 learners or it is common to learners from other L1 backgrounds.

In a similar study with two sorts of tasks, Farghal and Obiedat (1995) undertook research into the use of collocations by studying English learners in Jordan. They provided them with an English 'fill-in-the-blank' task and a translation task from Arabic into English involving 22 common "adjective + noun" collocations relating to core topics such as food, colour and the weather. The English list of fill-in-the-blank items was given to 34 L2 Arab university students, while the Arabic translation list of items was given to learners of English who had experience in teaching English in Jordan. The scores of the two groups were quite low at 18.3% and 5.3% while two L1 speakers scored 100% in the same list of items. Farghal and Obiedat (1995) concluded that some participants used the strategies such as avoidance, transfer, synonymy, and paraphrasing, which language learners tend to adopt when facing difficulties. Although it was not investigated in detail, they mentioned that when there is 'convergence'[5] between L1 and L2, learners answered correctly, while when there is divergence between L1 and L2, they do not answer accurately. It seems that most of the collocations they selected were "adjective + noun" collocations, the procedures of selecting the collocations they used were not explicitly mentioned.

In addition to the use of translation tasks, Howarth (1998a) studied the "verb + noun" combinations produced by learners from different L1 backgrounds with the use of learners' written data coming from ten essays (totalling about 25,000 words) written by masters' course students in Linguistics and

---

[5] 'Convergence' in the study of Farghal and Obiedat (1995) is used as the same meaning as 'congruence' in Yamashita and Jiang (2010).

English Language Teaching at British universities, nine of whom were teachers of English as a second or foreign language, coming from seven countries. The total number of collocations extracted from the three corpora for analysis was more than 6,500: over 5,000 from the L1 corpora and more than 1,000 from the learner material (*ibid.*:177). According to his study, the learners use less collocations and idioms than L1 speakers. The results of his study are similar to the Granger's in that less frequent use of collocations by the L2 learners than that of the L1 speakers. Here, Howarth (1998a) uses the term 'restricted collocations' originally defined by Cowie (1981, 1994) who is a typical representative of the phraseological approach and whose categorisations are often used by several researchers (e.g. Nesselhauf 2005; Fernando 1996).

Moreover, it is particularly significant for the present study that he also noted some clear cases of direct confusion in delexicalized verbs in such as "do attempts", "do a measurement", "get contact with", "make a reaction". According to Chi *et al.* (1994:158), delexicalized verbs are the verbs whose 'original meanings …gradually lose their significance'. Thus, for example, when considering the phrase "have a shower", they suggest the original meaning of the verb "have", meaning "to possess", or "to receive", etc., has disappeared into the noun "shower". These kinds of verbs include "give", "have", "make", "take", "do", "hold", "keep" and "set".

Chi *et al.* (1994) focused on the area of lexical collocation, as defined by Benson, Benson, and Ilson (1997) in *The BBI Combinatory Dictionary of English*, specifically as the delexicalization of verbs, or what Carter & McCarthy (1988:153) describe as 'the tendency of certain commoner transitive verbs to carry particular nouns or adjectives which can in most cases themselves be transitive verbs'.

Chi *et al.*'s study is based on a 1,000,000-word extract from the HKUST (Hong Kong University of Science and Technology) Learner Corpus, which consists of two assignments of approximately 500 words each, written by first-year students[6] on an English language enhancement course at the university. The topics include a recommendation report based on a given set of criteria and a letter to a newspaper arguing for or against a particular point of view. Delexicalized verbs such as *"have"*, *"make"*, *"take"*, *"do"* and *"get"* were selected for the analysis. Chi *et al.* produced a list of faulty collocations using MicroConcord and three other dictionaries to identify the faulty collocations. The results show that delexicalised verbs were difficult to produce for the students in their study. For example, the preference for using one verb over another when employing guessing strategies was noted, such as selecting "take (an) interview" due to transfer from the learners' L1 rather than "make (an) interview" or "do (an) interview" instead of the verb "interview". Also, they argue that there is L1 transfer on learners' production, as in "do an effort" rather than "make an effort" since Chinese use "do" rather than "make". However, Chi *et al.* also warn that the misuse of verbs is not only derived from 'the fact that the verb does not carry any meaning in itself but takes its meaning from the noun which follows it' (Chi *et al.* 1994:164) but is also caused by other factors.

While they identify transfer from the learners' L1, other factors still remain unresolved. It is not persuasive enough to claim that there is language transfer from Chinese because delexicalised verbs seem to be hard to acquire for learners of any L1 background. The present study will include delexicalised verbs to investigate further in terms of French and Japanese learners who have never been studied before concerning their knowledge of delexicalised verbs.

A recent study on the use of learners' collocations conducted by Nesselhauf (2003) focused on [verb+noun] collocations specifically, such as "take a picture "or "draw up a list". Thirty-two German-speaking at an advanced level in third- or fourth-year university students of English were selected, and they wrote essays for the research. The average length of each essay was about 500

---

[6] The L1 of these Chinese students are not mentioned in their study and it is not sure their L1 is Mandarin or Cantonese. However, it is said that 89% of the population in Hong Kong use Cantonese as their L1 (Miyazoe 2002).

words. The extracted [verb-noun] collocations were classified into several categories based on the degree of restriction, such as free combination, restricted combination and idiom. Although she adopted categorization similar to combinability of collocations adopted in the current study, her study did not deal with the collocations in terms of transparency. Her focus was on 1,072 "verb + noun" combinations from the learner essays, of which 213 were classified as collocations, 846 as free combinations and 13 as idioms. According to her analysis (*ibid.*:233), a largest number of mistakes were found in the collocations which have several possibilities of combinability and the smallest number of mistakes was found in terms of the collocations with a few possibilities of combinability. Nesselhauf suggested that highly restricted ([+Restricted Combinability]) collocations are more often acquired and produced as wholes.

By investigating whether this influence was different according to the degree of restriction of a combination, she confirmed that: 1) L1 influence played a significant role in word combination mistakes and concluded that L1 influence in collocations seems to be considerably stronger than even those researchers who have suspected its importance have assumed; and 2) the combination mistakes observed more often in less restricted combinability (*ibid.*: 237).

More recently, some studies on collocations were carried out with the use of corpora consisting of essays of the learners (Altenberg & Granger 2001; Biber & Barbieri 2007; Siyanova & Schmitt 2008; Durrant & Schmitt 2009; Liu 2010;). By comparing their corpus of essays written by advanced learners of several L1 backgrounds, such as Turkish, Mandarin, Arabic, and Korean, with that of L1 speakers, the tendency to use high-frequency collocations than L1 speakers was indicated (Durrant & Schimitt 2009). While De Cock *et al.* (1998) studied spoken data of French learners, these recent studies examined written data of L2 learners. The investigated collocations were modifier-noun combinations, including both adjective-noun and noun-noun combinations, because they were particularly common in the texts analysed. Siyanova &

Schmitt (2008) investigated adjective-noun collocations extracted from 31 essays from Russian advanced learners and found that 45% of the collocations were appropriate collocations. However, their acceptability judgement tests given to the learners showed that the learners had more difficulties in correctly recognizing the infrequent collocations than the frequent collocations. These previous studies showed that different task types can shed light on different aspects of learners' difficulties in collocations. Thus, in the present study, two task types, Multiple Choice Question Tasks and Translation Tasks are adopted. Also, in Translation Tasks in the present study, the morphological errors are judged less serious than inappropriate collocational combinations by British native speakers. However, since the judgments are affected by the socio-cultural factors of those British native speakers, the judgments in the present study are provisional.

The claims made in previous research on L1 transfer in acquiring collocations are not consistent. Some studies conclude that L1 influence is very weak. Biskup (1992) investigated German L2 learners with her translation test, and L1 influence was found in 21% of the inappropriate collocations produced by German learners. She also found L1 influence in 48% of the inappropriate collocations with Polish learners and claims that there is strong L1 influence on inappropriate collocations. Nesselhauf (2003) observes L1 influence in about two-thirds of the inappropriate collocations when she studied "make" and "take" in the German learners' corpus. Nesselhauf (2005) claims that L1 influence is found in about half of the L2 collocations and found to be particularly strong with respect to minor lexical[7] and non-lexical elements. Accordingly, the fact that having participants with only one L1 background and claiming that their errors are due to L1 influence is observed across many previous studies. The present study can contribute to the studies of L2 learners' collocations by hav-

---

[7] Minor lexical elements are those elements such as the number of noun (singular/plural) and determiner, rather than the major lexical elements such as verbs and nouns.

73

ing participants with two different L1 backgrounds and examining whether their errors were due to L1 influence.

3.4 Summary

This chapter discussed the collocations in the field of second language acquisition. Firstly, the studies on the prefabs and its relevance to collocations were presented. Also, the studies on cognitive approaches in relation to collocations were introduced. Then, it is presented that there are two types of knowledge, receptive and productive, both of which the present study investigates.

While a range of studies have focused on learners of single language L1 background, the present study adopts learners of two different L1 backgrounds in order to clarify the knowledge and use of collocations in written language. Moreover, since the present study deals with L2 learners from different L1 backgrounds, French and Japanese, syntactic differences between French/Japanese and English and cognates in French and English were discussed. It is particularly important to examine whether their errors are due to L1 influence, including cognates, since it has been indicated that there are important roles of cognates in L2 vocabulary acquisition when the learners' L1 and L2 belong to the same language family, such as French and English. The existence of cognates can affect the knowledge and use of collocations by French learners. Further, the previous studies on the use of collocations by French, Japanese and other L1 backgrounds were presented. In particular, previous studies on "verb + noun" collocations and "delexicalised verb + noun" ones were presented since half of the collocations the present study adopts include them.

In the next chapter, research questions and the tasks adopted for the current research will be presented.

Chapter 4

RESEARCH QUESTIONS AND
DATA COLLECTION INSTRUMENTS

4.1 Introduction

In spite of the importance of collocations for the successful mastery of reading/listening/oral/writing skills, it is difficult for L2 learners to learn them. Sufficient research has not been performed thus far comparing learners of different L1 backgrounds. Thus, the present study performs cross-linguistic comparison of French and Japanese speakers learning English.

This chapter presents the research questions of the present study and the data collection instruments adopted to answer the questions. Firstly, the research questions which investigate the knowledge and use of L2 English collocations by French and Japanese learners of English are presented. Secondly, the collocation categories and collocation types selected in the present study are described. Thirdly, the procedure of selecting collocations and the pilot studies carried out to the L1 speakers of English and French L2 learners are presented. Fourthly, the participants and procedures of the tasks are explained. Lastly, the three types of data collection instruments adopted in the study are described in detail: Multiple Choice Questions (MCQ) Tasks, Translation Tasks and Learner Corpus Investigation.

4.2 Research Questions

French and Japanese are classified into typologically different groups; French is included in the group of Indo-European, Romance languages whereas Japanese is a non-Indo-European in the unidentified language group (Tsunoda 1991). As it was indicated in the previous chapters, earlier studies on the use of collocations by L2 learners have focused mainly on those learners with Indo-European language backgrounds such as French, German and Polish, while research into learners with non-Indo-European backgrounds such as Japanese, Chinese, Korean is still scarce.

The previous studies have not fully investigated the followings:

1) whether and to what extent the learners' L1 influences their receptive and productive knowledge of collocations; and
2) the differences and/or similarities between learners of different L1s in their knowledge and use of English collocations.

Therefore, the present study investigates learners' knowledge and use of collocations by comparing two groups of learners with different L1s: Indo-European (French) students and non-Indo-European (Japanese) students. The 'knowledge' is used to mean 'receptive knowledge' and 'use' is used to mean 'productive knowledge' in the present study interchangeably.

Moreover, earlier research methodology depended on only one or two types of data elicitation instruments, such as cloze task and translation task. The present study addresses the following research questions using three different data elicitation instruments.

Research Question 1:

How different is the French and Japanese learners' L1 influence in their responses?

Research Question 2:

How different are the French and Japanese learners' responses depending on the two combinations of combinability and semantic transparency of collocations, i.e. [+Restricted Combinability, +Transparency] and [-Restricted Combinability, -Transparency]?

In order to answer the above research questions, a list of collocations were first selected based on the pilot study with the L1 speakers' of English, and the selected collocations were provided to French and Japanese learners in the form of both Multiple Choice Questions (MCQ) Tasks and Translation Tasks. The data from the two types of tasks are then analysed concerning respective categories of collocations in relation to their overall accuracy and their L1 influence. Moreover, the target collocations used in MCQ and Translation Tasks is adopted in the investigation of learner corpora. Thus, the two types of tasks and the French and Japanese learner corpora are the instruments to be used in the present study. MCQ Tasks are adopted predominantly for the investigation of receptive knowledge and Translation Tasks are mainly for the investigation of productive knowledge. Receptive knowledge of collocations was defined by Nation (1990) as the ability to recognize appropriate words that comes before or after another word. The following sections present the research methodology adopted in the present study more in detail.

4.3 Selection of Target Collocations

The collocations which the present study deals with are frequent collocations found in British National Corpus (BNC) and selected according to the two criteria: collocation categories and collocation types. Collocation categories indicate grammatical structures of collocations, such as "verb + noun", and collocation types are semantic types of collocations, such as [+/- Transparency], and possibilities of combinations with other collocates, such as [+/- Restricted Combinability]. They are discussed in the followings.

4.3.1 Lexical Categories of Collocations

The following four categories of collocations were selected for the present study:

Category 1:   [Verb + Noun]
Category 2:   [Delexicalised Verb + Noun]
Category 3:   [Adjective + Noun]
Category 4:   [Adverb + Adjective]

The nodes of each collocation type are: nouns in Category 1, Category 2, and Category 3, and adjectives in Category 4.

Category 1: [Verb + Noun]

It has been suggested that the [verb + noun] combinations 'tend to form the communicative core of utterances where the most important information is placed' (Altenberg, 1993:227). For example, "lose weight", "attend the meeting", and "cross the border" are included in the [verb + noun] lexical category.

Category 2: [Delexicalized Verb + Noun]

The significance and difficulties of learning [delexicalised verb + noun] collocations for learners have already been indicated by Biskup (1992), Chi *et al.* (1994) and Howarth (1996). Delexicalized verbs are verbs such as "have" in "have a look" or "make" in "make a promise" whose original meaning disappears when they combine with certain nouns.

Investigation into the use of these [delexicalised verb + noun] combinations by Chinese learners has been carried out by Chi *et al.* (1994) who examined the verbs "have", "make", "take", "do" and "get" from a one-million-word corpus based on essays. They found that using these combinations is difficult even for advanced level learners. (See Section 3.3.2)

Category 3: [Adjective + Noun]

[Adjective + noun] combinations are less frequently used by L1 speakers than [verb + noun] combinations but are identified as useful combinations by Benson (1985) since they are frequently used by L1 speakers, and frequency is considered to be one of the criteria of 'usefulness'. This category of collocations is beneficial for L2 learners and considered as one of the categories which should be included in dictionaries (Benson 1985). However, they have received scant coverage in previous research. For example, "next week", "poor health" and "tight control" are included in this category.

Category 4: [Adverb + Adjective]

As mentioned earlier in Section 3.3.2, the acquisition of [adverb + adjective] combinations among French learners of English has been studied (Granger 1998), but there has not been any study of the acquisition of this type of collocations among Japanese learners. [Adverb + adjective] collocations are considered to be difficult for learners, as studies with French learners have indicated (Granger 1998), but they have not yet fully studied. For example, "highly likely", "heavily involved" and "fully aware" are included in this lexical category.

4.3.2 Collocation Types

In order to answer the research questions described in Section 4.2, two types of collocations were selected based on the combinability and transparency of collocations by adopting: 1) [+/-Restricted Combinability] according to the possibility that a node in a collocation can combine with one or two/more than three words; and 2) [+/-Transparency] based on whether a word has its primary/dominant meaning in a collocation. In the present study, the primary meaning is determined to be the very first meaning among the list of meanings for a word in the dictionaries. However, as I will point out in the last chapter in the present study, the primacy in semantics is not mentioned in the present study in view of diachronic considerations. The definitions here, thus, are provisional. Similarly, the learners approach L2 collocations by trying to derive them from the original meaning is not a presupposition but a hypothesis in the present study. By examining the lexical characteristics of collocations, more definite tendencies in the knowledge and use of collocations by the French and Japanese learners will be revealed.

The present study examines the following two types of collocations among three types of collocations shown in Section 2.2.1 based on the two criteria: combinability and transparency.

1) + Restricted Combinability / + Transparency (literal in meaning)
2) – Restricted Combinability / -Transparency (figurative in meaning)

The first group contains those collocations in which the node can be combined only with one or two possible words ([+ResComb]) and in which a collocate has literal features in meaning (i.e. if a collocate, "verb" in a "verb + noun" collocation, for example, has a literal meaning, it is classified as [+Transp] even if a noun in a "verb + noun" collocation has figurative meaning). The second group holds collocations that are not restricted in combinability (i.e. the node can be combined with three or more possible words) with non-literal or figurative meaning (i.e. if a collocate, "verb" in a "verb + noun" collocation, for example, has a non-literal or figurative meaning, it is classified as [-Transp] even if a noun in a "verb + noun" collocation has literal meaning).

In the present study, whether the collocations are [+/-Transparency] was decided based on the definitions of a word in a collocation in several dictionaries such as the *Longman Dictionary of Contemporary English* (2003), the *Oxford Advanced Learner's Dictionary* (1990), and the *Cambridge Advanced Learner's Dictionary* (2005). These dictionaries contain the elements useful for learners[1]

---

[1] For example, the *Longman Dictionary of Contemporary English* (2003) includes the top 3,000 most frequent words so that learners can note their significance, as well as many examples to help learners understand words in context.

and are used frequently. A collocation is classed as [+Transparency] when one of the words are used in their primary literal sense, and as [-Transparency] when either of the words in the collocations are used in their figurative sense. For example, the verb "meet" has a meaning of "to go to a place where someone will be at a particular time, according to an arrangement, so that you can talk or do something together" as its literal sense in the *Longman Dictionary of Contemporary English* (2003), as can be seen in "Meet me at 8:00". On the other hand, when it is used in its figurative sense, such as in "meet a need", it is used in a figurative way: "to do something that someone wants, needs, or expects you to do or be as good as they need, expect, etc". Thus, collocations involving the figurative meaning of a component word cannot be readily derived from the original meaning of the word when it is used in combination with another word. It must be remembered that although the distinction between literal and figurative collocations may not be an either-or choice, the present study tries to find words that clearly have the primary sense versus those that clearly have figurative sense.

The method to determine [+/-Restricted Combinability] of collocations was based on 14 L1-speakers' answers in the pilot study data. For example, "tell the truth" is categorised into [+Restricted Combinability] since most of the L1 speakers answered "tell" to combine with "the truth" while few of them answered "say". On the other hand, in the case of "make a speech", L1 speakers' answers were divided as to whether they chose either "make", "give" or "write". Thus, this collocation is classified as [-Restricted Combinability].

The 71 collocations selected on the basis of the pilot study (to be discussed below) were classified into 4 lexical categories, and each category has two groups based on the collocation criteria as shown Table 4.1. The decision whether the collocations can be grouped into [+ResComb, +Transp] or [-ResComb, -Transp] was made. In addition, since one of the target language groups in this current study is Japanese learners whose English language education was greatly influenced by American English, data were also collected from two American L1 English speakers[2]. The comparison revealed that British and American data were mostly similar. The examples of the collocations in each group are shown below:

Table 4.1 List of Collocations by Collocation Category and Criteria

Group	Collocation Category	Collocation Criteria		No. of items	Examples
		Restricted Combinability	Transparency		
1-a	[Verb + Noun]	+	+	10	*attend the meeting*
1-b		-	-	8	*meet/answer the needs*
2-a	[Delexicalized	+	+	9	*keep records*
2-b	Verb + Noun]	-	-	10	*make/give a speech*
3-a	[Adjective +	+	+	10	*high fever*
3-b	Noun]	-	-	7	*heavy/thick fog*
4-a	[Adverb +	+	+	7	*terribly afraid*
4-b	Adjective]	-	-	10	*severely/badly affected*

Despite the 'fuzziness' between each of combinability and transparency, the present study tries to adopt values of [+/-Restricted Combinability] and [+/-Transparency] of the receptive knowledge of collocations and their production by learners of English. The decision of [+/-Transparency] is made based on the use of several dictionaries as mentioned above, while whether the collocation in question is [+/-Restricted Combinability] is defined based on Pilot Study 1 presented below.

---

[2] They are two Americans who teach English at a Japanese university.

4.4 Pilot Studies

4.4.1 Pilot Study 1: L1 Speakers of English

This section explains the pilot study with the L1 speakers of English carried out with the aim of selecting appropriate collocations.

1) Purpose

The main purpose of the Pilot Study 1 was to select the target collocations to be investigated with the L2 learners in Multiple Choice Questions Tasks and Translation Tasks. As it was discussed in the earlier chapters, only a small number of collocations have been investigated in the previous studies. (Bahns and Eldaw [1993], for example). Therefore, this Pilot Study 1 aimed to determine the appropriateness of the items of collocations of the investigation.

2) Participants

16 L1 speakers of English were asked to do a gap-fill of the target collocations with four choices given to each question. 14 of these participants were British undergraduate students at the University of London Institute in Paris aged 19-25 and 2 of them were British academics[3] who used to teach at University of London Institute in Paris. Although their length of stay in France and their French proficiency level were not collected, the students have studied French in Paris. It might be possible that they are affected by French language while they are in France.

3) Length of Time

It took 20-30 minutes to fill in the questionnaires.

---

[3] They are Dr. David Horner and Mr. Dennis Davy who used to teach at University of London Institute in Paris.

4) Procedure for Selecting Collocations for the Pilot Study 1

Among a large number of possible collocations, some 20 collocations (See Appendix 1) for each lexical category were selected for this pilot study. The first stage was to arbitrarily select some collocations consisting of [verb + noun], [delexicalized verb + noun], [adjective + noun] and [adverb + adjective]. These selected collocations were chosen from the same set of the dictionaries mentioned in Section 4.3.2 and *The BBI Dictionary of English Word Combinations* (Benson *et al.*: 1997). Among these dictionaries, *Oxford Collocations Dictionary for Students of English* (2005), for example, contains the 9,000 headwords most of which are the commonest words in the language. The main source used for *Oxford Collocations Dictionary for Students of English* (2005), for example, is the 100-million-word British National Corpus which contains both spoken and written data of British English. The collocations more commonly used in the written or spoken language were selected in this dictionary.

While the first selection of the collocations that was expected to be familiar and appropriate for intermediate learners was basically an arbitrary, subjective decision, they were then checked in the British National Corpus online (http://www.natcorp.ox.ac.uk), the largest L1 English speaker corpus which consists of a 100-million-word collection of samples of written and spoken language. The purpose at this stage was to ensure that the collocations intuitively selected are actually frequent in the British National Corpus (BNC). Thus, those collocations which scored more than fifty hits in the BNC were considered to be appropriate for the present study and many such collocations were included. Seventy one target collocations consist of 18 collocations of [verb + noun], 19 collocations of [delexicalised verb + noun], 17 collocations of [adjective + noun] and 17 collocations of [adverb + adjective] (See Appendix 1).

The selection of sentences used in the tasks was based on the BNC with some modification. The sentences had to be simplified on many occasions because of problems such as cognitive processing load, discourse, complexity, context and register. For example, when it was decided to include the collocation "tell the truth" the BNC had the sentence "You should tell the truth".[4] However, as this sentence without any context does not provide sufficient clue to answer for the participants, the sentence was modified with more context: "Parents should tell the truth to their children". Those modifications and simplifications were discussed and decided with the advice of two British L1 linguists. Many of the sentences were made up for the purpose of the present study. Once collocations to be included were selected, they were double-checked and distracters and unexpected answers were identified. Double-checking process involves checking the cognitive processing load, complexity and register of the modified and simplified sentences including the target collocations with the advice of the British L1 linguists.

5) Design

The 71 collocations presented in the sentences were given to 14 L1 speakers of English in the form of a gap-fill to be completed with an appropriate collocation. They were then asked to rate how confident they were about their responses by ticking "sure", "fairly sure", "not sure" or "guess". For example, "pick up/answer the phone" was classified as follows by a L1 speaker of English. Each L1 speaker was allowed to give more than one response to find frequent collocations common to these L1 speakers:

When you (   ) the phone, just say "hello" and do not give your name and number.

[pick up]   1. sure ☑   2. fairly sure ☐   3. not sure ☐   4. guess ☐   .
[answer]   1. sure ☐   2. fairly sure ☑   3. not sure ☐   4. guess ☐   .

---

[4] This is a written phrase in a novel adopted for the BNC.

In this case, the L1 speaker of English was sure of his use of "pick up" and fairly sure of the use of "answer" for this collocation. The list of questionnaires was presented in Appendix 2.

6) Results

The L1 speakers' answers were counted and represented in Appendix 3. Each of their answers was examined and evaluated by the afore-mentioned two British linguists as to whether they involved inappropriate use and/or spelling mistakes. For example, regarding "single room", a L1 speaker answered "quadruple room" with a high certainty, which were not considered to be included as appropriate collocations.   In terms of "lose weight", several L1 speakers made errors, such as "loose" instead of "lose", which were considered to be spelling mistakes.   Those collocations which were considered to be appropriate and answered frequency with high certainty were selected for L2 investigation.

There were 15 answers which were found to be inappropriate, and were therefore excluded from the list. For example, "flush the toilet" was meant to be [−ResComb, +Transp], but many L1 speakers answered other several words instead of "flush" to combine with "the toilet" because of the insufficient contextual information. Accordingly, the number of collocations on the revised version of list to be provided to the learners of English was reduced to 56, which are listed below. These 56 collocations were further tested in the Pilot Study 2, described in the next section.

Table 4.2 Selected Collocations after Pilot Study 1

1)-a: [Verb + Noun] / [+ResComb, +Transp]

1. tell the truth
2. draw a line
3. win the match
4. lose weight
5. read music
6. ask her a question
7. attend the meeting
8. play the violin
9. cross the border

1)-b: [Verb + Noun] / [-ResComb, -Transp]

10. blow/wipe/pick one's nose
11. answer/pick up the phone
12. offer/provide/give an opportunity
13. gain/get experiences
14. answer/meet/fulfil the needs
15. reach/arrive at/come to a conclusion

2)-a: [Delexicalized Verb + Noun] / [+ResComb, +Transp]

16. keep records
17. do you good
18. take a picture
19. keep a secret
20. do (me) a favour
21. have the (same) effect
22. give (me) a ring

2)-b: [Delexicalized Verb + Noun] / [-ResComb, -Transp]

23. keep/write a diary
24. make/give a speech
25. take/make notes
26. have/hold talks
27. make/arrange an appointment

28. receive/obtain an answer
29. have/keep good control
30. take/have a walk

3)-a: [Adjective + Noun] / [+ResComb, +Transp]

31. bad habit
32. long flight
33. high fever
34. main meal
35. next week
36. single room
37. common sense

3)-b: [Adjective + Noun] / [-ResComb, -Transp]

38. poor/ill/bad health
39. thick/heavy fog
40. high/large population
41. free/spare/leisure time
42. high/good standard
43. tight/strict control
44. poor/bad/low quality

4)-a: [Adverb + Adjective] / [+ResComb, +Transp]

45. only natural (to do)
46. extremely serious (about)
47. highly unlikely
48. terribly afraid (of)
49. highly recommended

4)-b: [Adverb + Adjective] / [-ResComb, -Transp]

50. terribly/completely lost
51. extremely/totally different
52. fully/certainly/perfectly aware
53. badly/severely affected
54. highly/extremely competent
55. deeply/heavily involved
56. bitterly/extremely cold

4.4.2 Pilot Study 2: French L2 Learners

In Pilot Study 1, the list of target collocations was fine-tuned by the results of L1 speakers of English. As the next step before the actual assessment of those target collocations to L2 learners, Pilot Study 2 was administered.

1) Purpose

It was necessary to confirm whether the tasks including the selected collocations would actually work with L2 learners without problems.

2) Participants

10 French learners of English participated. They were undergraduate students at the University of London Institute in Paris. Their level was indicated as intermediate by the teachers who were teaching them at that time. Since Japanese learners of English for Pilot Study 2 were not available at this point in time, only French learners participated. A potential problem of not having Japanese learners in the pilot study is that the questions may be difficult for them to answer. Thus, the collocations were chosen carefully based on the author's teaching experience of Japanese intermediate learners. The average length of studying English at the time of the experiment was 7 years. The use of a dictionary was not allowed.

3) Length of Time

It took 20-30 minutes to answer all the questions.

4) Design

The French L1 speakers were provided with the fifty-six collocations in the form of MCQ gap-fill tasks with four alternatives from which they were required to choose the appropriate item(s). The alternatives included English translations of possible French and Japanese equivalent collocations and the items obtained from the English L1-speaker in the pilot study discussed in the earlier sections. An example is shown below:

Parents should (   ) the truth to their children.

a) inform   b) say   c) tell   d) speak

In this case, "c) tell" is the most frequently-used likely answer, whereas "a) inform" and "b) say" did not appear in the English L1 speaker data, although "d) speak" did to a small degree. In this case, the French and Japanese L1 equivalents are "b) say" and/or "c) tell" individually.

5) Results

Since the French learners completed the task within the given time (25-30 minutes), at least in terms of time to finish the task, the 56 collocations were regarded as appropriate and were adopted in the Multiple Choice Question (MCQ) and Translation Tasks. These collocations were classified into four lexical categories with approximately the same number of collocations in each lexical category. The complete version of the collocations list is shown in Table 4.2.

4.5 Participants and Procedure of MCQ and Translation Tasks

4.5.1 Participants

1) French Learners

34 French learners participated in MCQ Tasks and 29 participated in Translation Tasks. The level of the French learners measured by the Association of Language Testers in Europe (ALTE) 5-point scale is 3, or using the Common European Framework of Reference (CEFR) level B2[5]. The author accepted the

---

[5] The CEFR provides six levels of language proficiency from A1/A2, B1/B2 to C1/C2. Learners in the A group are called 'Basic User', the B group, 'Independent User',

teacher's report that the students' levels were measured at the beginning of their academic year by the test which was designed in reference with CEFR. They were undergraduates studying English part-time at the University of London Institute in Paris (ULIP). In this regard, the status of the French participants is not exactly the same as the Japanese participants who are full-time students. All the French students are L1 speakers of French who live in France. Most of the French learners had studied English for 7 years before entering university. The number of years they studied in English is similar to that of the Japanese learners. The ages of the learners are from 19 to 45 years old.

As is mentioned earlier, the CEFR consists of not only spoken but also written language as a standard of measurements of learners' level. Among the 6 levels, which can be further divided depending on the purpose, i.e. understanding consisting of listening and reading, speaking, and writing, the French learners are categorised into B2 level. For the B2 level ability is described as 'I can write clear, detailed text on a wide range of subjects related to my interests. I can write an essay or report, passing on information or giving reasons in support of or against a particular point of view. I can write letters highlighting the personal significance of events and experiences' (Council of Europe 2001:27).

2) Japanese Learners

30 Japanese learners participated in MCQ Tasks and 38 Japanese learners in Translation Tasks. The numbers of years of studying English is from 6 to 7 years. They are third- or fourth-year non-English-major undergraduate students at two Japanese universities. All the Japanese learners had studied Eng-

---

and the C group, 'Proficient User'. Learners at B2 level can, for example, 'understand the main ideas of complex text on both concrete and abstract topic, including technical discussion in his/her field of specialisation' (Council of Europe 2001:24). They can also 'interact with a degree of fluency and spontaneity that makes regular interaction with L1 speakers quite possible without strain for either party' (*ibid.*) and can 'produce clear, detailed text on a wide range of subjects and explain a viewpoint on a topical issue giving the advantages and disadvantages of various options' (*ibid.*:24).

lish for 6 years before entering university since they started learning English at the age of 13. The ages of the learners are from 19 to 25 years old. The level of Japanese learners, on the other hand, is not measured by the same standard but by TOEIC (Test of English for International Communication) and/or the Test in Practical English Proficiency (Eiken), which is the major test taken by many Japanese students. Although CEFR has attracted many Japanese educational specialists, categorising learners based on CEFR has not yet been adopted for the Japanese learners. However, there are differences in the criteria of proficiency criteria between CEFR and TOEIC. One of the differences between CEFR and TOEIC is that CEFR is a framework of reference for languages which are designed to be used in learning, teaching and assessment in European countries, while TOEIC is one of the tests for L2 learners'. Thus, CEFR is used as a framework of reference for a curriculum design of an educational institution, for example.

But according to the equivalency table between CEFR, TOEIC, TOEFL and Eiken (Tannenbaum & Wylie 2004), those who are at the level of 2nd grade in Test in Practical English Proficiency in Japan are approximately equivalent to the B1 level of the CEFR. Thus the French participants in the present study were more proficient (B2) than the Japanese participants (B1). The learners at B1 level can 'understand the main point of clear standard input on familiar matters regularly encountered in work, school, leisure, etc.'(Council of Europe 2001: 24). They can also 'deal with most situations likely to arise whilst travelling in an area where the language is spoken' and can 'produce simple connected text on topics which are familiar or of personal interest'. They 'can describe experiences and events, dreams, hopes and ambitions and briefly give reasons and explanations for opinions and plans' (Council of Europe 2001:24).

Although the Japanese learners are considered as 'Independent User' of English by CEFR, the French learners belong to a higher level of group (B2 defined in CEFR) than the Japanese learners (equivalent to B1 defined in

CEFR). The possibility that this small difference of the participant levels may lead to different results are considered when analyzing the data.

4.5.2 Procedure

The tasks were carried out in the classrooms without the use of a dictionary. The time given for MCQ Tasks is 25 minutes whereas for Translation Tasks it took 30 minutes to complete all tasks in the questionnaires. These two types of tasks were carried out on a separate date by separate groups of each of French and Japanese participants.

4.6 Data Collection Instruments

The aim of applying the two types of tasks and learner corpus investigation is to compare the results found in the two types of tasks and those in learner corpus by French and Japanese learners. The reason for adopting the two tasks instead of just one is, as was previously mentioned, that learners react differently in different tasks (Larsen-Freeman & Long 1991; Källkvist 1999). Many recent studies on learners' collocations have not applied multiple tasks but adopted only one method, corpora. Only a few studies administered both cloze task and translation task to the same participants (Bahns and Eldaw 1993). However, as was mentioned earlier, one type of task can only allow the investigation of one aspect of learners' interlanguage. It is important to make comparisons between different types of tasks in order to discover the whole nature of the L1 influence from different points of view. Moreover, although translation task has been adopted by several researchers (Biscup 1992; Bahns 1993; Farghal and Obiedat 1995), they did not systematically consider the types of collocations in their studies. Thus, the present study uses two types of tasks and learner corpus investigation to answer the research questions.

4.6.1 Multiple Choice Question (MCQ) Tasks

1) Purposes and Outline of the Tasks

In order to investigate the learners' receptive knowledge of collocations, the present study used Multiple Choice Question (MCQ) Tasks. MCQ Tasks involve a series of gap-fills for four categories of lexical collocations: [verb+noun], [delexicalised verb+noun], [adjective+noun] and [adverb+adjective]. MCQ Tasks require learners to fill the gap by selecting possible answers from the four given alternatives.

Multiple-choice tests are one of the most widely used methods of vocabulary assessment (Read 2000; Nation 2001). One of the reasons for MCQ tasks being popular in language testing is that they are easy to score and, if the choices are not closely related to each other, learners can draw on partial knowledge (Nation 2001:349). According to Nist and Olejnik (1995), who measured learning from context and dictionary definitions using four different tests[6] for each word, multiple-choice tests were the easiest ones for college freshmen.

2) Format of the Questionnaires in the Tasks

MCQ tasks are designed to examine French and Japanese learners' receptive knowledge of the [+ResComb, +Transp] and [-ResComb, -Transp] collocations. The tasks contain a list of collocations with blanks to be filled in for each collocation. Each question has four possible answers from which one (sometimes more than one) must be selected. Each sentence was presented with a gap which had to be filled with one of the alternatives given for that sentence. For example, learners have to fill the gap with one of the four alternatives for the following sentence:

---

[6] 1) a multiple-choice test for meanings, 2) a multiple-choice tests of examples, 3) asking learners to write a sentence to illustrate the word and 4) sentence completion.

Can you (   ) a secret?

a. hold   b. guard   c. protect   d. keep

In this sentence, "keep" should be chosen as the correct answer since none of the other three alternatives are used with "a secret" to mean not to tell anyone about a secret that you know.

The advantage of this type of task is that it is possible to investigate whether the learners' L1 influences the chosen alternatives by looking at each of the incorrect answers. In most of the questions the distracters for each item include both congruent and incongruent translation equivalents of the learners' L1, French and Japanese, since it is assumed that the learners might be tempted to choose them because of their L1 influence. In the case of French L1 congruent alternative, the L1 congruent translation equivalent is selected in terms of either the formal or semantic convergence to English. For example, a [verb + noun] collocation, "answer the phone", the French L1 congruent translation equivalent is "répondre" in "répondre au téléphone", which is semantically congruent to French. For the words which are not formally congruent to English, semantically congruent words to English were selected. In the case of Japanese L1 congruent alternative, the semantic convergent words were selected because the formal convergence between English and Japanese does not necessarily exist[7].

These tasks are, therefore, useful both in analyzing the research questions which examine the receptive knowledge of [+ResComb, +Transp] and [-ResComb, -Transp] collocations by both French and Japanese learners and in investigating L1 influence on the results of the tasks.

Both formal and semantic equivalence to their L1s will be discussed when analysing the results obtained from MCQ Tasks. Each question in MCQ Tasks contains both French and Japanese L1 equivalent items in the four alternatives.

---

[7] There are a small number of cases in which loanwords are involved in collocations.

Despite the popularity of MCQ Tasks, there are some disadvantages as well. Constructing MCQ Tasks for the present study was not easy. Constructing MCQ Tasks required field-testing and refinement; it was necessary to examine the L1 speakers' results of collocations followed by piloting with a small number of French learners prior to the real investigation with French and Japanese learners. Wesche and Paribakht (1996:17) point out several limitations of multiple choice tests for assessing lexical knowledge. One of the limitations they suggest seems to apply to the MCQ in the present study that "this formats permits only a very limited sampling of the learner's total vocabulary (Wesche and Paribakht 1996: 17). In order to compensate for the limitations of MCQ Tasks, it is necessary to provide a different type of tasks to gain a more objective outcome from the results. Thus, the present study adopts Translation Tasks which is presented in the next section.

3) Methods of Analysis

The scoring of accuracy was carried out: 1) by counting the correct answers; 2) by extracting the number of wrong answers from the number of correct answers. Some of the questions in the [-ResComb, -Transp] group of collocations have more than one correct item. In the case the learners chose more than one correct answers, the number of the correct answers are counted as the scores. The number of incorrect answer(s) was extracted from the number of correct answers if there's any. Thus the raw numbers of correct answers in each collocation type is different depending on the collocation types.

The overall accuracy of the French and Japanese learners is calculated with respect to all the four lexical categories of collocations. One-way ANOVA was used for the comparison of overall means in each lexical category. In order to examine whether there are significant differences in their choices of alternatives between the French and Japanese learners, chi square test was conducted. The items of collocations which showed significant differences are discussed in terms of the likelihood of L1 influence.

In relation to influence of [+ResComb, +Transp] and [-ResComb, -Transp], the accuracy of French and Japanese learners in the [+ResComb, +Transp] and [-ResComb, -Transp] groups of collocations is examined with the use of two-way ANOVA with the accuracy as the dependent variable and the language group and collocation type ([+ResComb, +Transp] and [-ResComb, -Transp]) as the independent variables.

In addition to analyzing the differences of means of accuracy between the French and Japanese learners, the present study analyzes whether there is significant differences in the French and Japanese learners' choices of alternatives in MCQ Tasks. Thus, chi-square test is utilized to find the significant differences of the results by measuring the frequencies of categories (Field 2009:687-688). The French and Japanese learners are provided with the same alternatives in MCQ Tasks. Further data analysis is carried out in terms of the collocations which showed significant differences between French and Japanese learners, rather than to compare all 56 collocation results against one another.

4.6.2 Translation Tasks

1) Purposes and Outline of the Tasks

In order to investigate the learners' productive knowledge of collocations, the present study uses Translation Tasks for both French and Japanese learners. Translation Tasks involve a series of gap-fills for four categories of lexical collocations: [verb+noun], [delexicalised verb + noun], [adjective + noun] and [adverb + adjective]. The gaps the learners are required to fill are not the words in a collocations but collocations as unit. Translation Tasks will require the learners to translate their L1 collocations into English collocations. The difference between the MCQ Tasks and the translation task is that they are required to produce appropriate collocations and/or appropriate structures of word combinations in given sentences. Translation Tasks can compensate for the limitations of MCQ Tasks because they require learners to elicit their knowledge of collocations based on their L1 version of collocations in the tasks.

However, there is a limitation of Translation Tasks that the tasks are likely to invite L2 learners to use L1 knowledge because the tasks require L2 learners to translate from L1 to L2. Thus, learner corpora investigation analysis can rectify this limitation to a certain extent.

2) Format of the Questionnaires in the Tasks

Translation Tasks for the French and Japanese learners were designed to fill in the collocations in the parenthesis:

Les parents doivent dire la vérité à leur enfants.

Parents should (   ) to their children.

The L1 translation equivalents used on the questionnaires were the translation given by a L1 French academic and a L1 Japanese academic respectively.[8] Each version of Translation Tasks was then undertaken with about five French and Japanese people.

3) Methods of Analysis

The responses obtained from Translation Tasks are divided into three categories: 1) acceptable; 2) infelicitous; and 3) wrong answers. The decision is made with the support of two British L1 speakers[9]. Based on the categorization of the answers, a three-way ANOVA (2 levels of language group: French and Japanese, 2 levels of collocation type: [+ResComb, +Transp] and [-ResComb, -Transp], and 4 levels of lexical category: [verb + noun], [delexicalised verb + noun], [adjective + noun] and [adverb + adjective]) was performed. The dependent variable was the accuracy of the French and Japanese learners' responses. The independent variables were language group and collocation types,

---

[8] The expressions utilized in the test were checked by a French L1 professor of English. Thus, this is a French standard expression for the English sentence.
[9] They are mentioned in the footnote of Section 4.3.2.

i.e. [+ResComb, +Transp] and [-ResComb, -Transp] and lexical category of collocations, i.e. [verb + noun], [delexicalised verb + noun], [adjective + noun] and [adverb + adjective].

With the focus on the infelicitous and wrong answers, the types of mistakes are divided into seven categories: 'wrong choice of verbs'; 'wrong choice of nouns'; 'adding or losing determiners'; and 'singular/plural forms' and so forth. Then the tendencies found in the individual lexical category of collocations are discussed and analyzed.

4.6.3 Learner Corpus Investigation

1) Purposes

In addition to the two kinds of tasks requiring, the present study investigates the productive use of collocations in learner corpora, available in a published CD-ROM and on a website. The aim of the present study is to investigate whether the features or tendencies of learners' use of collocations found in MCQ and Translation Tasks will be also found in learner corpora, i.e. in practical language use.

2) The Use of *International Corpus of Learner English (ICLE)*

The learner corpus used in the present study was compiled by the *International Corpus of Learner English (ICLE)* which is the largest publicly available learner corpus to date, consisting of two million words of EFL (English as a Foreign Language) learners' writings from many different countries, mainly in Europe. This corpus contains eleven sub-corpora consisting of English written by learners from eleven different L1s. They currently include Bulgarian, Czech, Dutch, Finnish, French, German, Italian, Polish, Russian, Spanish and Swedish. Founded and coordinated by Granger at the University of Louvain in Belgium, the ICLE project has been collecting learners' writing since 1990 and Japanese has been added recently. The level of the target learners in this corpus are defined as ranging from higher intermediate to advanced learners (approximately B2 and higher level of CEFR) according to the description of the ICLE[10] though any basis for measuring their levels is not demonstrated. The French learners in the sub-corpus are 88% female and are all university undergraduates in their early twenties and they have been studying English at University for three to four years. The written material collected was mainly essay material in which students set out to defend a given opinion, having an average length of 657 words.[11] Covering a wide range of topics, essays were given with titles asking for opinions about a place for dreaming and imagination, rather than science, technology and industrialization, for example.

The Japanese sub-corpus has not yet been officially included in the above-mentioned ICLE learner corpus at the time of the present study. In the present study, therefore, another Japanese sub-corpus is used, compiled by Dr. Kaneko Tomoko at Showa Women's University and working as one of the branch groups of the ICLE project. She offers her data of Japanese university undergraduate writings for non-commercial use on her website (www.tomoko-kaneko.com). The procedures taken for compiling these data are exactly the same as those in the ICLE project.

The advantage of using a learner corpus is that it contains a large amount of data which allows as many collocations as possible to be analysed. Also, essays require more productive skills from learners than in MCQ Tasks and Translation Tasks. No kind of clue is provided in the essay but learners need to produce the language by themselves by accessing their mental lexicon as much as possible. L1 is less likely to influence the use of English collocations than the translation tasks, and thus it helps to verify the findings obtained in the translation tasks. In spite of the time consumed digitizing the data, essays have been

---

[10] Granger *et al.* (2002:14) indicates that because 'a quick look at some sample essays shows that the corpus displays differences in proficiency level,… it seems therefore more appropriate to say that the proficiency level ranges from higher intermediate to advanced'.

[11] Although the collocations investigated in the present study are not necessarily likely to be featured in written expository texts, this ICLE was the only French and Japanese learner corpora available at this time.

a popular method of examining learners' productive written language. Because of these advantages, previously, researchers have studied the use of collocations by learners from different L1 backgrounds (see Section 3.4), and indeed this is now the most popular method, associated with the rise of corpus linguistics.

The frequency of the items of collocations used in both the MCQ and Translation Tasks in the learner corpora was counted. The frequency of the collocations of each lexical category, such as "verb + noun", "delexicalised verb + noun" etc., in each French and Japanese corpus was compared.

4.7 Summary

This chapter presented the procedures of this present study, including the research questions, selection of target collocations, the format of the question-naires in the tasks, and two Pilot Studies.

Since the previous studies have not fully investigated the knowledge and use of collocations by L2 learners in relation to their L1 influence of different L1 backgrounds, the present study examines them by comparing French and Japanese learners whose L2 backgrounds are typologically different. Also, the previous studies have not fully examined the L2 learners' knowledge and use of collocations by considering the properties of collocations such as combinability and semantic transparency. Then the two research questions to be investigated are presented in Section 4.2: 1) How different is the French and Japanese learners' L1 influence in their responses?; 2) How different are the French and Japanese learners' responses depending on the two combinations of combinability and semantic transparency of collocations, i.e. [+Restricted Combinability, +Transparency] and [-Restricted Combinability, -Transparency]?

Following the research questions, the procedures of selecting target collo-cations were presented, and showed the significance of the processes of devel-oping, validating and refining the target collocations to be given to the L2 learners. Before the implementation of the tasks with the L2 learners, two pilot studies were carried out. In Pilot Study 1, the 71 randomly selected collocations were given to L1 speakers of English to examine the L1 speakers' choice of words to complete the collocation in gap-fill sentences and their confidence in their choice. Their responses are examined to exclude problematic items. The revised version of fifty-six collocations was then administered to French learners of English in Pilot Study 2 to determine the appropriateness of the items of collocations.

The descriptions of the three selected types of instruments were presented: MCQ Tasks, Translation Tasks and Learner Corpus Investigation. MCQ Tasks investigate learners' responses to the target collocations in the form of gap-fill items, whereas Translation Tasks will require learners to produce the target collocations that correspond to their L1 translations. Learner Corpus Investigation uses both French and Japanese learner corpora to examine whether the target collocations were actually used in free essay writing. In the following chapters, the results and analysis of the tasks are presented.

Chapter 5

RESULTS AND ANALYSIS OF
MULTIPLE CHOICE QUESTIONS TASKS

5.1 Introduction

In the previous chapter, the research questions and data collection instruments to be investigated in the present study were presented. It was shown that most of the previous research written in English have focused mainly on learners from Indo-European language backgrounds but not on the learners from non-Indo-European language backgrounds, such as Japanese, and any contrastive study of the knowledge and use of collocations by learners from different L1 backgrounds has not been carried out. Moreover, with regard to the data collection instruments adopted for the studies on the learners' knowledge and use of collocations, most of the research already undertaken has chosen only one type of task, such as translation tasks. However, research on task-type effects has shown that learners can show different reactions depending on the types of tasks (Ellis 1994; Källkvist 1999). In order to compensate for the gap between different types of tasks with respect to the learners' knowledge and use of collocations, two types of data collection instruments were used in the present study: Multiple Choice Questions (MCQ) and Translation Tasks. MCQ Tasks were used to investigate receptive knowledge and Translation Tasks were used to study productive knowledge of collocations. This chapter presents the results obtained from MCQ tasks by both French and Japanese learners. The results of the descriptive statistics will be firstly presented based on the raw scores obtained from the tasks which are then analyzed in more detail using ANOVA.

Firstly, the overall comparative accuracy between the French and Japanese learners with respect to all the four lexical categories of collocations is presented. One-way ANOVA was used for the comparison of overall means in each lexical category. Secondly, in order to examine whether there are significant differences in their choices of alternatives between the French and Japanese learners, chi square test was conducted. Then, the items of collocations which showed significant differences were examined in terms of the likelihood of L1 influence. Thirdly, the accuracy of French and Japanese learners in the [+ResComb, +Transp] and [-ResComb, -Transp] groups of collocations is presented respectively. This question is examined with the use of two-way ANOVA with the accuracy as the dependent variable and the language group and collocation type ([+ResComb, +Transp] and [-ResComb, -Transp]) as the independent variables. Finally, this analysis investigates whether and how the learners' L1 and combinability/transparency influence the learners' recognition of collocations.

5.2 Overall Results of French and Japanese Learners

The overall raw scores and the percentages of the responses by French and Japanese learners are computed as shown in Appendix 5. Based on the overall results of the raw scores, more detailed analysis of the responses of French and Japanese learners is performed using statistical tests. The calculation of overall accuracy was carried out: 1) by counting the correct answers; 2) by dividing them by the total number of answers by each of the French and Japanese learners. Some of the questions in the [-ResComb, -Transp] group of collocations have more than one correct item. In the case the learners chose more than one correct answers, the number of the correct answers were counted as the scores. The number of incorrect answer(s) was extracted from the number of correct

answers if there's any. Thus the raw numbers of correct answers in each collocation type is different depending on the collocation types.

Firstly, the mean scores of overall accuracy of French and Japanese learners
by lexical category, as shown in Table 5.1, shows how the accuracy of the
French and Japanese learners differ depending on the lexical categories of
collocations.

Table 5.1 Mean Scores of Overall Accuracy by Lexical Category

Lexical Category	Language Group	Number of students	Mean Scores
1) Verb + Noun	French	34	12.15
	Japanese	30	12.70
2) Delexicalised Verb + Noun	French	34	12.21
	Japanese	30	12.90
3) Adjective + Noun	French	34	12.65
	Japanese	30	12.50
4) Adverb + Adjective	French	34	8.82
	Japanese	30	7.83

The one-way ANOVA shows that none of the four lexical categories
shows significant differences between the responses of French and Japanese
learners:

1) [verb + noun] group of collocations: $F(1,62)= 0.86, p= .36.$

2) [delexicalised verb + noun] group of collocations: $F(1,62)=1.12, p= .29.$

3) [adjective + noun] group of collocations: $F(1,62)= .057, p= .81.$

4) [adverb + adjective] group of collocations: $F(1,62)=2.73, p= .10.$

5.3 Results of Chi Square Test

This section discusses whether the responses in the MCQ Tasks show significant differences between the results of the French and Japanese learners. The comparison was made in terms of the different choices made by French and Japanese learners respectively by the use of the chi-square test. The chi square test was performed for all the 56 items of collocations. The dependent variable was the number of alternatives the learners chose in each item of collocations. The items with significant difference are listed as follows in each of the four lexical categories.

1)-a. Verb + Noun: [+ ResComb, + Transp] group

Among the 9 items of collocations in this category, observed response proportions differ significantly from the hypothesized proportions in the results of:

no. 5 "read music" (x^2 (3, $N=74$)$=12.9, p< .05$).

1)-b. Verb + Noun: [-ResComb, - Transp] group

Among the 6 items of collocations in this category, observed response proportions differ significantly from the hypothesized proportions in the results of:

no. 13 "gain/get experiences" ($x^2(3, N=89)=19.0, p< .05$); and

no.14 "meet/answer the needs" ($x^2(3, N=78)=7.9, p< .05$).

2)-a. Delexicalised Verb + Noun: [+ ResComb, + Transp] group

Among the 7 items of collocations, significant difference between observed response proportions and the hypothesized proportions was shown in:

no. 16 "keep records" ($x^2(3)=11.0, p< .05$);

no. 20 "do me a favour" ($x^2(3)=9.3, p< .05$); and

no.21 "has the same effect" ($x^2(3) =9.4, p< .05$).

2)-b. Delexicalised Verb + Noun: [- ResComb, - Transp] group

Among the 8 items of collocations in this category, significant difference between observed response proportions and the hypothesized proportions was found in:

no.23 "keep/write a diary" $(x^2(3) = 20.6, p < .05)$;

no.27 "make/arrange/book an appointment" $(x^2(3) = 14.2, p < .05)$; and

no. 29 "keep a good control" $(x^2(3) = 16.4, p < .05)$.

3)-a. Adjective + Noun: [+ ResComb, + Transp] group

Among the 7 items of collocations in this category, significant difference between observed response proportions and the hypothesized proportions was found in:

no. 34 "main meal" $(x^2(3) = 9.5, p < .05)$; and

no. 37. "common sense" $(x^2(3) = 10.4, p < .05)$.

3)-b. Adjective + Noun: [- ResComb, - Transp] group

Among the 7 items of collocations in this category, significant difference between observed response proportions and the hypothesized proportions was identified in:

no. 38 "poor/bad health" $(x^2(3) = 18.9, p < .05)$;

no. 39 "thick/dense fog" $(x^2(3) = 8.9, p < .05)$; and

no.40 "large/high population" $(x^2(3) = 10.8, p < .05)$.

4)-a. Adverb + Adjective: [+ ResComb, + Transp] group

Among the 5 items of collocations in this category, significant difference between observed response proportions and the hypothesized proportions was identified in:

no. 45 "only natural" $(x^2(3) = 14.9, p < .05)$; and

no.46 "extremely serious" $(x^2(3) = 11.2, p < .05)$.

4)-b. Adverb + Adjective: [- ResComb, - Transp] group

Among the 7 items of collocations in this category, significant difference between observed response proportions and the hypothesized proportions was identified in:

no. 50 "entirely/completely lost" $(x^2(2)=10.1, p< .05)$;

no.52 "fully/quite aware" $(x^2(3) =15.7, p< .05)$;

no. 54 "highly/extremely competent" $(x^2(3)=8.0, p< .05)$; and

no. 55 "deeply/heavily involved" $(x^2(3)=11.4, p< .05)$.

Since the collocations which showed significant differences are the primary focus of interest, the next sections examine the results from the following points of view:

1) whether significant differences occur due to the L1 influence of French and Japanese;

2) whether significant differences occur due to the combinability/transparency of collocations.

One of the research questions in the present study is whether there are differences and/or similarities concerning L1 influence on the choice of target collocations. As it was mentioned in Chapter 3, the discussion of L1 influence on the choice of collocations has been one of the main issues in the previous research (e.g. Granger 1998; Holmes and Ramos 1993) which assumed that L2 learners are likely to be influenced by their L1. However, few studies have been carried out as to the comparative of L1 influence between L2 learners from different L1 backgrounds. Thus, the present study intends to clarify the respective tendencies of the French and Japanese learners.

The following sections will analyse each lexical category of collocations, i.e. [verb + noun], [delexicalised verb + noun], [adjective + noun] and [adverb + adjective]. The analysis aims to clarify, in terms of L1 influence, the tendencies in relation to the receptive knowledge of collocations by the French and Japanese learners.

5.4 Learners' L1 Influence on the Collocations

The following section presents the collocations which showed significant differences between the French and Japanese learners. The likelihood of their L1 influences is discussed for each lexical category of collocations. The check mark (✓) in the tables represents the L1 equivalent likely alternative.

5.4.1 Category 1: [Verb + Noun] Collocations

With respect to the [verb + noun] category of collocations, it was found that, among the 15 collocations, 3 collocations, "read music", "gain/get experiences", "meet/answer/satisfy the needs", showed significant differences between the French and Japanese learners' responses. The data for these 3 examples are shown in Tables 5.2-5.4.

1) MCQ Task No. 5: "read music"

Whereas 71.1% of the French participants chose the correct collocate, "read", to combine with the node "music", only 30.6% of the Japanese answers were target-like. Rather, 30.6% of the Japanese answers were "understand", while only 13.2% of the French answers were found for this verb. From the viewpoint of L1 equivalent, while the French L1 equivalent, "lire la musique" corresponds exactly to "read music" semantically and syntactically, they seemed to be influenced by their L1 and their accuracy was high. The Japanese version of this collocation is "gakuhu (score) - wo (object particle) - yomu (read)," and it seemed that the Japanese learners did not recognize "music" to mean "a set of written marks representing music" but rather interpreted this term to mean the sound and melodies of music. It is likely that they showed divergence in their choice of verb because some of the Japanese learners did not have certainty in recognizing the appropriate meaning of a noun in the collocation. While both Japanese and French learners may have been influenced by their L1s, L1 influence was found to be beneficial for French learners in this case.

Table 5.2 Comparison of Tasks No. 5: "read music"

Task No.5	French Learners			Japanese Learners		
read music	raw score	%	L1 equivalent	raw score	%	L1 equivalent
read*	27	71.1	✓	11	30.6	✓
seize	2	5.3		8	22.2	
understand	5	13.2		11	30.6	
know	4	10.5		6	16.7	

*: targeted correct choice

2) MCQ Task No. 13: "gain/get experiences"

The second collocation which shows significant differences between the French and Japanese learners' responses is "gain/get experiences". The French version of this collocation is "acquérir de l'experience" and 41.9% of the French answers were found in their L1 equivalent, "acquire". The Japanese version of this collocation is "keiken (experience)-wo (object particle)-tsumu (accumulate)" and no Japanese answer was their L1 equivalent, "accumulate". It is clear that the L1 influence of the French learners is much greater than that of the Japanese learners. The most frequent verb that both French and Japanese learners chose was "get": almost half of the French learners (46.5%) and the Japanese learners (45.7%) chose this collocate. It is likely that both L2 learners, as intermediate level learners, assumed that "get" is a multipurpose verb. However, in terms of "gain", only 9.3% of the French learners chose it in comparison to 43.5% of the Japanese learners. For many of the French learners, "gain" does not seem to be their L1 equivalent, nor a synonym of "get". In addition to the Japanese version of this collocation "keiken (experience)-wo (object particle)-tsumu (pile)", it is also possible to say "keiken (experience)-wo (object particle)-eru (gain)". It seems that this alternative collocation is transferred by the Japanese learners to choose "gain" to the higher percentages. In this case, though both Japanese and French learners might have been influenced by their L1s, L1 influence was found to be beneficial for Japanese learners.

Table 5.3 Comparison of Tasks No. 13: "gain/get experiences"

Task No.13	French Learners			Japanese Learners		
gain/ get experiences	raw score	%	L1 equivalent	raw score	%	L1 equivalent
gain*	4	9.3		20	43.5	✓
acquire	18	41.9	✓	5	10.9	
get*	20	46.5		21	45.7	
pile	1	2.3		0	0	✓

*: targeted correct choice

3) MCQ Task No. 14: "meet/answer/satisfy the needs"

With regard to the collocation, "meet/answer/satisfy the needs", 60.5% of the French answers were "satisfy", 18.6% for "answer" and 9.3% for "meet". The French version of this collocation is "répondre aux besoins" or "satisfaire les besoins"; the verb "répondre" is equivalent to "answer" and "satisfaire" is equivalent to "satisfy". In this case, more French learners chose "satisfy" than "answer" despite the fact that both are semantically equivalent to their L1. In one of the French equivalent collocation, "répondre aux besoins", "aux" is used as a combination of preposition, "à" and the plural form of article, "les". It is likely that the French learners were aware of the missing part of this collocation in the English version and did not choose "answer". Also, "satisfy" is one of the 'parographs', i.e. words which are cognate, but not identically written, as discussed in 3.3.1. The French learners may have chosen "satisfy" because of the close resemblance

between "satisfaire" and "satisfy". As for "meet", only 9.3% of the French responses were correct. The Japanese learners' choices were somewhat different from
that of the French learners: their L1 equivalent is "kotaeru (answer)", and 31.4%
of their answers were "answer". It is likely that the many Japanese learners do
not choose "meet", since Japanese L1 equivalent, "au (meet)", does not mean
"answer". Only 17.1% of the Japanese answers were "meet". The verb most frequently selected by the Japanese participants is "answer," which matches their
L1 equivalent, "kotaeru (answer)". However, while the percentage of the L1
equivalent answers chosen by the French answers was 60.5%, the Japanese
counterpart was 31.4%. This finding indicates that it is likely that the French
learners tend to be influenced more by their L1 than the Japanese learners. In
this case, the accuracy is higher in the French learners' responses (88.4%) than
that in the Japanese learners' responses (77.1%). The French L1 equivalent of
this collocation appears to be beneficial for their accuracy of the French learners, while the Japanese L1 equivalent was not for the Japanese learners.

Table 5.4 Comparison of Tasks No. 14: "meet/answer/satisfy the needs"

Task No.14	French Learners			Japanese Learners		
meet/answer/ satisfy the needs	raw score	%	L1 equivalent	raw score	%	L1 equivalent
meet*	4	9.3		6	17.1	
satisfy*	26	60.5	✓	10	28.6	
answer*	8	18.6	✓	11	31.4	✓
fill	5	11.6		8	22.9	

*: targeted correct choice

4) Summary

In the [verb + noun] category of collocations, a greater L1 influence among French
learners than the Japanese learners was found in "meet/answer/satisfy the
needs". In other 2 items, "read music" and "gain/get experiences", neither the

French nor Japanese learners showed greater L1 influence. In this category, there was no statistically significant difference between the accuracy by the French and Japanese learners. Thus, the learners' L1 influence does not always have the effects on their accuracy.

5.4.2 Category 2: [Delexicalised Verb + Noun] Collocations

With respect to the [delexicalised verb+noun] category, as many as six collocations showed significant differences between the Japanese and French learners as shown in Tables 5.5-5.10.

1) MCQ Task No. 16: "keep records"

In the first collocation, "keep records", 42.4% of the French learners and 36.8% of the Japanese learners chose the correct verb "keep". However, as many as 42.4 % of the French learners chose "note" and 31.6% of the Japanese learners "make". Since the French verb, "noter" means to "write down" in English[1], it is likely that the French learners are influenced by their L1 and combine "note" with "records" because of the formal similarity between "note" in English and "noter" in French. The French learners chose "keep" and their L1 equivalent, "note", equally in numbers. The French learners seemed to have learned this collocation as a chunk. But at the same time, they may have been influenced by their L1. In the case of the Japanese learners, they chose "make" not because it is equivalent to the Japanese L1 but because they used their inaccurate knowledge of collocations. It is likely that although they recognized that delexicalised verbs are used for this collocation, they were not confident of appropriate delexicalised verb for this collocation. The Japanese L1 collocation for "keep records" is "kiroku (records)-wo (objective particle)-tsukeru (attach)" and "keep", "make" or "note" does not match the meaning of the Japanese L1 meaning to "attach". It is likely that they recognize this collocation as a chunk and regard

---

[1] The definition of "noter" is referred to *Collins Robert French Dictionary* (2005).

"keep" and "make" as the verbs which can go together well in this collocation, because quite a few Japanese chose one of the delexicalised verbs, "make", in addition to "keep".

Table 5.5 Comparison of Tasks No. 16: "keep records"

Task No.16	French Learners			Japanese Learners		
keep records	raw score	%	L1 equivalent	raw score	%	L1 equivalent
keep*	14	42.4		14	36.8	
make	2	6.1		12	31.6	
note	14	42.4	✓	6	15.8	
take	3	9.1		6	15.8	

*: targeted correct choice

2) MCQ Task No. 20: "do me a favour"

Similarly in the case of "do me a favour", the verb most frequently chosen by the French learners were "make" (42.9%) followed by "do" (28.6%). Many French learners may have been influenced by their L1, "faire" which means "to make" or "to do", while in French they use "rendre" for this collocation. While the French verb, "rendre" means to "make" or "give back", only 17.1% of the French learners' responses were "give" due to the difference in meaning from "give back", and instead chose "make" and "do". The Japanese learners, on the other hand, chose "give" as the second most frequent answer. The Japanese L1 equivalent for "do" is "kiku (ask)" and 26.5% chose "ask", while 32.4% of their answers were "do" and 29.4% chose "give". It is likely that the Japanese learners may have recognized this collocation as a chunk rather than being influenced by their L1. In terms of this collocation, the Japanese learners' accuracy (32.4%) is higher than that of the French learners' (28.6%).

Table 5.6 Comparison of Tasks No. 20: "do me a favour"

Task No.20	French Learners			Japanese Learners		
do me a favour	raw score	%	L1 equivalent	raw score	%	L1 equivalent
do*	10	28.6		11	32.4	
give	6	17.1	✓	10	29.4	
ask	4	11.4		9	26.5	
make	15	42.9		4	11.8	

*: targeted correct choice

3) MCQ Task No. 21: "has the (same) effect"

The third collocation, "has the same effect", shows significant differences between the French and Japanese learners. 72.2% of the French learners and 58.5% of the Japanese learners chose the correct verb, "has". This gap between the French and Japanese learners on the choice of "has" is greater than any other collocations in the [delexicalised verb + noun] category. The French L1 equivalent of this collocation is "avoir le même effet" and the verb "avoir" means "to have" in English. On the other hand, the Japanese equivalent collocation is "onaji (the same)-kouka (effects)-ga (subjective particle)- aru (have/ is/ exist). While the verbs such as "brings" and "affects" do not match the Japanese L1 equivalent semantically, some of the Japanese learners selected them. The lack of knowledge of this collocation as a chunk by the Japanese and the greater L1 influence by the French learners seems to have led to the difference between the French and Japanese learners' choice of "has" in this case.

Table 5.7 Comparison of Tasks No. 21: "has the (same) effect"

Task No.21	French Learners			Japanese Learners		
has the (same) effect	raw score	%	L1 equivalent	raw score	%	L1 equivalent
has*	26	72.2	✓	24	58.5	✓
affects	0	0		8	19.5	
brings	5	13.9		7	17.1	
does	5	13.9		2	4.9	

*: targeted correct choice

4) MCQ Task No. 23: "keep/write a diary"

In the fourth collocation, "keep/write a diary", although the French L1 equivalent of this collocation is expressed as "tenir un journal" and the meaning of "tenir" exactly corresponds to "keep", only 18.2% of the French learners chose "keep". The most frequent verb they chose was "write", which is not a delexialised verb, and the percentage for this verb of their answers was 78.8%. The French learners may have preferred "write" instead of "keep" because "write" was a lexical verb whose meaning they may have been sure of. This case seems to agree with Kellerman (1978)'s theory that learners are not able to transfer words with non-literal meaning whereas they are willing to transfer those with literal meaning. The French learners seem to have preferred "write" because of its literal meaning to "keep" with non-literal meaning. On the other hand, as many as 61.5% of the Japanese answers were "keep", which has a non-literal meaning, while only 25.6% of them chose "write", which has a literal meaning. The Japanese learners' responses cannot be accounted for by Kellerman's theory that L2 learners are not willing to transfer non-literal meaning of verbs. In addition, the Japanese version of this collocation is "nikki (journal)–wo (object particle)–tsukeru (attach/mark)" and 25.6% of the Japanese learners chose "write", which is different from their L1, "mark". This suggests that the Japanese learners are not necessarily influenced by their L1 but they may have learned this collocation as a chunk. The accuracy between the French and Japanese learners is not statistically significant: $F(1,70)=2.25, p= .14$.

Table 5.8 Comparison of Tasks No. 23: "keep/write a diary"

Task No.23	French Learners			Japanese Learners		
keep/write a diary	raw score	%	L1 equivalent	raw score	%	L1 equivalent
keep*	6	18.2	✓	24	61.5	
write*	26	78.8		10	25.6	✓
note	1	3.0		3	7.7	
mark	0	0		2	5.1	

*: targeted correct choice

5) MCQ Task No. 27: "make/arrange an appointment"

In the fifth collocation, "make/arrange an appointment", the most frequent verb the participants chose was the delexicalised verb, "make", which is correct. Also, quite a few of the French answers were another correct verb, "arrange". While the French L1 equivalent is "prendre" meaning "take", it was not included in the alternatives by mistake. On the other hand, the Japanese learners were successful in recognizing this collocation. The Japanese L1 equivalent collocation is "yoyaku-suru (make an appointment)" and "suru" works as a light verb which has no significant contribution to the meaning of the collocation. The most frequent verb they chose was one of the correct ones, "make", but only a few chose the other correct verbs, "arrange" and "book". It is shown that they were aware that "an appointment" can go together well with "make" as a collocation. That is, they may have been able to recognize this collocation as a chunk rather than by relying on their L1. This result shows that the available range of verbs the Japanese learners have is not as wide as that of the French learners. The accuracy was not statistically different between the results of the Japanese and the French learners: $F(1, 72)= .74, p= .39$.

Table 5.9 Comparison of Tasks No. 27: "make/arrange an appointment"

Task No.27	French Learners			Japanese Learners		
make/arrange/book an appointment	raw score	%	L1 equivalent (not included)	raw score	%	L1 equivalent
make*	15	40.5		29	78.4	
arrange*	13	35.1		2	5.4	
book	8	21.6		4	10.8	
do	1	2.7		2	5.4	

*: targeted correct choice

6) MCQ Task No.29: "keeps/has good control"

The French version of this collocation, "keeps/has good control", is expressed as "tenir bien", which does not exactly match the English version of collocation. While the French verb, "tenir", is semantically the same as the English verb, "keep", the larger number of the French answers were "has" (56.4%) than "keeps" (41.0%). The higher percentage of "has" instead of their L1 equivalent, "keep", indicates that the French learners are not only influenced by their L1 but also by their knowledge of this collocation including delexicalised verbs. The Japanese version of this collocation is "yoku (well)–kanri-suru(control)" and it does not exactly match the English collocation. The Japanese version includes a light verb, "suru", which has no significant contribution to the meaning of the collocation. Neither of the most frequently selected delexicalised verb, "keeps" (41.7%) and the second one, "takes", (30.6%) are Japanese L1 equivalents. Thus, the Japanese learners are not likely to be influenced by their L1 equivalent but they may have learned this collocation as chunks. However, since the availability of the Japanese learners' use of delexicalised verb, "has", is smaller than the French learners, there was a significant difference in the accuracy between the French and Japanese learners: $F(1,74)=13.801$, $p= .00$. Thus, the influence of the learners' L1 by the French and Japanese learners is not highly likely with regard to this collocation.

Table 5.10 Comparison of Tasks No. 29 "keeps/has good control"

Task No.29	French Learners			Japanese Learners		
keeps/ has good control	raw score	%	L1 equivalent	raw score	%	L1 equivalent (not included)
keeps*	16	41.0	✓	15	41.7	
has*	22	56.4		9	25.0	
takes	0	0		11	30.6	
exercises	1	2.6		1	2.8	

*: targeted correct choice

7) Summary

This section identified that both French and Japanese learners are likely to have learned this [delexicalised verb + noun] category of collocations as a chunk regardless of their L1s. However, a slightly greater L1 influence of the French learners than that of the Japanese learners was found in this category of collocations. The Japanese learners seemed less influenced by their L1 when they had no L1 equivalent in the case of collocations with delexicalised verbs. Also, the French learners seemed to have a wider range of availability of the use of delexicalised verbs.

5.4.3 Category 3: [Adjective + Noun] Collocations

With regard to the [adjective+noun] category of collocations, five collocations, "main meal", "common sense", "poor/bad health", "thick/heavy/dense fog" and "large/dense population" showed significant differences between the French and Japanese learners. The close examination is given from Table 5.11 to Table 5.15.

1) MCQ Task No. 34: "main meal"

In the case of "main meal", French and Japanese learners chose "main" most frequently among the four alternatives: 75.7% of the French answers and 66.7% of the Japanese answers. The divergence between the two is due to the second most frequently chosen adjectives: 18.9 % of the French answers were "principal" while only 6.7% of the Japanese answers was this adjective; 20.0% of the Japanese answers was "major" whereas none of the French chose this. The French learners who chose "principal", the French L1 equivalent, was 18.9%, which indicates that the French learners are not necessarily influenced by their L1. On the other hand, 20.0% of the Japanese learners chose "major" which primarily means "important, serious, or significant," while the correct adjective, "main" means "chief in size or importance". It is likely that some of the Japanese learners recognized the approximate meaning of "main" and "major", not distinguishing "main" from "major" which combines with the noun "meal".

Table 5.11 Comparison of Tasks No. 34 "main meal"

Task No.34	French Learners			Japanese Learners		
main meal	raw score	%	L1 equivalent	raw score	%	L1 equivalent
main*	28	75.7		20	66.7	✓
principal	7	18.9	✓	2	6.7	
favourite	2	5.4		2	6.7	
major	0	0		6	20.0	✓

*: targeted correct choice

120

2) MCQ Task No. 37: "common sense"

Similarly, in the case of the collocation, "common sense", as many as 65.6% of the Japanese answers was the correct adjective, "common", while 51.4% of the French answers was this adjective. While the accuracy is quite high, the divergence between them can be found: as many as 48.6% of the French answers were "good", whereas 18.8% of the Japanese answers were this adjective. This divergence seems to have resulted from greater L1 influence by the French L1, "good", even though some of the French learners are able to recognize the correct adjective. The Japanese learners recognized this adjective most likely because "common sense" is used as a loan-word, "komon-sensu" in Japanese, which may affect the frequent choice by the Japanese learners. Thus, it is considered that the loan word in their L1 may have a positive influence on their accuracy.

Table 5.12 Comparison of Tasks No. 37 "common sense"

Task No.37	French Learners			Japanese Learners		
common sense	raw score	%	L1 equivalent	raw score	%	L1 equivalent
common*	18	51.4		21	65.6	✓
good	17	48.6	✓	6	18.8	
balanced	0	0		2	6.3	
ordinary	0	0		3	9.4	

*: targeted correct choice

3) MCQ Task No. 38: "poor/bad health"

In the case of "poor/bad health", almost all the French learners chose "bad" and only 6.1% of their answers were "poor". However, 45.9% of the Japanese answers were "bad" and 37.8% of them were "poor". The Japanese L1 equivalent does not match this collocation involving either "bad" or "poor", because "poor/bad health" is expressed as "hu-kenkou (being unhealthy)" which is not a collocation consisting of [adjective + noun]. The French L1 equivalent is "mauvais sante" and "mauvais" means "bad", which explains "bad" (93.9%). In "poor/bad health", although the accuracy of both French and Japanese learners was quite high, the accuracy of the French learners was higher (100%) than that of the Japanese learners (83.7%) and there was a significance differences in the accuracy between the French and Japanese learners: $F(1, 68)=6.205, p= .02$. The L1 influence in the French learners' responses was greater than that of the Japanese learners because the French L1 equivalent collocation has the adjective semantically similar to the English collocation.

Table 5.13 Comparison of Tasks No. 38 "poor/bad health"

Task No.38	French Learners			Japanese Learners		
poor/bad health	raw score	%	L1 equivalent	raw score	%	L1 equivalent (not included)
poor*	2	6.1		14	37.8	
bad*	31	93.9	✓	17	45.9	
inferior	0	0		5	13.5	
ill	0	0		1	2.7	

*: targeted correct choice

4) MCQ Task No. 39: "thick/heavy fog"

In "thick/heavy/dense fog", while the French L1 equivalent is "épais(thick/deep)" and as many as 31.4% of their answers was "deep", 22.9% of them was "thick", and 28.6% of them was "dense". The French learners prefer L1 semantic equivalent, "thick" or "deep." On the other hand, as many as 45.9% of the Japanese answers was "deep" and 8.1% of them was "dense" which corresponds to the Japanese adjective, "fukai (deep)" and "koi (dense)" to combine with "fog". 35.1% of them recognized "heavy" correctly. Since the literal meaning of "heavy" is used to express the weight of something rather than the density of fog, more Japanese learners seemed to be influenced by their L1 equivalents.

Thus, Japanese learners were more likely to be influenced by their L1 than the French learners with regard to this collocation. However, the accuracy between the French and Japanese learners shows no significant differences. Also, the accuracy of the French learners (68.6%) and that of the Japanese learners (54.0%) indicates that they were able to recognize the adjectives with figurative meaning.

Table 5.14 Comparison of Tasks No. 39 "thick/heavy/dense fog"

Task No.39	French Learners			Japanese Learners		
thick/heavy/ dense fog	raw score	%	L1 equivalent	raw score	%	L1 equivalent
dense*	10	28.6	✓	3	8.1	✓
thick*	8	22.9	✓	4	10.8	
heavy*	6	17.1		13	35.1	
deep	11	31.4	✓	17	45.9	✓

*: targeted correct choice

5) MCQ Task No. 40: "large/dense/high population"

In "large/dense population", the accuracy of the French learners was 100% while that of the Japanese was 86.7%. Although the Japanese L1 equivalent is "ooi (many)", only 13.3% of them chose "many" and the adjective which they chose most frequently was "large". While the French version of this collocation is "importante population", their most frequently selected adjective was "large", followed by "dense". The French learners' availability of adjectives for this collocation is larger than the Japanese learners'. Only a few Japanese learners recognize "dense population" is possible. These results indicate that the Japanese learners are influenced by their L1 only to a small extent and both French and Japanese learners recognized the adjectives with figurative meaning.

Table 5.15 Comparison of Tasks No. 40 "large/dense/high population"

Task No.40	French Learners			Japanese Learners		
large/dense/ high population	Raw score	%	L1 equivalent (not included)	raw score	%	L1 equivalent
large*	22	57.9		20	66.7	
dense*	10	26.3		1	3.3	
high*	6	15.8		5	16.7	
many	0	0		4	13.3	✓

*: targeted correct choice

6) Summary

In the above items of collocations, it was found that both French and Japanese learners refer to their knowledge of collocations as chunks, while they often refer to their L1s. Especially, the Japanese learners showed greater L1 influence than the French learners. The accuracy of French learners' responses is higher than that of Japanese learners' even though both French and Japanese learners' were influenced by their L1 equivalent collocations. Particularly the French learners were not necessarily influenced by their formal L1 equivalent. They also have a wider availability of collocations than the Japanese learners for [adjective + noun] category of collocations.

5.4.4 Category 4: [Adverb + Adjective] Collocations

In terms of [adverb + adjective] category, six collocations showed significant differences: "only natural", "extremely serious", "entirely/completely lost", "fully/quite aware", "highly/extremely competent" and "deeply/heavily involved". The analysis of these collocations is shown from Table 5.16 to Table 5.19. For these two collocations, participants needed to select appropriate adjectives while for the other items they needed to select appropriate adverbs. The nodes for these two collocations are adverbs, while for the other items the nodes are adjectives. Thus, the results of the six items of collocations are not necessarily comparable. The first two items, "only natural" and "extremely serious" may not be appropriate for this analysis because of the nature of questions, thus these two collocations were excluded from the analysis in this section since the adverb should have been questioned, in these two items, the adjective were in question.

1) MCQ Task No. 50: "entirely/completely lost"

In the collocation, "completely/entirely lost", "completely" was chosen most frequently by both the French and Japanese learners. The French L1 equivalent for this collocation is "complétement perdu", and they chose "completely" the most frequently (88.6%) but chose "entirely" which is also a correct adverb to use in this collocation, infrequently (11.4%). Thus, they may have learned this collocation as a chunk or they may be influenced by their L1 in this case. Though the Japanese learners chose "completely" (47.2%) and perfectly (16.7%), both of which correspond to the L1 equivalent (kanzen ni), they also chose the other two alternatives, "entirely" (22.2%) and "extremely" (13.9%). Thus, they were not necessarily influenced by their L1 equivalent adverbs.

Table 5.16 Comparison of Tasks No. 50 "completely/entirely lost"

Task No.50	French Learners			Japanese Learners		
entirely/ completely lost	raw score	%	L1 equivalent	raw score	%	L1 equivalent
completely*	31	88.6	✓	17	47.2	✓
entirely*	4	11.4		8	22.2	
extremely	0	0		5	13.9	
perfectly	0	0		6	16.7	✓

*: targeted correct choice

2) MCQ Task No. 52: "fully/quite aware"

In the fourth collocation, "fully/quite aware", the French L1 equivalent, "par-faitement", which has the formal similarity, was not included in the alternatives. The most frequent adverbs they chose were "fully" and "quite", both of which are correct. Though the Japanese L1 equivalent ("yoku" or "jyuubun-ni") is considered to have the same meaning as "fully" and "sufficiently", the Japanese learners were not necessarily influenced by their L1.

Table 5.17 Comparison of Tasks No. 52 "fully/quite aware"

Task No.52	French Learners			Japanese Learners		
fully/quite aware	raw score	%	L1 equivalent (not included)	raw score	%	L1 equivalent
fully*	17	43.6		5	16.1	✓
quite*	21	53.8		15	48.4	
sufficiently	1	2.6		6	19.4	✓
amply	0	0		5	16.1	

*: targeted correct choice

3) MCQ Task No.54: "highly/extremely competent"

In the collocation, "highly/extremely competent", the adverb most frequently chosen by the French learners is "highly" (51.4%). The French L1 equivalent is "hautement", which exactly semantically coincides with "highly" in English. The French L1 equivalent for "extremely" is semantically the same or close to "highly". As they chose either "highly" or "extremely" frequently, the French learners were likely to be influenced by their L1. On the other hand, the most frequent adverb that the Japanese learners chose is "highly" (45.2%). While the Japanese semantically L1 equivalent can be translated into "hijyou-ni (extremely)", 35.5% of the Japanese learners chose it. It is not likely that the Japanese learners are influenced by their L1 but have learned them as a chunk.

Table 5.18 Comparison of Tasks No. 54 "highly/extremely competent"

Task No.54	French Learners			Japanese Learners		
highly/ extremely competent	raw score	%	L1 equivalent	raw score	%	L1 equivalent
extremely*	13	35.1		11	35.5	✓
highly*	19	51.4	✓	14	45.2	
completely	1	2.7		6	19.4	
fully	4	10.8		0	0	

*: targeted correct choice

4) MCQ Task No. 55: "deeply/completely involved"

In a collocation, "deeply/completely involved", the Japanese semantically L1 equivalent is "fukaku", which means "deeply" and "profoundly", which are the most frequently selected adverbs. However, they also chose "completely" (15.2%). The Japanese learners were not really influenced by their L1 but may have learned this collocation as a chunk. On the other hand, since the French L1 equivalent, "seriously", was not included in the alternatives, there was no alternatives that would directly suggest L1 influence. Thus, the French learners' L1 influence was not obviously indicated in terms of this item.

Table 5.19 Comparison of Tasks No. 55 "heavily/deeply/completely involved"

Task No.55	French Learners			Japanese Learners		
deeply/completely/ heavily involved	raw score	%	L1 equivalent (not included)	raw score	%	L1 equivalent
completely*	15	46.9		5	15.2	
deeply*	13	40.6		13	39.4	✓
profoundly	3	9.4		12	36.4	✓
heavily*	1	3.1		3	9.1	

*: targeted correct choice

5) Summary

The results showed that there seems to be more L1 influence by the French learners than the Japanese learners for "completely/entirely lost" and "highly competent" among the 4 collocations, but not for the other 2 collocations. Although the L1 influence was expected to be higher among French learners than among the Japanese learners, it was not always the case with the [adverb + adjective] category of collocation.

5.4.5 Conclusion

As shown above, the French and Japanese learners' responses to the 20 collocations in the four lexical categories of collocations demonstrated significant differences. Among them, the results showed a slightly greater L1 influence by the French learners in the [verb + noun] and [delexicalised verb + noun] categories. The L1 influence in the [adverb + adjective] category was not definitely demonstrated. Different from the original expectation, in the [adjective + noun] category, the Japanese answers showed a slightly greater L1 influence than the French learners. In the [adverb + adjective] category, the French answers were more influenced by their L1 in terms of 2 items out of 4 items. Even in the [verb + noun], [delexicalised verb + noun] and [adverb + adjective] categories, learners are not necessarily influenced by their L1s but may have learned the collocations as chunks.

Because of the formal similarity between French and English, it was expected that the L1 influence would be higher in the results of the French learners than that of the Japanese. However, it was found that, among the four lexical categories, the [adjective + noun] category showed a greater L1 influence by the Japanese learners.

In addition, by examining the items which showed significant differences between the French and Japanese learners, the differences between them were not necessarily caused by L1 influence but by other reasons. The larger availability of collocations by French learners than that of Japanese learners was found, which may have affected the differences between them. There may be some developmental errors unique to learning collocations by both French and Japanese learners. Because the factors which caused the differences in addition to their L1 are not clear at this stage, further investigation will be required.

In the next section, whether the recognition of collocations by learners of different L1 are different depending on the combinability and transparency of collocations is examined.

5.5 Combinability and Transparency Influence on the Collocations

The second research question raised in Chapter 4 was whether combinability and transparency affects the French and Japanese learners' recognition of collocations. The mean scores of accuracy in the [+ResComb, +Transp] and the [-ResComb, -Transp] groups of collocations by French and Japanese learners did not show statistically significant difference between the [+ResComb, +Transp] and the [-ResComb, -Transp] groups of collocations.

Table 5.20 Mean Scores of Overall Accuracy: [+ResComb, +Transp] and [-ResComb, -Transp] Collocations

Group of Collocations	Language Group	Number of Students	Mean Scores
1) [+ResComb, +Transp]	French	34	17.65
	Japanese	30	16.67
2) [-ResComb, -Transp]	French	34	27.41
	Japanese	30	26.20

As shown in Table 5.20, the mean of French learners' overall accuracy was 17.65 while that of Japanese learners was 16.67 in terms of the [+ResComb, +Transp] group of collocations. According to one-way ANOVA, in the

[+ResComb, +Transp] group of collocations, there was no significant difference between the French and Japanese learners: $F(1,62)= 2.20$, $p= .14$. Similarly, in relation to the [-ResComb, -Transp] group of collocations, the mean of French learners' overall accuracy was 27.41 while that of Japanese learners was 26.20. There was no significant difference between the French and Japanese learners: $F(1,62)=1.12$, $p= .29$.

Moreover, in order to examine the accuracy between the French and Japanese learners in four lexical categories, a two-way ANOVA (2 levels of language group: French and Japanese, 2 levels of collocation type: [+ResComb, +Transp] and [-ResComb, -Transp] for each lexical category was performed. Since the statistical calculation was carried out in terms of each lexical category, a two-way ANOVA was performed instead of three-way ANOVA. The dependent variable was the accuracy of the French and Japanese learners' responses. The results are as follows:

Table 5.21 Significant Differences found in two-way ANOVA

Lexical Category	Significant Differences between Collocation Types	Interaction between Language Group & Collocation Type
1) verb + noun	$F(3,124)=83.37$, $p= .00$	$F(3,124)=2.89$, $p= .09$
2) del. verb + noun	$F(3,124)=200.66$, $p= .00$	$F(3,124)=1.50$, $p= .22$
3) adjective + noun	$F(3,124)=25.8$, $p= .00$	$F(3,124)=1.16$, $p= .28$
4) adverb + adjective	$F(3,124)=142.56$, $p= .00$	$F(3,124)=4.34$, $p= .04$

In all of the four lexical categories of collocations, the main effect of language group was not significant as examined in Section 5.2 (Table 5.1). However, the main effect of collocation type was significant in all of the lexical categories. Also, with regard to the [verb + noun], [delexicalised verb + noun] and [adjective + noun] categories of collocations, the interaction between language group and collocation type was not significant, while it was significant in the [adverb + adjective] category of collocations. These results suggest that there are effects of collocation types (i.e. [+ResComb, +Transp] and [-ResComb, -Transp][2]) on the accuracy of the learners' recognition of collocations with regard to all of the four lexical categories of collocations (i.e. [verb + noun], [delexicalised verb + noun], [adjective + noun] and [adverb + adjective]).

5.6 Summary

In this chapter, recognition of collocations by the French and Japanese learners was investigated by implementing MCQ Tasks. The analysis was carried out in order to examine the research questions: whether the L1 and the combinability and transparency have the influence on the learners' recognition of collocations.

While the L1 influence was expected to be found in all four lexical categories of collocations, a slightly greater L1 influence was found in the responses of the French learners in terms of the [verb + noun], [delexicalised verb + noun] categories. However, a greater L1 influence by the French learners did not necessarily occur in every item of collocations in these lexical categories because significant differences between the responses of the French and Japanese learners were not exclusively caused by L1 influence. Moreover, a greater L1 influence by the Japanese learners than the French learners was identified in the [adjective + noun] category, which is different from the original expectation. In terms of the [adverb + adjective] category, any conclusive result was found since a greater L1 influence by the French learners was identified in half of the collocations.

In addition, this chapter showed that the [+ResComb, +Transp] and [-ResComb, -Transp] similarly influenced the recognition of collocations by

---

[2] As discussed in Section 4.3.2., [+ResComb, +Transp] contains those collocations in which the node can be combined only with one or two possible words and in which both of the elements have literal features in meaning. The [-ResComb, -Transp] holds collocations that are not restricted in combinability (i.e. the node can be combined with three or more possible words) with non-literal or figurative meaning (i.e. either or both word in the collocation has non-literal or figurative meaning).

the French and Japanese learners. By examining the effect of collocation types in each lexical category of collocations, their accuracy showed no distinct differences depending on the learners' L1s. However, there were significant differences between the responses of the French learners and that of the Japanese learners by the types of collocations, i.e., [+ResComb, +Transp] or [-ResComb, -Transp]. With regard to the [adverb + adjective] category, significant differences were found in the interaction between the language group, i.e. French and Japanese, and collocation types, i.e. [+ResComb, +Transp] and [-ResComb, -Transp].

Chapter 6

RESULTS AND ANALYSIS
OF TRANSLATION TASKS

6.1 Introduction

This chapter presents the results from Translation Tasks in order to clarify the tendencies and specificities which the French and Japanese learners have in the translation of the target collocations. The main purpose of these tasks is to examine the learners' production of collocations.

Translation Tasks were adopted in previous studies. For example, Bahns and Eldaw (1993) studied the [verb+noun] and [noun+verb] collocations of German learners, while Biskup (1992) investigated Polish and German learners. Both conclude that there was reliance on the L1s, though the kinds of reliance were different: German learners depended on formal similarity whereas Polish learners were dependent on transfer or extension of L2 meaning on the basis of the L1 word[1].

To test the robustness of the findings through MCQ Tasks, i.e. the recognition of collocations, and to test another type of knowledge of collocations, i.e. the production of collocations, the present study adopted a different type of task. In order to clarify the findings identified in MCQ Tasks, the collocations to be translated were exactly the same as those given in MCQ Tasks. The French and Japanese sentences involving 56 target

---

[1] Biskup (1992:91) mentioned that extension of L2 meaning is an interference error, resulting from assumed identity of semantic structures. In his study, Polish students made errors such as "to lead a bookshop", "to drive a bookshop", etc. to mean "to run a bookshop" caused by their L1 equivalent.

collocations were provided for the learners. Learners were required to fill in the missing words in the blank space for the target collocations which match the meaning of their L1 collocations. The learners' responses of Translation Tasks are classified into three categories, i.e. acceptable, infelicitous and non-target collocations, and were analysed in terms of L1 influence and combinability/transparency effects.

6.2 Overall Results of French and Japanese Learners

6.2.1 Classification of the Results

Unlike MCQ Tasks which required learners to select one or a few alternatives among the four given, Translation Tasks elicited various types of answers produced by French and Japanese learners who are required to translate from their L1 into L2 collocations. In the first step of the analysis, the learners' various answers to the translations were split into three types of categories: acceptable, infelicitous and non-target collocations. This categorization of responses was implemented with a view to assessing the learners' knowledge of the collocation and their capacity to reproduce an appropriate L2 equivalent. The judgements on the acceptability of the collocations produced by the learners were made with the support of the two British linguists who also helped to analyze the MCQ data. They were asked to judge the collocations learners produced according to the following standards of judgement:

1) **Target/acceptable collocations**: when the learners' answers are exactly the same as the target collocations, or they differ only slightly from the target collocations, they are assigned to this group;

2) **Infelicitous collocations**: when the collocations produced by the learners are close to the original collocations but infelicitous, those answers are assigned to this group. The infelicitous aspects include syntactic problems

such as a plural noun, an article or determiner where the collocation does not allow them. This would imply that the learners have some knowledge of the collocation or have to try to reconstruct it from its constituents;

3) **Non-Target/wrong collocations**: when the learners' answers are obviously deviant from target collocations, they are included in this group. These results show that the learners do not have the knowledge of the target collocations and translated an L1 equivalent or searched for a circumlocution instead.

Because of the variation in the norms of the native British linguists[2] who judged the collocations produced by the learners, these results of categorisation should be considered as an approximation rather than as an absolute judgement. The results of the answers of the French and Japanese learners are presented in Appendix 7. It has their answers of collocations in English, which were translated from their L1 equivalent collocations in each lexical category.

6.2.2 Overall Results of Accuracy

Firstly, the overall accuracy of the French and Japanese learners is presented in order to make comparison and hence identify any tendencies in the results of each of the L1 learners. As shown in Table 6.1, the overall accuracy of French and Japanese learners indicates that the percentage of accuracy is greater in the responses of the French learners than in those of the Japanese learners.

---

[2] Though they agreed on most of the cases, some variation was found in terms of a few collocations.

Table 6.1 Overall Accuracy of French and Japanese Learners
in Translation Tasks

(1) [Verb + Noun] Group of Collocations (15 collocations)

Lang. Group	Types of Answers				Total
	acceptable	infelicitous	non-target	non-response	
French	150	32	87	166	435
(n=29)	34.5%	7.4%	20.0%	38.2%	100%
Japanese	152	56	154	208	570
(n=38)	26.7%	9.8%	27.0%	36.5%	100%

(2) [Delexicalised Verb + Noun] Group of Collocations (15 collocations)

Lang. Group	Types of Answers				Total
	acceptable	infelicitous	non-target	non-response	
French	169	15	118	133	435
(n=29)	38.9%	3.4%	27.1%	30.6.%	100%
Japanese	183	39	125	223	570
(n=38)	32.1%	6.8%	21.9%	39.1%	100%

(3) [Adjective+ Noun] Group of Collocations (14 collocations)

Lang. Group	Types of Answers				Total
	acceptable	infelicitous	non-target	non-response	
French	198	10	117	81	406
(n=29)	48.8%	2.5%	28.8%	20.0%	100%
Japanese	269	6	121	136	532
(n=38)	50.6%	1.1%	22.7%	25.6%	100%

(4) [Adverb + Adjective] Group of Collocations (12 collocations)

Lang. Group	Types of Answers				Total
	acceptable	infelicitous	non-target	non-response	
French	54	10	145	139	348
(n=29)	15.5%	2.9%	41.7%	39.9%	100%
Japanese	31	7	140	278	456
(n=38)	6.8%	1.5%	30.7%	61.0%	100%

Based on the above responses, a three-way ANOVA (2 levels of language group: French and Japanese, 2 levels of collocation type: [+ResComb, +Transp] and [-ResComb, -Transp], and 4 levels of lexical category: [verb +

noun], [delexicalised verb + noun], [adjective + noun] and [adverb + adjective]) was performed. The dependent variable was the accuracy of the French and Japanese learners' responses. The independent variables were language group and collocation types, i.e. [+ResComb, +Transp] and [-ResComb, -Transp] and lexical category of collocations, i.e. [verb + noun], [delexicalised verb + noun], [adjective + noun] and [adverb + adjective]. The results are as follows:

(1) The main effect of language group was significant: $F(15, 520)=11.2$, $p= .00$.

(2) The main effect of lexical type, i.e. [verb + noun], [delexicalised verb + noun], [adjective + noun] and [adverb + adjective], was significant: $F(15, 520)=87.6, p= .00$.

(3) The main effect of collocation type, i.e. [+ResComb, +Transp] and [-ResComb, -Transp], was not significant: $F(15, 520)=0.64, p= .42$.

(4) The interaction of language group and lexical type, i.e. [verb + noun], [delexicalised verb + noun], [adjective + noun] and [adverb + adjective], was not significant: $F(15, 520)=2.53, p= .06$.

(5) The interaction of language group and collocation type, i.e. [+ResComb, +Transp] and [-ResComb, -Transp], was significant: $F(15,520)=8.7$, $p= .00$.

(6) The interaction of lexical type, i.e. [verb + noun], [delexicalised verb + noun], [adjective + noun] and [adverb + adjective], and collocation type, i.e. [+ResComb, +Transp] and [-ResComb, -Transp], was significant: $F(15,520)=34.4, p= .00$.

(7) The interaction of language group, lexical type and collocation type was significant: $F(15,520)=4.4, p= .00$.

As indicated above, the main effects of language groups and lexical types, i.e. [verb + noun], [delexicalised verb + noun], [adjective + noun] and [adverb

+ adjective], were significant, and three interactions of: 1) language group and collocation type; 2) lexical type and collocation type; 3) language group, lexical type and collocation type, were significant. Thus, the following sections will reveal the nature of these significances by looking at the errors of words of different grammatical categories in each lexical category.

In the next section, the discussion in relation to the learners' L1 and [+ResComb, +Transp] and [-ResComb, -Transp] is demonstrated.

6.3 Learners' L1 Influence on the Collocations

6.3.1 Types of Errors

In the second step of the analysis, the learners' responses were analyzed in relation to the types of errors the French and Japanese learners made and the analysis tries to clarify the differences between them. Similarly to the MCQ Tasks, the nodes of the collocations are: nouns in [verb + noun], [delexicalised verb + noun] and [adjective + noun] categories of collocations and adjectives in the [adverb + adjective] category of collocations. The collocates are: verbs in [verb + noun], delexicalised verbs in [delexicalised verb + noun], adjectives in [adjective + noun] and adverbs in [adverb + adjective] categories of collocations.

The collocations in the present study were divided into four lexical categories and the errors in each lexical category were classified into seven types based on the translation responses by the French and Japanese learners in order to closely examine the comparative tendencies of the French and Japanese learners. Seven types of errors for each of [verb + noun], [delexicalised verb + noun], [adjective + noun], and [adverb + adjective] categories are presented. With respect to the [verb + noun] category, for example, the following seven types of errors are identified. The collocations with an asterisk (*) indicates the non-target collocations produced by French and Japanese learners:

1) **Verb**: The verb in a collocation is wrong.

Example: *cross the border* (French: *pass the border*)

2) **Noun**: The noun in a collocation is wrong.

Example: *reach any conclusion* (Japanese: *reach the consequence[3]*)

3) **Determiners**: The article or possessive pronoun is missing or added.

Example: meet the needs (Japanese: *meet needs*)

4) **Structure**: Syntactic structure is wrong.

Example: *ask her a question* (Japanese: *question[4]*)

5) **Preposition**: Preposition is added through unnecessary or wrong choice.

Example: *attend the meeting* (French: *assist to the meeting*)

6) **Different expression**: Translation does not include a collocation and/or consists of a circumlocution.

Example: *won the match* (Japanese: *became a champion*)

7) **Number**: Noun is used in singular instead of plural or vice versa.

Example: *gain experience* (French: *have experiences*)

In terms of the [delexicalised verb + noun], [adjective + noun] and [adverb + adjective] categories, "verb" and/or "noun" are respectively replaced according to each lexical category. Thus, for example, in the [adjective + noun] category, we have "wrong choice of adjective" and in the [adverb + adjective] category, "wrong choice of adverb" and "wrong choice of adjective". Since the translation results do not necessarily contain one type of error but a few, counting was carried out with regard to all possible types of errors in a translated collocation. The occurrences of all type of errors were then presented as percentages because of the different amount of errors between the Japanese and French learners.

---

[3] In this case, the determiner, 'the' is classified into 3) in addition to 2).

[4] In this case, the learner seems to use 'question' as a verb instead of the target collocation, 'ask her a question'.

The following section examines whether there are differences in the production of collocations by the French and Japanese learners. In addition, it will attempt to answer the two research questions raised in Section 4.2: 1) L1 influence on the collocations; and 2) the influence of combinability/ transparency on the collocations.

Based on the responses in the following tables of wrong and infelicitous occurrences and L1 likely errors' occurrences, one-way ANOVA with the proportion of L1 likely errors within the wrong/infelicitous occurrences of each of French and Japanese learners as the dependent variable and the language group as the independent variable was conducted. The tables are shown for each lexical category below and the analysis of the tables and the responses of the learners are carried out.

6.3.2 Category 1: [Verb + Noun] Collocations

Among the previous studies on the L2 learners' knowledge of collocations, it has been indicated that verb errors are more noticeable than other types of errors in terms of the [verb + noun] category in relation to German learners (Nesselhauf 2003). Similarly, in the present study, both among French and Japanese learners the occurrences of incorrect verb choices were considerably higher than those of other types of errors (See Table 6.2).

However, the French and Japanese learners were quite different in their answers regarding the other types of errors, such as determiners, prepositions and different expressions. While Japanese learners' errors with missed or added determiners, such as articles or pronouns, were as high as 23.7%, similar errors were far less frequent with French learners, showing only 13.4 %. In terms of prepositions, the French learners present a higher level of errors, at 8.2%, while only 1.9% of the Japanese learners made errors with prepositions. As for errors concerning different expressions, the errors made by the Japanese learners (13.8%) exceed those made by the French learners (2.2%). In the following tables, "W/I occurrences" refers to the wrong or infelicitous choice of words in collocations. Whether given errors were likely to be due to their L1 was determined based on the difference between the learners' L1 and English. For example, when a Japanese learner did not use a determiner in a collocation in which it should be, the error was considered to be due to their L1. Similarly, when a French learner used a preposition in a collocation in which it should not be but their L1 equivalent collocation has one, the error was considered to be due to their L1.

Table 6.2 Distribution of Types of Errors, W/I Occurrences & L1 likely Errors by the French and Japanese Learners ([Verb + Noun] collocations)

[verb + noun]	French Learners (n=29)			Japanese Learners (n=38)		
	W/I Occurrences* (a)	L1 likely Errors (b)	% (b) / (a)	W/I Occurrences* (a)	L1 likely Errors (b)	% (b) / (a)
(1) verbs	70 (52.2%)	34 (70.8%)	48.6	108 (34.6%)	59 (62.1%)	54.6
(2) nouns	27 (20.1%)	5 (10.4%)	18.5	35 (11.2%)	15 (15.8%)	42.9
(3) determiners	18 (13.4%)	2 (4.2%)	11.1	74 (23.7%)	15 (15.8%)	20.3
(4) structure	3 (2.2%)	0 (0.0%)	0.0	17 (5.4%)	0	0.0
(5) different expressions	3 (2.2%)	2 (4.2%)	66.7	43 (13.8%)	11 (11.6%)	23.4
(6) prepositions	11 (8.2%)	5 (10.4%)	45.5	6 (1.9%)	4 (4.2%)	66.7
(7) numbers	2 (1.5.%)	0 (0.0%)	0.0	29 (9.3%)	0 (0.0%)	0.0
TOTAL	134 (100%)	48 (100%)	35.8	312 (100%)	104 (100%)	33.3

The one-way ANOVA based on the above responses was conducted and the test was not significant: $F(1,65)=1.11$, $p= .30$. Regarding the L1 influence on the collocations found in the wrong or infelicitous choice of words in collocations, the results are shown in the Table 6.2. L1 influence in the responses of the French learners (35.8%) is higher than in the responses of the Japanese learners (33.3%). It is notable that these results coincide with those identified in MCQ Tasks; the L1 reliance of the French learners was greater than that of the Japanese learners in [verb + noun] collocations.

Through examining the types of errors made by the French learners more closely, a higher degree of L1 influence was identified particularly in "prepositions" and "different expressions" among the seven types of errors. One particular example can be seen in the collocation, "attend the meeting", for which as many as 42.1% of the French learners used "assist to/at the meeting". Not only the choice of verb was wrong but also they added a preposition to the verb because of the reference to their L1 collocation, "assister à la réunion". Another example is "answer the phone", for which as many as 21.7% of the French learners translated as "answer to the phone". Since their L1 collocation is expressed as "répondre au téléphone", it is likely that they added the preposition to the verb in the English version of the collocation (See Appendix 7). Thus, although a moderate number of the French correctly used these collocations which do not require prepositions, it is likely that some learners tend to be influenced by their L1 when they come across these types of collocations.

Although the number of occurrences is fairly small, the L1 influence was identified in the other collocations produced by the French learners. For example, the collocation, "read music", the French L1 equivalent collocation is "faire du solfège" and "faire" is usually translated into "do" in English. They may have translated it into "do/play solfège" from their L1 equivalent collocation. In terms of this collocation, no correct translation was produced, but "read music notes", "do/play solfège" and "write music" were produced. The collocation, "write music" may be produced because the French L1 equivalent noun, "solfège," partly refers to write music. Although the number of occurrences is small, it is likely that they tend to be influenced by their L1 in cases where they do not know the correct collocation.

The L1 influence seen in verb errors is particularly noteworthy and this tendency echoes with the discussion in the previous studies that L2 learners rely heavily on their L1 particularly with regard to verbs. The percentage of French learners showing L1 influence seen in verbs is 70.8% which is higher than that of the Japanese learners (62.1%) (See Table 6.2). From the results of the present study, concerning verbs, the French learners tend to be influenced by their L1 more than the Japanese learners.

With respect to the Japanese learners, the greatest L1 influence was found in the preposition errors. One of the collocations which showed their L1 influence in relation to this type of error is "attend to the meeting" for "attend the meeting". The Japanese L1 for this collocation includes a dative particle, 'ni', which has a role similar to that of the preposition "to" in some contexts; this could explain why a small number of the Japanese learners added the preposition to the verb. While the number of the preposition errors by the Japanese learners is found to be smaller than the ones by the French learners, both of them are likely to add prepositions when they have ones in their L1 equivalent collocations.

With respect to determiners, the results showed that the Japanese learners tend to make errors in the production of determiners (23.7%) more often than the French learners (13.4%). Since the Japanese language does not have determiners, unlike English and many Indo-European languages, it is expected that this fact lead to the different results between the Japanese and French learners. They are also likely to miss necessary articles and/or pronouns or add unnecessary ones. This type of error is scarce in the responses of the French learners who have determiners in their L1, French.

Regarding noun errors, the Japanese learners showed greater L1 influence than the French learners. While there is no formal similarity of nouns between Japanese and English, the Japanese learners tend to make errors by choosing nouns which should not combine with the verb in a collocation.

A remarkable difference in the L1 influence seen in errors was found in respect of prepositions. The French learners showed greater L1 influence in the choice of prepositions than the Japanese learners. Further studies on French learners' use of prepositions will be interesting. Another difference is in relation to the determiners. The Japanese learners tend to make the error of missing and/or adding determiners because of the lack of the notion of determiners in their L1.

As discussed above, the L1 had some influence on the results of both the French and Japanese learners.

6.3.3 Category 2: [Delexicalised Verb + Noun] Collocations

Similarly to the [verb + noun] collocations, the French and Japanese learners frequently made errors in the [delexicalised verbs + noun] collocations as well. The one-way ANOVA based on the above responses was conducted and the test was not significant: $F(1,65)=0.35, p= .56$.

In previous studies, while it has been indicated that delexicalised verbs are difficult for the L2 learners (Chi, et al. 1994), the results in the current study do not necessarily uphold such a conclusion. Rather, in terms of the French learners, as compared with the [verb + noun] category of collocations as shown in Table 6.3 below, the percentage showing the wrong choice of delexicalised verb is lower (34.6%) than that of the [verb + noun] category of collocations (48.2%). For the French learners, it has been shown through the translation tasks that translating verbs is more difficult in terms of the [verb + noun] category of collocations than in terms of the [delexicalised verb + noun] one. Also, it is probable that the French learners guessed and provided one of the delexicalized verbs (which is a limited set) when they were not sure.

Table 6.3 Distribution of Types of Errors, W/I Occurrences &

L1 likely Errors by the French and Japanese Learners

([Delexicalised Verb + Noun] collocations)

[delexicalised verb + noun]	French Learners (n=29)			Japanese Learners (n=38)		
	W/I Occurrences* (a)	L1 likely Errors (b)	% (b) / (a)	W/I Occurrences* (a)	L1 likely Errors (b)	% (b) / (a)
(1) delexicalised verbs	48 (40.0%)	31 (46.8%)	64.6%	66 (34.6%)	20 (51.3%)	30.3%
(2) nouns	41 (34.2%)	24 (27.8%)	58.5%	21 (11.0%)	6 (15.4%)	28.6%
(3) determiners	2 (1.7%)	0 (0.0%)	0.0%	51 (26.7%)	0 (0.0%)	0.0%
(4) structure	0 (0.0%)	0 (0.0%)	0.0%	1 (0.5%)	0 (0.0%)	0.0%
(5) different expressions	25 (20.8%)	17 (25.3%)	68.0%	44 (23.0%)	13 (33.3%)	29.5%
(6) prepositions	4 (3.3%)	2 (0.0%)	50.0%	1 (0.5%)	0 (0.0%)	0.0%
(7) numbers	0 (0.0%)	0 (0.0%)	0.0%	7 (3.7%)	0 (0.0%)	0.0%
TOTAL	120 (100%)	74 (100%)	61.7%	191 (100%)	39 (100%)	20.4%

(*: "W/I occurrences" refers to the number of wrong or infelicitous collocations.)

Concerning the overall errors that the Japanese learners made, the percentage of the wrong choice of verb is slightly higher (40.0%) than the [verb + noun] category (34.6%). It is presented that the Japanese learners face similar level of difficulty in relation to the verbs of the [verb + noun] and the [delexicalised verb + noun] category of collocations.

Unlike the [verb + noun] category of collocations, both the French and Japanese learners showed different expressions for the [delexicalised verb + noun] category of collocations and the French learners revealed higher percentages of L1 likely errors than the Japanese learners. For example, both the French and Japanese learners use a similar verb, "meet", instead of a collocation, "have/hold talks" based on the French L1, 's'entretenir' and the Japanese L1, "au". This tendency may have resulted from the greater influence on their L1, as will be discussed in more detail below. A larger number of errors in terms of determiners are identified in the responses of the Japanese learners than in those of the French learners. This tendency agrees with the results found in the [verb + noun] category of collocations, and this is likely to be because of the lack of notion of determiners in the Japanese language. In other words, French learners' higher accuracy is due to their L1 influence, since L1 influence is not a negative factor but a positive factor for the L2 learners.

While delexicalised verb errors did not show considerable differences between the French and Japanese learners, the overall percentages of L1 influence on the errors were particularly higher in the responses of the French learners (61.7%) than in those of the Japanese learners (20.4%) as shown in Table 6.3.

The differences between the L1 influence of the French and Japanese learners are identified in the wrong choice of delexicalised verbs, nouns and different expressions. In terms of the wrong choice of delexicalised verbs, while the percentage of the total errors made by the French learners is approximately the same as that of the Japanese learners, the L1 influence of the French learners is found to be higher than that of the Japanese learners.

A distinctive difference between the results of the French learners and those of the Japanese learners is also found in the wrong choice of nouns. A higher percentage of L1 influence on the errors is identified in the results of the French learners (58.5%) than that of the Japanese learners (28.6%). The French learners seem to rely on the formal similarity between French nouns and English ones. For example, the French version of the collocation, "keep records", is "garder une trace écrite" and more than 70% of them translated it as "keep a written proof" which is nearly the word-to-word translation of the French version. Because of the nature of the translation tasks which invite the learners to use their L1, the French learners may have answered as they were asked to translate rather than using their knowledge of collocations. In a collocation, "keep a diary", more than half of the French learners' wrong translation was "a newspaper" for "a diary" because of their L1 version of this collocation, "tenir un journal". Although "un journal" can be translated into "a newspaper", in a collocation, "tenir un journal", it is natural to translate it to "a diary" in this context.[5] Based on the investigation into the characteristics of types of errors by the French learners, the L1 influence by the French learners played a greater role than by their Japanese counterparts with regard to the results of the wrong choice of nouns.

6.3.4 Category 3: [Adjective + Noun] Collocations

The one-way ANOVA based on the above responses was conducted and the test was not significant: $F(1,65)=0.44$, $p= .51$. The responses of the learners show that there are distinct differences between the French and Japanese learners in their responses of the [adjective + noun] category of collocations as shown in Table 6.4 below. The percentage of errors in the choice of adjective is higher in the responses of the French learners than in those of the Japanese learners, whereas the percentage of the errors in the choice of noun is lower in

---

[5] The sentence for this question is "I am going to (   ) next year" with the French L1 equivalent sentence.

the responses of the French learners than in those of the Japanese learners. Table 6.4 below also shows whether these differences have resulted from the L1 influence.

**Table 6.4 Distribution of Types of Errors, W/I Occurrences &
L1 likely Errors by the French and Japanese Learners
([Adjective + Noun] collocations)**

[adjective + noun]	French Learners (n=29)			Japanese Learners (n=38)		
	W/I Occurrences* (a)	L1 likely Errors (b)	% (b) / (a)	W/I Occurrences* (a)	L1 likely Errors (b)	% (b) / (a)
(1) adjectives	79 (61.2%)	42 (53.8%)	53.2	44 (31.9%)	30 (32.6%)	68.2
(2) nouns	50 (38.8%)	36 (46.2%)	72.0	91 (65.9%)	62 (67.4%)	68.1
(3) determiners	0 (0.0%)	0 (0.0%)	0.0	0 (0.0%)	0 (0.0%)	0.0
(4) structure	0 (0.0%)	0 (0.0%)	0.0	0 (0.0%)	0 (0.0%)	0.0
(5) different expressions	1 (0.8%)	0 (0.0%)	0.0	3 (2.2%)	0 (0.0%)	0.0
(6) prepositions	0 (0.0%)	0 (0.0%)	0.0	0 (0.0%)	0 (0.0%)	0.0
(7) numbers	0 (0.0%)	0 (0.0%)	0.0	0 (0.0%)	0 (0.0%)	0.0
TOTAL	129 (100%)	78 (100%)	60.5	138 (100%)	92 (100%)	66.6

(*: "W/I occurrences" refers to the number of wrong or infelicitous collocations.)

As it was shown in MCQ Tasks in this [adjective+noun] category, the French learners showed more extent of the L1 influence in their choice of wrong/infelicitous adjectives, though the difference is not large in Translation Tasks.

The results of Translation Tasks showed the similar responses concerning their choice of adjectives and nouns. The overall accuracy between them shows that the French (60.5%) and Japanese learners (66.6%) are likely to be influenced by their L1 to a similar extent. Since the word order of the [adjective + noun] category of collocations in English and French, English and Japanese is similar in many cases, the L1 influence is easily found. For example, in the collocation, "main meal", about half of the French learners' wrong translation was "principal meal" because of the French version of this collocation, "repas principal". However, because of the nature of the translation tasks which require the learners to translate their L1 equivalent collocation into English, the French learners may have translated it literally. Nearly 53.0% of the French learners' wrong translation was "strong fever" instead of "high fever" because of the French version "une forte fièvre" in which "forte" means "strong". The Japanese learners' errors in the choice of nouns are evident in the collocation, "high fever" in which more than half of the wrong translation was "high heat" since "heat" and "fever" can be both translated as "netsu" in Japanese. In the collocation, "bad habit", more than 33.0% of the Japanese learners' wrong translation was "bad custom" because both "habit" and "custom" are translated as "shuukan" in Japanese.

6.3.5 Category 4: [Adverb + Adjective] Collocations

Among the four lexical categories of collocations the present study investigates, the level of acceptable answers is the lowest for [Adverb + Adjective] in the responses of both the French and Japanese learners: only 10.0% of the French learners and 5.7% of the Japanese learners' translations were acceptable collocations (See Table 6.1 above). Such results indicate that the [adverb + adjective] category of collocations is extremely difficult for learners regardless of their L1. The one-way ANOVA based on the above responses was conducted and the test was significant: $F(1,65)=4.84$, $p=.03$.

In terms of the errors both French and Japanese learners made, the number of the wrong choices is higher in relation to adverbs than to adjectives and the adverbs were the collocates on which the present study focuses. The following section investigates to what extent the wrong choice of adverbs was influenced by the learners' L1.

Table 6.5 Distribution of Types of Errors, W/I Occurrences &

L1 likely Errors by the French and Japanese Learners

([Adverb + Adjective] collocations)

[adverb + adjective]	French Learners (n=29)			Japanese Learners (n=38)		
	W/I Occurrences* (a)	L1 likely Errors (b)	% (b) / (a)	W/I Occurrences* (a)	L1 likely Errors (b)	% (b) / (a)
(1) adverbs	110 (58.8%)	40(56.3%)	36.4	127 (76.5%)	22 (62.9%)	17.3
(2) adjectives	71 (38.0%)	30(42.3%)	42.3	35 (21.1%)	13 (37.1%)	37.1
(3) determiners	0 (0.0%)	0 (0.0%)	0	0 (0.0%)	0 (0.0%)	0.0
(4) structure	0 (0.0%)	0 (0.0%)	0	0 (0.0%)	0 (0.0%)	0.0
(5) different expressions	6 (3.2%)	0 (0.0%)	0	4 (2.4%)	0 (0.0%)	0.0
(6) prepositions	0 (0.0%)	0 (0.0%)	0	0 (0.0%)	0 (0.0%)	0.0
(7) numbers	0 (0.0%)	0 (0.0%)	0	0 (0.0%)	0 (0.0%)	0.0
TOTAL	187 (100%)	71(100%)	38.0	166 (100%)	35(100%)	21.1

(*: "W/I occurrences" refers to the number of wrong or infelicitous collocations.)

As shown in Table 6.5, the extent of the L1 influence on the wrong choice of adverbs is greater in the responses of the Japanese learners than those of the French learners. The average percentages of L1 likely errors of the French and Japanese learners in relation to adverbs and/or adjectives are not quite similar, i.e. 38.0% in French learners, and 21.1% in Japanese learners, which indicates that the French learners are likely to be influenced by their L1 than the Japanese learners. At the same time, this result may suggest the effect of the translation tasks itself which needs to be taken into account. Since the translation tasks present the learners' L1 equivalent collocations, their L1 influence is likely to be triggered. In terms of the Japanese learners, this percentage (49.4%) is almost as high as the L1 influence shown in the [adjective + noun] collocations, and other categories, [verb + noun] and [delexicalised verb + noun] collocations, showed less percentage of L1 influence.

149

6.3.6 Conclusion

While L1 influence is apparent in the results of both the French and Japanese learners, the extent of the L1 influence depends on the lexical categories. The analysis of the types of errors found in the responses with regard to all the four lexical categories of collocations showed greater L1 influence among the French learners than the Japanese learners especially in the [verb + noun], [delexicalised verb + noun] and [adverb + adjective] categories. A relatively large degree of L1 influence is observed in relation to the use of prepositions by the French learners and the use of nouns by the Japanese learners, the L1 influence on verbs is generally greater in the responses of both the French and Japanese learners than that on other types of errors.

The responses of the different expressions, which involve circumlocution rather than using collocations, were shared by the French and Japanese learners in the [delexicalised verb + noun] categories. Both of them used different expressions when they encountered the collocations they do not know. These findings about [delexicalised verb + noun] suggest a number of possible causes for the errors occurring in the learner' production of collocations: 1) learners tend to add prepositions in producing L2 collocations when the verbs in their L1 collocations include prepositions; 2) learners tend to confuse nouns with different meaning in their L1s (notably French learners' translation of "a newspaper" for "a diary", for example).

Concerning the [adjective + noun] category of collocations, though French learners also showed large extent of L1 influence on wrong/infelicitous collocations, Japanese learners showed greater extent of L1 influence in Translation Tasks. Regarding the collocations in the former category, this tendency was also found in MCQ Task.

Both the French and Japanese learners showed L1 influence in terms of the [adjective + noun] category of collocations. In some cases, L1 influence may have led to the correct answer both by the French and Japanese learners in terms of the [adjective + noun] category of collocations.

6.4 Combinability and Transparency Influence on the Collocations

This section investigates whether the combinability and transparency of collocations affect the L2 learners' production of collocations. Though it has been previously indicated that the L2 learners tend to be influenced by their L1 in choosing correct collocations, no study has been carried out from the viewpoint of the L2 learners' of collocations with combinability and transparency. Since the collocations in the Translation Tasks in the present study are divided into two groups, [+ Restricted Combinability, + Transparency] and [- Restriceted Combinability, - Transparency], analyses are performed for each group.

It is true that the main effect of collocation type, i.e. [+ ResComb, + Transp] and [- ResComb, - Transp] of collocations, was not significant as shown in Section 6.2.2. However, the interactions of language group and collocation type, and those of lexical type and collocation type, and those of language group, lexical type and collocation type were significant. Thus, the following discussion will reveal the nature of these significances.

The overall acceptable, infelicitous and wrong answers of all four lexical categories are classified in Table 6.6 by the [+ResComb, +Transp] and the [-ResComb, -Transp] groups.

In terms of the [verb + noun] category of collocations, both French and Japanese learners show higher accuracy in language production in the [+ResComb, +Transp] group than in the [-ResComb, -Transp] group of collocations.

Table 6.6 Number of the Responses of Translation Tasks in the [+ResComb, +Transp] and [-ResComb, -Transp] Groups of Collocations

(1) [Verb + Noun] Group of Collocations

(15 collocations: 9 for [+ResComb, +Transp] and 6 for [-ResComb, -Transp])

Lang. Group	Types of Collocation	Types of Answers				Total
		acceptable	infelicitous	non-target	non-response	
French (n=29)	[+,+]:score	107	14	45	95	261
	%	41.0%	5.4%	17.2%	36.4%	100%
	[-, -]: score	43	18	42	71	174
	%	24.7%	10.3%	24.1%	40.8%	100%
Japanese (n=38)	[+,+]:score	114	38	94	96	342
		33.3%	11.1%	27.5%	28.1%	100%
	[-, -]: score	38	18	60	112	228
		16.7%	7.9%	26.3%	49.1%	100%

(2) [Delexicalised Verb + Noun] Group of Collocations:

(15 collocations: 7 for [+ResComb, +Transp]; 8 for [-ResComb, -Transp])

Lang. Group	Types of Collocation	Types of Answers				Total
		acceptable	infelicitous	non-target	non-response	
French (n=29)	[+,+]:score	90	4	50	59	203
	%	44.3%	2.0%	24.6%	29.1%	100%
	[-, -]: score	79	11	68	74	232
	%	34.1%	4.7%	29.3%	31.9%	100%
Japanese (n=38)	[+,+]:score	96	14	55	101	266
		36.1%	5.3%	20.7%	38.0%	100%
	[-, -]: score	87	25	70	122	304
		28.6%	8.2%	23.0%	40.1%	100%

Similarly to the [verb + noun] category of collocations discussed above, with respect to the [delexicalised verb + noun] category of collocations, the French learners show higher accuracy in the responses of the [+ResComb, +Transp] (44.3%) than those in the [-ResComb, -Transp] groups of collocations (34.1%). Similar tendency is found in the results of the Japanese learners who show a higher percentage of acceptable answers in the [+ResComb, +Transp] group (36.1%) than in the [-ResComb, -Transp] group of collocations (28.6%). Thus, the results indicate that both the French and Japanese learners showed higher accuracy in the [+ResComb, +Transp] group of collocations than in the [-ResComb, -Transp] group of collocations for [verb + noun] collocations regardless of the learners' L1s.

(3) [Adjective+ Noun] Group of Collocations:

(14 collocations: 7 for each of [+ResComb, +Transp] and [-ResComb, -Transp])

Lang. Group	Types of Collocation	Types of Answers				Total
		acceptable	infelicitous	non-target	non-response	
French (n=29)	[+,+]:score	97	7	58	41	203
	%	47.8%	3.4%	28.6%	20.2%	100%
	[-, -]: score	101	3	59	40	203
	%	49.8%	1.5%	29.1%	19.7%	100%
Japanese (n=38)	[+,+]:score	177	3	39	47	266
		66.5%	1.1%	14.7%	17.7%	100%
	[-, -]: score	92	3	82	89	266
		34.6%	1.1%	30.8%	33.5%	100%

While in terms of the [verb + noun] and [delexicalised verb + noun] categories of collocations, the tendency to show higher accuracy in the [+ResComb, +Transp] group of collocations was common to both French and Japanese learners, this was not the case for the [adjective + noun] category of collocations. While the Japanese learners show higher accuracy (66.5%) in producing the [+ResComb, +Transp] than in the [-ResComb, -Transp] group of collocations (34.6%), the French learners show slightly lower accuracy (47.8%) in the [+ResComb, +Transp] than in the [-ResComb, -Transp] group of collocations (49.8%). The accuracy of the Japanese learners (66.5%) in the [+ResComb, +Transp] group of collocations exceeds the French learners' accuracy in the [+ResComb, +Transp] (47.8%) and even the [-ResComb, -Transp] group of collocations (49.8%). The [+ResComb, +Transp] and [-

ResComb, -Transp] do not seem to affect the accuracy of answers provided by French learners in this category of collocations.

(4) [Adverb + Adjective] Group of Collocations:

(12 collocations: 5 for [+ResComb, +Transp]; 7 for [-ResComb, -Transp])

Lang. Group	Types of Collocation	Types of Answers				Total
		acceptable	infelicitous	non-target	Non-response	
French (n=29)	[+,+]:score	10	10	67	58	145
	%	6.9%	6.9%	46.2%	40.0%	100%
	[-, -]: score	44	0	78	81	203
	%	21.7%	0.0%	38.4%	39.9%	100%
Japanese (n=38)	[+,+]:score	2	1	75	112	190
		1.1%	0.5%	39.5%	58.9%	100%
	[-, -]: score	29	6	65	166	266
		10.9%	2.3%	24.4%	62.4%	100%

Lastly, in terms of the results in the [adverb + adjective] category of collocations, unlike the results of the other lexical categories, the accuracy of both the French and Japanese learners' responses was lower in the [+ResComb, +Transp] group than in the [-ResComb, -Transp] group of collocations. The accuracy of this category of collocations by both the French and Japanese learners is considerably lower than the one in the results of the other three lexical categories. Thus, the collocations in the [adverb + adjective] category may be particularly difficult for the L2 learners. As shown in Table 6.6-(4), the number of acceptable answers with regard to both the French and Japanese learners in the [-ResComb, -Transp] group was larger than that of the [+ResComb, +Transp] group of collocations. The influence of the [+ResComb, +Transp] and [-ResComb, -Transp] for this category of collocations may not have operated in the same way as they did in the other lexical categories of collocations. Unlike the other three lexical categories of collocations, producing the [+ResComb, +Transp] group of collocations were not easier than the [-ResComb, -Transp] group of collocations by both French and Japanese learners. Also, the number of the non-responses by both the French and Japanese learners was considerably large in this category of collocations.

6.5 Summary

In this chapter, the production of collocations was investigated through the use of Translation Tasks. The results were categorized into three types, namely 1) acceptable, 2) infelicitous and 3) non-target, based on the judgment of two British linguists.

Firstly, as shown in Table 6.1 on overall accuracy of Translation Tasks, the French learners showed higher accuracy in the three lexical categories of collocations: [verb + noun], [delexicalised verb + noun] and [adverb + adjective] categories of collocations.

The main effects of the language groups, i.e. French and Japanese, and lexical types, i.e. [verb + noun], [delexicalised verb + noun], [adjective + noun] and [adverb + adjective], were significant. Based on the responses of the learners, the L1 influence was investigated by looking at the errors of words of different grammatical categories in each lexical category. All the errors made by the French and Japanese learners were then categorized and analyzed in terms of the seven types of errors defined, such as verbs, nouns, adjectives, adverbs, determiners, prepositions, different expressions, structure and numbers, in order to show how L1 influenced the errors in different types (grammatical categories) of words. With respect to the [verb + noun], [delexicalised verb + noun] and [adverb + adjective] categories of collocations, the French learners demonstrated greater L1 influence than the Japanese learners. The results of Translation Tasks indicate that it is likely that there is a difference in the L1 influence between learners from different L1 backgrounds.

Thirdly, it was investigated that the discussion on the [+ResComb, +Transp] and [-ResComb, -Transp] influence on the production of collocations by the French and Japanese learners was shown. While there was no significant difference between the responses in the [+ResComb, +Transp] and those in the [-ResComb, -Transp] groups of collocations in each lexical category, the French learners showed a higher accuracy in the [+ResComb, +Transp] than that of the [-ResComb, -Transp] of collocations in terms of the [verb + noun], [delexicalised verb + noun] and [adjective + noun] categories. Both the French and Japanese learners showed a higher accuracy in the [-ResComb, -Transp] than the [+ResComb, +Transp] collocations with regard to [adverb + adjective] category of collocations. The effect of the interaction between the language group and collocation type was found in the [adjective + noun] but not in the [verb + noun], [delexicalised verb + noun] and [adverb + adjective] categories of collocations.

The next chapter investigates the use of collocations by the French and Japanese learners through utilizing the learner corpora.

Chapter 7

RESULTS AND ANALYSIS OF LEARNER CORPORA

7.1 Introduction

In this chapter, the results from the investigation into both French and Japanese learner corpora will be reported. In the preceding two chapters, the learners' responses in MCQ and Translation Tasks responses were analyzed so as to clarify the specificities of French and Japanese learners' knowledge and use of English collocations. The two types of tasks were formulated based on the [+/- Restricted Combinability] and [+/- Transparency] particular to the present study. In addition to MCQ and Translation Tasks, an investigation of both French and Japanese learner corpora were carried out to ensure the objectivity of the results obtained in MCQ and Translation Tasks. The investigation of the learner corpora is expected to reveal any trends in French and Japanese learners' use of English collocations in totally free production. The two learner corpora, French and Japanese learner corpora, are made up from learners' written essays containing completely free production of English, whereas MCQ and Translation Tasks required learners to respond to the particular target collocations chosen for the tasks in the present study.

7.2 Outline of the Learner Corpora

In order to focus on the collocations targeted in the two earlier tasks, the frequencies of occurrences of the target collocations were counted in the French and Japanese learner corpus respectively. The raw occurrences of the target collocations are presented in the following sections.

The number of texts included in the present study is 267 for French learners and 175 for Japanese learners. 160,079 word tokens are included in the French learner corpus, while there are 84,799 tokens in the Japanese one.

Table 7.1 Numbers of Texts and Words for French and Japanese Learner Corpora

	French	Japanese
Total Number of Essays	267	175
Total Number of Words	160,079	84,779
Average Number of Words per Text	599	484

The Japanese learner corpus was from the unpublished corpus of written essays by Japanese university students collected by the International Corpus of Learner English (ICLE) project group. These unpublished essays were obtained from Professor Kaneko Tomoko, the organizer of the Japan branch of the ICLE project. The detailed Japanese learner profiles are not available in the Japanese learner corpus.

On the other hand, the French learner corpus used in this investigation was selected from the published ICLE (2002). The learners' L1 is French and length of experience in English-speaking countries is 12 months maximum.

The age of the learners is between 18 and 24 and the samples were collected from university students with French and Japanese L1 backgrounds. The concordance tool WordSmith 4.0 was used for the investigation of all 56 target collocations.

The detailed backgrounds of the French and Japanese learners are not exactly the same as the learners examined in MCQ and Translation Tasks. For example, the age of the French learners for this learner corpus is younger than that of the French learners who participated in MCQ and Translation Tasks. The learners' level is indicated as "higher intermediate to advanced" (Granger *et al.* 2002:14) but any standard measurements were not used. This investigation aims to reveal the tendency that French and Japanese learners show in the form of totally free production of collocations.

Both the French corpus in the ICLE and the Japanese corpus were downloaded in WordSmith 4.0 analysis. An investigation was carried out in the French and Japanese corpora for all the target collocations and the infelicitous and unacceptable collocations found in Translation Tasks in order to investigate to what extent such collocations occur in free production. Both Translation Tasks and the learner corpus require learners to produce collocations rather than recognize them as was the case in MCQ Tasks. For example, in the case of "common sense", the occurrences of all the collocations produced by learners in Translation Tasks, i.e. "good sense", "good mind", "good feelings", "rational raison", "good knowledge", "logical thinking" and "logical sense", were investigated in the French learner corpus. Despite the productive nature of tasks in both data sets, i.e. Translation Tasks and Learner Corpus, they are essentially quite different. The degree of restriction in production is higher in Translation Tasks than in the essay writing. Because the L1 equivalents are given to the learners, the likelihood of L1 influence is greater for translation tasks than for essay writing. This analysis of corpus clarifies whether any of the findings of the Translation Tasks were artifacts of the tasks. On the other hand, there is a limitation with this dataset: the learners can usually consult with a dictionary in essay writing without time limit, thus a wider variety of expressions is available for them than in translation tasks.

7.3 Results of the Learner Corpora Investigation

7.3.1 Results of the French Learner Corpus Investigation

Table 7.2 below shows the details of relevant collocations identified in the French corpus. The occurrences refer to the number of hits found in each learner corpus. The sentences or phrases with the asterisk (*) indicate that they show either infelicitous or unacceptable collocations judged by the two native

Table 7.2 Raw Occurrences of Collocations by Lexical Category
(French Learners)

No	Collocations found in French Learner Corpus	Occurrence
(1)	**[Verb + Noun] Collocations**	
1	(*Target Collocation*: ask her/him a question)	
	One can *ask oneself the question* whether it is…	1
	Everybody should *ask* himself *the* following *questions*: "Is…?	1
	The public opinion *ask* the same *question*: how efficient…	1
2	(*Target Collocation*: reach/arrive at/come to a conclusion)	
	what *conclusions* may be *drawn* from all this?	1
	we inevitably *come to the conclusion* that…	1
3	(*Target Collocation*: give/provide/offer an opportunity)	
	A solution would be to *give* them *the opportunity* to follow…	1
	Everybody should be *given the opportunity* of studying at …	1
	It *gives* them *the opportunity* to have a nice dream	1
	They *give* us *the opportunity* to transforms the…	1
	* Educational systems don't *give* many *possibilities* to the practice of …	1
	* Television also *gives the possibility* to discover other horizons.	1
	* *give* to young people *the possibility* to enrich their…	1
	Let us *give* Europe *a chance!*	1
	They are not *offered* a second *chance.*	1
	(a) Sub Total	14
(2)	**[Delexicalised Verb + Noun] Collocations**	
4	(*Target Collocation*: take/have/go for a walk)	
	we have to *go* out *for a walk.*	1
5	(*Target Collocation*: take/make notes)	
	who is conscientiously *taking notes.*	1
6	(*Target Collocation*: have the (same) effect)	
	watch anything *has an harmful effect.*	1
	often accused of *having* harmful *effects*	1
	Its usage *has* negative *effects.*	1
	Sociologists argue that television *has* a cathartic *effect* on people.	1
7	(*Target Collocation*: receive/obtain an answer)	
	We shall *have the answer* tomorrow…	1
8	(*Target Collocation*: have/keep good control)	
	have some *control*	1
	industrialization *is the master* of the modern world	1
	* we are masters of our lives	1
	(b) Sub Total	10

(3) [Adjective + Noun] Collocations		
9	(*Target Collocation*: bad/poor/low quality)	
	The real reason for buying such *bad quality* is that …	1
	This is mainly due to the *bad quality* of the programs	1
10	(*Target Collocation*: common sense)	
	a lot of *common sense* will be required.	1
11	(*Target Collocation*: free/spare/leisure time)	
	leisure time can be most enriching to …	1
	some people waste their *leisure time* on senseless occupations like…	1
	found it difficult to occupy our *free time*.	1
	Now all our *free time* is regulated by…	1
	(c) Sub Total	7
(4) [Adverb + Adjective] Collocations		
12	(*Target Collocation*: extremely serious)	
	they did something that was *really serious*	1
13	(*Target Collocation*: highly unlikely)	
	this is *very unlikely* to happen	1
14	(*Target Collocation*: fully/certainly/perfectly aware)	
	I am *perfectly aware* that it is much easier to imagine…	1
	(d) Sub Total	3
Total (a) + (b) + (c) + (d)		**34**

speakers of English. Except for the following 14 collocations for French learner corpus and 12 collocations for Japanese learner corpus, there were no hits for the other collocations in each of the French and Japanese learner corpora.

The total number of relevant occurrences found in the French learner corpus is considerably smaller than originally expected. In total, the number of relevant occurrences that the French learners produced is 34 which represented 14 collocations in total out of the 56 collocations used in MCQ and Translation Tasks in the present study. Among them, relatively frequent occurrences, including infelicitous and unacceptable collocations, were found in the three lexical groups, i.e., the [verb + noun], [delexicalised verb + noun] and [adjective + noun]. Only a small variety of adverbs were identified in the [adverb + adjective] group, because it is likely that the learners use safe adverbs, such as "very" and "really", to avoid potential mistakes.

7.3.2 Results of the Japanese Learner Corpus Investigation

The results found in the Japanese learner corpus are presented as in Table 7.3 below. The details of relevant collocations are shown with the number of occurrences, and the asterisks (*) indicate that the sentences/phrases include either infelicitous or unacceptable collocation, which is similar to Table 7.2.

Table 7.3 Raw Occurrences of Target Collocations by Lexical Category (Japanese learners)

No	Collocations found in French Learner Corpus	Occurrence
(1) [Verb + Noun] Collocations		
1	(Target Collocation: tell the truth)	
	Doctors have to tell the truth.	1
2	(Target Collocation: lose weight)	
	* I reduce my weight.	1
3	(Target Collocation: ask her/him a question)	
	I was asked a question	1
	we would buy goods order meal and asked the question	1
	* I want to ask more question to teacher	1
	* English teacher asked some question to us.	1
	If you have a chance to ask them the same question,	1
4	(Target Collocation: give/provide/offer an opportunity)	
	It gives us a chance to be more good international person.	1
	The criminals should be given chances to reform himself.	1
	* it continues to give me chance of meeting.	1
5	(Target Collocation: win the game)	
	Our team won the championship.	1
	(a) Sub Total	**11**
(2) [Delexicalised Verb + Noun] Collocations		
6	(Target Collocation: take/have/go for a walk)	
	I took a walk with Koro	1
	neighbor who wants to take a walk with them.	1
	owner don't have to take a walk with him	1
7	(Target Collocation: receive/obtain an answer)	
	I was glad that I get the answer mail soon…	1
	we need time to get an answer…	1
	(b) Sub Total	**5**

(3) [Adjective + Noun] Collocations		
8	(*Target Collocation*: common sense)	
	who don't have culture and *common sense*.	1
	In point of *common sense*	1
	assailant's boys lack *common sense*	1
	we have a chance to learn *common sense*	1
	we can't say he has *common sense*	1
	* to insist of oneself opinion is very important or *common knowledge*.	1
9	(*Target Collocation*: free/spare/leisure time)	
	I can do anything during the *free time*	1
	I can have a lot of *free time*	1
	While I had much *free time*	1
	There is no *free time* in my daily life	1
	There is a lot of *free time*	1
	students send their abundant *spare time*	1
	Many students spend their abundant *spare time* working at…	1
	(c) Sub Total	13
(4) [Adverb + Adjective] Collocations		
10	(*Target Collocation*: extremely serious)	
	Japanese depression is *very serious* problem	1
11	(*Target Collocation*: terribly afraid)	
	I was *very afraid* to make a mistake	1
12	(*Target Collocation*: extremely/totally different)	
	children and adults are *completely different*	1
	America is *very different* from Japan.	1
	English which is *very different* from Japanese	1
	Japanese English and English is *very different*	1
	very different types of listeners	1
	very different types of musicians	1
	(d) Sub Total	8
Total (a) + (b) + (c) + (d)		37

In total, the number of relevant collocations that the Japanese learners produced is 37, which represent 12 collocations in total out of the 56 collocations used in MCQ and Translation Tasks in the present study. Among them, frequent occurrences were found in three lexical groups of [verb + noun], [adjective + noun] and [adverb + adjective] groups, but not in the [delexicalised verb + noun] group. The number of the occurrences in the [delexicalised verb + noun] group is much smaller than that of the French learners, which appears

163

to indicate that the Japanese learners may not often use this category of collocations when the restriction of production is totally free. When the Japanese learners' results in the four lexical groups are compared with those of the French learners, the number of occurrences of the collocations in the [adverb + adjective] group by the Japanese learners is larger than that of the French learners. Yet, the variety of collocations does not show a great difference between the French learners and the Japanese learners' corpora. As indicated in the results of the French learners, the use of the adverbs is limited to "very" rather than the variety of adverbs partly because they seem to prefer to use "very" rather than using other adverbs.

7.4 Analysis of the Results

7.4.1 Learners' L1 Influence on the Collocations

Though the limited number of the collocations was identified in the French and Japanese learner corpora, this section tries to discuss the L1 influence by investigating respective lexical category of collocations, and examine the L1 influence which may affect the learners' production of collocations.

With regard to the [verb + noun] category of collocations produced by the French learners, 3 collocations were found with 14 occurrences in total (See Table 7.2): "ask a question", "draw a conclusion" and "offer/give the opportunity". The collocation, "offer/give the opportunity", whose L1 French equivalent is "donner(=give) sa chance", occurred 9 times, and 8 out of 9 occurrences used "give". The learners used "the possibility", "the opportunity" and "chance" as the nouns to go with "give". Their frequent use of "give" seems to suggest that the French learners are either influenced by their L1 in this collocation or they have learned this collocation as a chunk. The frequent use of "give" by the French learners indicates the use of safe and simple verbs to avoid mistakes.

With respect to the Japanese learners' corpus, 5 collocations were found with 11 occurrences in the [verb + noun] category of collocations. Among them, "tell the truth", "lose weight" and "give/offer the opportunity" do not seem to be the consequence of the influence of their L1. Similarly to the French learners, in the collocation "give/offer the opportunity", whose Japanese equivalent is "kikai(chance) wo(object particle) teikyousuru(provide/offer)" more frequent use of the verb, "give", was found rather than other possible verbs such as "provide" and "offer". Because L1 Japanese equivalent uses a different type of verb, this may indicate that the Japanese learners may have learned the collocation as a chunk, and/or their frequent use of "give" implies their intention to avoid a risk of mistake by using safe and simple verbs. In case of "ask someone a question", whose Japanese equivalent it "shitsumon(a question) wo(object particle) suru(do)", 5 occurrences were found. The Japanese learners do not use the target collocation, "ask someone a question", due to L1 influence, since the Japanese equivalent collocation does not contain the verb meaning to "ask"(=kiku,tazuneru) but to "do"(=suru). The Japanese learners' frequent use of this collocation seems to indicate that they are not necessarily influenced by their L1.

The considerable differences between the French and the Japanese learners' corpora were found in the number of occurrences in the [delexicalised verb + noun] category (F: 10, J: 5). However, because the size of the French learners corpus is twice as large as that of the Japanese learner corpus, the number of occurrences of this category of collocations is considered equal. The French learners produced 5 types of collocations: "go out for a walk", "take notes", "have (harmful) effects", "have the answer" and "have (some) control". Except for "go out for a walk", all of the 5 types of collocations have the possibilities of being influenced by their L1, French, which has the equivalent word orders and the delexicalised verbs and nouns.

On the other hand, the Japanese learners produced 2 collocations, "take a walk" and "receive/obtain an answer". The L1 equivalents of these collocations are: "sanpo suru" for "take a walk" and "kotae wo morau" for "receive/obtain an answer". They use the collocation, "take a walk", though the Japanese L1 equivalent collocation involves the verb meaning "do" instead of the one meaning "take". Thus, whereas the Japanese learners produce 5 occurrences of 2 collocations, the 10 occurrences of 5 collocations may be the consequence of the L1 influence as in the French learner corpus. This suggests that the L2 learners who do not have the L1 equivalent collocations produce the [delexicalised verb + noun] group of collocations by using their knowledge of collocations which were stored as a chunk.

With regard to the [adjective + noun] category of collocations, 3 collocations, such as "bad quality", "common sense" and "leisure time", were produced with 7 occurrences by the French learners. 2 of them, "bad quality" and "common sense", have the equivalent collocations in their L1. In the results of the Japanese learner corpus, all of the 2 collocations with 13 occurrences in "common sense" and "free time" have the L1 equivalents. However, based on the limited number of collocations in this category, it is not clear whether the French and Japanese learners tend to produce such collocations due to L1 influence. Moreover, the number of occurrences found in this category of collocations by the Japanese learners is larger than that of the French learners despite the smaller size of the Japanese learner corpora. This suggests that the Japanese learners have a better access to this category of collocations than other lexical categories of collocations.

Lastly, in relation to the results from the collocations produced in the [adverb + adjective] category of collocations, it is likely that the learners use only familiar adverbs to combine with the adjectives in order to avoid making mistakes by using the adverbs which are not familiar enough with them. The French learners produced "really serious", "very unlikely", and "perfectly aware" with only 3 occurrences while the Japanese learners produce "very serious", "very afraid", "very different" with 8 occurrences. Although the number of occurrences is larger in the Japanese learners' corpus than the French learners', the variety of the adverbs is considerably small in both groups of learners.

In summary, despite the limited number of occurrences found in the French and Japanese learner corpora, the likelihood of L1 influence in all the four lexical categories of collocations was identified.

7.4.2 Combinability and Transparency Influence on the Collocations

This section examines whether the combinability and transparency affects their production of collocations. The following table shows the number of occurrences depending on the combinability and transparency of collocations. It shows that both the French and Japanese learners produce the [-ResComb, -Transp] group of collocations more often than the [+ ResComb, +Transp] one.

Table 7.4 Number of Occurrences of Collocations by the [+ResComb, +Transp] and [-ResComb, -Transp]

French learners	[+ResComb, +Transp]	[-ResComb, -Transp]
Verb + Noun	3	11
Delexicalized Verb + Noun	8	2
Adjective + Noun	1	6
Adverb + Adjective	1	2
Total	13	21
Japanese learners	[+ResComb, +Transp]	[-ResComb, -Transp]
Verb + Noun	2	9
Delexicalised Verb + Noun	0	5
Adjective + Noun	6	7
Adverb + Adjective	2	6
Total	10	27

Compared with [+ResComb, +Transp] group, a larger number of the occurrences is found in the [-ResComb, -Transp] group of collocations in the [verb + noun], [adjective + noun] and [adverb + adjective] categories of the French learner corpus. This may suggest the French learners find it easier to produce the [-ResComb, -Transp] groups of collocations. In this respect, the results of the French learners may not correspond to the previous discussion by Kellerman (1978) who asserts that the L1 learners are not willing to transfer words with non-literal or figurative meaning, i.e. [-Transp] as represented in the present study, while they are willing to transfer the words with literal meaning, i.e. [+Transp] as represented in the present study. The French learners are willing to produce collocations with non-literal or figurative meaning, i.e. [-Transp], and produce a larger number of [-ResComb, -Transp] collocations than the collocations with literal meaning, i.e. [+Transp]. In the Japanese learner corpus, the tendency to produce a larger number of the [-ResComb, -Transp] collocations is more robust than the one discussed in the French learner corpus; the larger number of occurrences in the [-ResComb, -Transp] group is identified in all 4 lexical categories of collocations than in the [+ResComb, +Transp] group of collocations.

However, it is not apparent whether these differences have arisen either due to [+/- ResComb] or [+/-Transp]. Because the current study did not examine the [+ResComb, -Transp] group of collocations where [ResComb] value is not constant with [+ResComb, +Transp] group of collocations, the effects of [+/-Transp] that is independent from the effect of [ResComb] cannot be discussed. The discussion in the present study is limited to the effect of [+ResComb, +Transp] and [-ResComb, -Transp] groups of collocations rather than the effect of [+/-Transp] by itself.

Although the numbers of occurrences found in both French and Japanese learner corpora were small, the present study showed that both L2 learners demonstrate the tendency to produce more collocations which have more figurativeness and more possibilities of combinability, which may disagree with the previous argument by Kellerman (*ibid.*) though. The present study is limited to the influence of the combinations of the two variables, i.e. [+/-ResComb] and [+/-Transp].

7.5 Summary

As discussed above, despite the limited number of collocations, this chapter tried to investigate the differences of L1 and combinability/transparency influence on the target collocations between the French and Japanese learner corpora. The overall results indicate that both the French and Japanese frequently use those collocations which have the equivalent meaning to their L1 equivalents, suggesting the L1 influence. In general, the differences of the L1 influence between French and Japanese learners were not identified clearly mainly because of the limited number of relevant occurrences found in the French and Japanese corpora.

With regard to the effect of the combinability and transparency on the production of collocations, the number of the relevant occurrences in the corpora showed that both French and Japanese learners were able to produce more collocations with more figurativeness and more possibilities of combinability with other words than the collocations with less figurativeness and less possibilities of combinability. These results may partly contrast the previous remark made by Kellerman (1978) who argues that the L2 learners are not able to transfer words with non-literal or figurative meaning. However, the influence of [+/-Transp], independent of the effect of [+/-ResComb] could not be examined because the current study focused on the influence of the two combinations, i.e. [+ResComb, +Transp] and [-ResComb, -Transp]. Moreover, since the number of the collocations investigated in this chapter is limited, the future research with a larger number of collocations into the learner corpus is necessary for the generalization of the L2 learners' production of collocations.

Chapter 8

CONCLUSION, IMPLICATIONS FOR TEACHING AND FURTHER RESEARCH

8.1 Introduction

While it has been recognized that the use of collocations is significant for L2 learners, a small number of research has been carried out on the knowledge and use of learners' collocations. Among the few studies on L2 learners' knowledge and use of collocations, the majority of them focused on the English learners with Indo-European L1 backgrounds, such as German and French, and the research on the learners of non-Indo-European L1 backgrounds is scarce. It was expected that the knowledge and use of the L2 learners from different L1 backgrounds, i.e. Indo-European and non-Indo-European, might be different because of the difference in their L1 backgrounds. Thus, the French learners who have Indo-European L1 background and the Japanese learners who have non-Indo-European L1 background were compared to investigate their knowledge and use of collocations.

Although most of the previous studies on learners' use of collocations have adopted one type of data elicitation instrument, the present study adopted three different types of data collection instruments to examine the knowledge and use of the collocations by the French and Japanese learners in detail. The three types are MCQ Tasks, Translation Tasks and Learner Corpora. The target collocations for investigation to be investigated were selected based on the L1 speakers' data and these target collocations were provided to the learners in the form of MCQ and Translation Tasks, and the collocations used in these two tasks were also examined in the French and Japanese Learner Corpora.

This chapter begins with the summary of the findings presented in Chapters 5, 6 and 7 in which the analyses of the two types of tasks and learner corpora data were carried out. The findings were presented in relation to: 1) learners' L1 influence on the collocations; 2) [+ResComb, +Transp] and [-ResComb, -Transp] influence on the collocations. In addition to the findings in the present study, some implications for teaching collocations are discussed in this chapter. Then, some suggestions will be made for further research related to the study of learners' knowledge and use of collocations based on the results and findings of the present study. Lastly, the final remarks are given.

8.2 Summary of Findings

Because of the syntactic and/or lexical differences in their L1s, French and Japanese learners' knowledge and use of collocations may not necessarily be similar to each other. Based on this assumption, the analysis of the data by two major types of tasks, i.e. MCQ and Translation Tasks, were undertaken and learner corpus is also investigated in the present study. This section summarizes the findings and the discussions about them. Firstly, the findings and discussions regarding learners' L1 influence on the recognition and production of collocations are presented. Then, those regarding the influence by the [+ResComb, +Transp] and [-ResComb, -Transp] on the collocations are presented.

8.2.1 Learners' L1 Influence on the Collocations

The first research question was whether there were any L1 influence on the knowledge and use of collocations by French and Japanese. If there were, the study investigated what kind of differences and/or similarities occur. Although the L1 is not the primary factor which has the influence on L2 learning, the present study examined the likelihood of L1 influence on their L2 collocations because of different L1 backgrounds of the French and Japanese learners. In the present study, L1 influence was operationalized by including the alternatives which were equivalent to the learners' L1s in the MCQ Tasks and by providing learners' L1 sentences in Translation tasks, which may trigger L1 influence. It was expected that the L1 influence in the French and Japanese learners was different because of their different L1 backgrounds. This section summarizes how the French and Japanese learners performed in the three types of data collection tasks in relation to the L1 influence.

In the MCQ Tasks, while the L1 influence was commonly found in their responses in both of the French and Japanese learners, it was not necessarily the primary source of their statistically significant differences. Many of the responses in all of the four lexical categories of collocations by the French and Japanese learners showed that they must have learned the collocations as chunks rather than by being influenced by their L1s. On the other hand, as Table 8.1, the French learners were more likely to be influenced by their L1 in the [verb + noun] and [delexicalised verb + noun] categories of collocations. In Translation Tasks, a greater L1 influence by the French learners was found in the [adverb + adjective] category.

Table 8.1 Results of L1 Influence by French and Japanese Learners

Lexical Category	MCQ Tasks	Translation Tasks	Learner Corpora *
1) [Verb + Noun]	✓	✓	(✓)
2) [Delexicalised Verb + Noun]	✓	✓	(✓)
3) [Adjective + Noun]			
4) [Adverb + Adjective]	(✓)	✓	

✓ :L1 influence of French learners is found to be slightly greater than that of Japanese learners.

* : Since the number of relevant collocations are a few, the comparison is not sufficient.

French and English share a number of cognate words. Because of the cognate words, it was expected that L1 influence of the French learners would be higher in all of the four lexical collocations than that of Japanese learners, who have non-Indo-European L1 backgrounds. However, in the Translation Tasks, the overall responses indicated that both the French and Japanese learners were likely to produce those collocations when they had the equivalent meaning to their L1s. As it was indicated above, the Japanese learners showed a greater L1 influence in the [adjective + noun] category not only in MCQ Tasks but also in other data collection instruments. Since Translation Tasks involve L1 equivalents of target English collocations in the tasks to be filled in with the English collocations, it is likely that the French learners were triggered to be influenced by their L1.

Concerning the [verb + noun] categories of collocations, L1 influence was identified not only in the verbs but also in the other lexical parts:

1) The results of the French learners showed L1 influence in the prepositions. Since the French L1 equivalent collocations often involve prepositions, they tended to produce verbs with the prepositions which correspond to their L1 equivalents.

2) The results of the Japanese learners showed L1 influence on the nouns of collocations. In the case of the Japanese learners, they were likely to translate Japanese nouns into English directly from their L1 nouns.

Accordingly, the L1 influence by the French and Japanese learners was not apparent in all of the three types of data collection instruments. The responses of many of the collocations in the respective four lexical categories showed that the learners must have learned as chunks rather than by being influenced by their L1s. However, in the L1 influence identified in the three types of data collection instruments, a greater L1 influence by the French learners than the Japanese learners was commonly found particularly in the [verb + noun] and [delexicalised verb + noun] groups. There is another similarity identified across the three different types of data instruments: a greater L1 influence by the Japanese learners than the French learners with regard to the [adjective + noun] category of collocations.

8.2.2 *Combinability and Transparency Influence on the Collocations*

The second research question was whether the L2 learners' knowledge and use of collocations depend on the combinability of collocations and semantic transparency in collocations. The collocations were categorized into [+Restricted Combinability, +Transparency] and [-Restricted Combinability, -Transparency] as to answer this second research question. [+/-Restricted Combinability] refers to the possibility that a node in a collocation can combine with one or two/more than three words. When the node is restricted to be combined with one or two word, the collocation is defined as [+ Restricted Combinability] or [+ResComb] and when the node is not restricted to be combined with another word (i.e. the node can be combined with three or more possible words), it is defined as [−Restricted Combinability] or [-ResComb]. [+/-Transparency] refers to the possibility whether a collocate in collocation (a verb in a [verb + noun] collocation, for example) has its literal/non-literal meaning in a collocation. When a collocate in a collocation has literal features in meaning, the collocation is defined as [+Transparency] or [+Transp] and when a collocate in a collocation has figurative features in meaning, the collocation is defined as [−Transparency] or [-Transp]. Thus, for example, a verb in a [verb + noun] collocation has a literal meaning, it is classified as [+Transp] even if a noun in a [verb + noun] collocation has a non-literal meaning. A verb in a [verb + noun] collocation has a non-literal meaning, it is classified as [-Trasnp] even if a noun in a [verb + noun] collocation has a literal meaning.

The comparison between these two types of collocations, i.e. [+ResComb, +Transp] and [-ResComb, -Transp], was carried out within each of four lexical categories. In the MCQ Tasks, no significant difference in the means of overall accuracy was found between the [+ResComb, +Transp] and [-ResComb, -Transp] groups of collocations. On the other hand, within each lexical category of collocations, i.e. [verb + noun], [delexicalised noun + noun], [adjective + noun] and [adverb + noun], the MCQ Tasks show that there were significant differences between the [+ResComb, +Transp] and [-ResComb, -Transp] groups of collocations, but no differences between the language groups. Thus, the MCQ Tasks suggest that the [+ResComb, +Transp] and [-ResComb, -Transp] has the influence on the learners' recognition of collocations.

In Translation Tasks, the main effect of the [+ResComb, +Transp] and [-ResComb, -Transp] groups of collocations was not significant. The interaction effect between the language group and collocation type was significantly different. Thus, the Translation Tasks suggest that the [+ResComb, +Transp] and [-ResComb, -Transp] does not have the influence on the learners' production of collocations.

In the learner corpora, however, the number of occurrences of collocations found in the [-ResComb, -Transp] group of collocations was larger than that of the [+ResComb, +Transp] ones though this analysis was based on the small number of collocations found in each of the French and Japanese learner corpora. The larger number in the [-ResComb, -Transp] group of collocations suggest that the learners are able to produce this group of collocations better than the [+ResComb, +Transp] ones. Thus, the learner corpora investigation indicates that the [+ResComb, +Transp] and [-ResComb, -Transp] of collocations has some effects on the learners' production of collocations.

Accordingly, all of the two types of data collection instruments, i.e. the MCQ Tasks, and the learner corpora investigation, showed that the [+ResComb, +Transp] and [-ResComb, -Transp] of collocations has some influence on the learners' knowledge and use of collocations. In the MCQ Tasks, which examined learners' recognition of collocations, and in the learner corpora investigation, which examined learners' production of collocations, the learners were likely to recognize and produce the [-ResComb, -Transp] group of collocations than the [+ResComb, +Transp] group of collocations. In the Translation Tasks, the influence of [+ResComb, +Transp] and [-ResComb, -Transp] was not identified. The different results between the other two types of tasks and the Translation Tasks may have caused because of the nature of the tasks that the L1 influence is triggered in translation tasks. However, unfortunately, it was not clear whether it occurred due to either [+/-Restricted Combinability] or [+/-Transparency] in the present study since either one of the variables was not constant.

8.3 Implications for Teaching Collocations

This section suggests four points which can be improved in teaching collocations in the classrooms based on the findings in the present study.

Firstly, based on the investigation into the influence of the combinability and transparency of the collocations, the present study suggested that there is a significant difference in accuracy between the [+ResComb, +Transp] and [-ResComb, -Transp]. Because one of the focuses of the present study is limited to the influence of [+/-Restricted Comibinability] and [+/-Transparency] in combination rather than the influence of one variable, it is not possible to claim that the results in the present study is in opposition to Kellerman's (1978) theory that learners are unwilling to transfer words with figurative meanings. However, it is possible to suggest that teachers should be aware that the learners are likely to recognize and produce the [+ResComb, +Transp] group of collocations less accurately.

Secondly, teachers should remember that the intermediate level learners are not familiar with [adverb + adjective] collocations. The results of MCQ and Translation Tasks suggest that the lowest accuracy among the four lexical categories is the one found in the [adverb + adjective] category by both the French and Japanese learners. It is important to explicitly teach this category of collocations. To enhance their stored memory of collocations, presenting collocations as wholes rather than as individual building blocks is considered important. In learning collocations, the importance of input also needs to be considered in classroom teaching situation, for example, since the input is not only received from the teachers but also from the peers (Adinolfi 2011).

8.4 Suggestions for Further Research

The present study has contributed to the understanding concerning the tendencies of the knowledge and use of collocations by L2 learners from different L1 backgrounds. For the further advancements of research in the collocations, the following directions in the further research are suggested based on the results of the present study.

The present study investigated the L2 learners' knowledge and use of collocations by means of the categorisation in terms of the combinability and transparency. Unlike other previous studies, the present study attempted to categorize collocations by applying the combinability and transparency. Nevertheless, it was extremely difficult to divide the collocations into the [+ResComb, +Transp] and [-ResComb, -Transp] groups. The effects obtained in the present study are considered to be either due to the combinability/transparency or both. In the further research, categorizing collocations by making one of the two variables consistent may expand research into the knowledge and use of the collocations by L2 learners.

Due to the limited number of collocations for the two tasks, i.e. MCQ Tasks and Translation Tasks, the number of the concerned collocations found in the learner corpora was considerably small, though it was originally expected that a larger number of collocations might be obtained in the learner corpora. In the further research, a larger number of collocations should be examined in the learner corpora.

Among the four lexical categories of collocations, the [adverb + adjective] category of collocations showed considerably low accuracy in both MCQ and Translation Tasks by both French and Japanese learners. In the learner corpora, merely a small range of adverbs were found, such as "very" and "really". Further research on the learners' knowledge and use of this category of collocations ought to be developed. The limited use of adverbs was found to be common in the French and Japanese learners and which may also be observable in the L2 learners of various L1 backgrounds.

Although the previous studies on collocations have discussed teaching collocations mainly to advanced L2 learners, the present study investigated the intermediate L2 learners. The present study showed that the French and Japanese learners at intermediate level of English are able to recognize and produce some collocations. It can be suggested that it is beneficial for the learners to learn collocations from the early stage of their learning. The L2 learners' tendency to be influenced by their L1s in particular lexical categories can be indicated at an early stage of their learning. Learning and teaching collocations as well as the research into their knowledge and use of collocations by the intermediate learners may be useful for the learners.

8.5 Final Remarks

Making comparison of the knowledge and use of collocations by the learners from different L1 backgrounds, i.e. the learners from Indo-European and non-Indo-European backgrounds, was expected to be unique because of their syntactic and/or lexical differences between the two language groups.

Certainly, both French and Japanese learners showed L1 influence, such as direct translation from their L1 equivalents, although French and English belong to Indo-European background languages and share a number of cognate words. In the present study, the Japanese learners showed a greater L1 influence in a certain collocations such as those in [adjective+noun] category, while the French learners showed a greater L1 influence in the [verb + noun] and [delexicalised verb + noun] categories. L1 influence depends not only on the learners' L1 but also on the lexical categories of collocations. Also, it was found that L1 influence is not the primary factor which affects accuracy between the French and Japanese learners but that the other factors may work in their recognition and production of collocations.

The present study also examined the [+ResComb, +Transp] and [-ResComb, -Transp] influence on the learners' collocations. In general, the results of French learners partly follow the discussion of Kellerman (1978) who indicated that the L2 learners are willing to transfer words with literal meanings. Nevertheless, since the two variables were both inconsistent in the present study, the conclusive analysis regarding the transparency itself was not carried out. Due to the same reason, the results of the Japanese learners partly contrasted the previous discussion, and partly found that they are able to transfer collocations with more figurativeness and more possibilities of combinations than the French learners. Thus, there remain possibilities that the Kellerman's (ibid.) theory is not necessarily applicable to the learners from non-Indo-European L1 backgrounds.

There is a potential to improve the teaching method of English collocations based on the analysis presented above. It is hoped that the present study not only deepened the knowledge and use of English collocation by the learners from the different L1 backgrounds, but also makes a contribution to improve teaching/learning method of English through recognizing the learners' L1 influence and combinability and transparency influence on the collocations.

Chapter 9

LIMITATIONS OF THE STUDY

9.1 Relation of a Socio-cultural Dimension to the Linguistic Description of Collocations

9.1.1 The Diachrony of Transparency of Collocations

The present study has categorized collocations based on two parameters, combinability and transparency, but a different approach to the operationalization of transparency needs to be considered from the viewpoint of the semantic change of words in historical linguistics. The diachrony of transparency of words means the evolution or change of the meanings of words over time; a non-transparent meaning today might have had a transparency meaning before.

In the field of semantics, it is indicated that the change in meanings of a word over time (Traugott & Dasher 2005) since words are constantly used and what is intended by speakers is not exactly the same each time. There are different types of semantic change. With regards to polysemous words, for instance, which have a basic and a related figurative meaning, there are cases that the original basic meaning is lost and the secondary meaning is developed in the course of time. For example, 'board' originally means 'plank' and 'table' in Old English, which developed into two different meanings: 'a piece of wood' and 'a council' (Minkova & Stockwell 2009). In a collocation, 'advisory board', 'board' means 'a council'. Also, there are cases in which a word becomes opaque in a later generation and its meaning changes. For example, 'obnoxious' which originally meant 'vulnerable to harm' in 16th century changed its meaning to 'extremely unpleasant' in the course of time (Oxford Dictionary of English 2003). For example, one of the collocations including 'obnoxious', whose meaning is 'extremely unpleasant', is 'obnoxious behavior'.

Thus, the diachronic or historical perspective on the semantic change of the meanings of words needs to be considered for a more critical understanding of transparency of collocations. The results of the L2 learners' understanding of collocations can be affected by a different operationalization of transparency of collocations. If a word in a collocation is used in transparent meaning today but was used in non-transparent meaning before, it is worth investigating to what extent the L2 learners understand such collocations in terms of transparency and non-transparency.

9.1.2 The Socio-cultural Dimension of Collocations

The socio-cultural dimension of 'transparency' also needs to be considered for better understanding of knowledge and use of collocations. Although the present study depends the decision of transparency of words in collocations on specific dictionaries, the socio-cultural dimension such as, for example, ideological and practical choices for compiling dictionaries needs to be considered in defining the transparency of collocations.

Dictionaries are compiled based on a variety of ideological or practical choices, which can be identified in different types of dictionaries. For example, one of the monolingual dictionaries compiled for L2 learners is *Longman Dictionary of Contemporary English* (LDCE 5th edition 2009). It involves 230,000 words based on Longman Corpus Network consisting of 330 million words from a wide range of real-life sources, such as books, newspapers and magazines. Since it is aimed for the use of L2 learners, over 65,000 collocations and the information about the difference of spoken and written English are provided. Unlike *Longman Dictionary of Contemporary English* (2009), *Oxford English Dictionary* (OED) (1989) is not compiled for L2 learners. Containing more than 600,000 words, *OED* is based on over 2 billion-word-corpus (The Oxford English Corpus) of real 21st century English. The type of English included in the Oxford English Corpus is from literary novels and specialist journals to everyday newspapers, magazines, the language of blogs, emails, and Internet message boards. The Oxford English Corpus consists of the language not only from the UK and the United States but also from Ireland, Australia, New Zealand, the Caribbean, Canada, India, Singapore, and South Africa (http://oxforddictionaries.com/words/about-the-oxford-english-corpus).

Thus, the socio-cultural dimensions of reference dictionaries need to be considered in defining the transparency of collocations since different dictionaries are compiled based on different ideas and practical selections.

9.1.3 Psycho-social Dimension of Collocation Use

The psycho-social dimension, such as the L2 learners' affective domain in their social context, can also affect the use of collocations by L2 learners. The future study needs to consider to what degree, which collocations and in which speech community the L2 learners use collocations to be a member of the speech community they are interested in.

Wray (2002:119) points out that

> it is in the interest of the speaker to anticipate which chunks are familiar and likely to result in a desired response on the part of the hearer. This will encourage individuals to accommodate their speech patterns to those of the groups that they prioritise for interaction, thus generally promoting cohesion in the linguistic behaviour of speech communities.

Her claim suggests that L1 and/or L2 learners can make use of their speech patterns, such as collocations, to be a member of the speech communities that they would like to belong to. The purpose of using collocations and the types of collocations that L1 and L2 learners are likely to

183

use, for example, needs to be considered in analyzing the data and in selecting items for experiments from the viewpoint of psycho-social aspect of collocation use. In their early stages of studying, the L2 learners studying English in Paris, such as the students at the University of London Institute in Paris in the present study, might be likely to use the collocations which are frequently used by L1 students and/or the L1 teachers at the university because they would like to adapt to the university community where they are studying.

Moreover, the motivation of learning collocations by L2 learners needs to be considered in analyzing the data because motivation is one of the key learner variables (Schmitt 2002). For instance, it is worth examining whether the L2 learners were motivated to learn collocations with fun value of learning collocations. Whether the fun value of learning collocations affects their knowledge and use of collocations in what level of L2 learners is also important to investigate in future study.

9.1.4 Sociolinguistic Factors Determining the Reference Corpus

The sociolinguistic factors determining the contents of the reference corpus can also affect the results of knowledge and use by L2 learners. Sociolinguistic factors are the factors which are relevant to linguistic variation and its social significance (Chambers 2009). For example, the frequently used collocation types might be different depending on the sociolinguistic factors of the reference corpus. The present study selected collocations which have more than 50 hits in British National Corpus as stimuli since they are frequently used by L1 speakers. However, the genres of material that have been included in the BNC are specific. BNC includes 90% of written part, which consists of, for example, extracts from regional and national newspapers, specialist periodicals and journals, academic books and popular fiction, published and unpublished letters, school and university essays, and so on, and 10% of spoken part, which consists of orthographic transcriptions of unscripted informal conversations and spoken language collected in different contexts. Since the source of the collocations was not available on the website of BNC, whether the collocations are used in either spoken or written forms and in what social context were not mentioned. Since the collocations selected in the present study were extracted from BNC, the social context which the collocations are used is not obvious. Whether the collocations are used at home, work, school, for example, is relevant in understanding the use of collocations because the speakers use different variety of language choice depending on the settings they participate in. Future study needs to investigate the types of collocations frequently used at school, for example, by recording and transcribing the classes.

Moreover, in relation to the use of BNC in the present study, one of the sociolinguistic factors, the participants, needs to be considered in analyzing the data. The participants of BNC are the speakers of modern British English, thus the collocations included are the ones frequently used by British L1 speakers of English. However, when the participants differ in their age, gender, ethnicity, social class and educational backgrounds, the collocations they use can vary. For example, if the participants are the ethnic minorities who are from Jamaica, for example, they use what is called British Black English including a variety of Jamaican Creole as well as a variety of English (Holmes 2008:189). The collocations frequently used by British Black English can differ from those used by other groups of British English since many ethnic groups use a distinctive language associated with their ethnic identity (Holmes 2008:184).

Similarly, if the participants are aged, for instance, the knowledge and use of collocations might be different from that of the younger participants since it is indicated that school children speak more like their peers than like their elders (Chambers 2009:170). The young groups of participants might have more casual types of collocations than the aged groups because young people are likely to show friendship or friendliness in interaction with people. Although the use of collocations by young people has not yet been investigated, in the field of phonetics, schoolchildren speak like their playmates and not like their parents (Chambers 2009: 171).

Based on the consideration of sociolinguistic factors such as language variation and social context, in the instructional context, a variety of collocations needs to be taught in order to raise awareness of various types of collocations. Also, what words come before or after the words they use needs to be included in the instruction because it will develop awareness about the L2 learners' use of collocations. Durrant and Schmitt (2009) warn that frequency of occurrence in the BNC should not be assumed to mirror levels of exposure in instructional contexts.

9.2 Relation of a Socio-cultural Dimension to the Learning Model and Learner Profiles Presented

In addition to the dimensions above, the learner profiles would also affect the knowledge and use of collocations among learners because their knowledge and use of collocations can be different depending on the types of instruction and cultural values of collocations in their L1 the learners have been exposed to.

Firstly, the information about the subjects' prior educational culture and current instructional context needs to be examined in future study, such as the methods of instruction French and Japanese learners were exposed to for learning collocations. With an interview to learners or a list of questionnaires, it would be possible to include the learners' learning models such as, for example, memory-based, structural, audio-lingual, or functional. Since the French and Japanese L2 learners are expected to have been exposed to structural and/or functional instruction, which were both popular in actual teaching situation especially for speaking and listening courses in EFL environment (Richards 2006), they might have been exposed to the target collocations in the tasks in the present study. If either French or Japanese learners were taught in different instructional method, the amount of exposure to collocations would be different depending on the types of approach. In addition, the information about whether the French and Japanese learners were exposed to explicit collocation teaching needs to be included in future study.

Secondly, the cultural value of collocation use in L1 French and L1 Japanese native cultures needs to be investigated for the future study. The significance of the learners' perception of collocations in their L1s can affect their knowledge and use of L2 collocations. If the collocation use is perceived as a proof of rhetorical skills and/or triggering motivations to learn by either French or Japanese learners, there may be differences between the French and Japanese learners in their accuracy and/or varieties of expression in collocations in the tasks in the present study.

Thirdly, the style and type of input the L2 learners have already been exposed to need to be examined since the knowledge and use of collocations of the L2 learners can vary according to the types of input they have been provided. By means of an interview, for example, the variety of collocations the learners produce can be investigated based on the information about how much informal/formal input the learners received. In particular, with regard to informal input, the information on whether and to what extent the L2 learners were exposed to, for example, films, internet, or other media tools is the data worth collecting to study the source of input for learning collocations.

Finally, in relation to learner corpora, whether learners were provided with a set of prescribed reading that they might have integrated into their own writing is also important to investigate. If the participants who were required to write essays for learner corpora were provided with any prescribed reading, it is possible that they use the collocations that appeared in the reading, but if they were not, the results would be examined without such presupposition. Since there would be some requirements for essay-writing for the collecting the data for learner corpora, the types of instruction the participants were given need to be examined for better understanding of the learner corpora.

9.3 Future Directions

Although the present study considered knowledge and use of collocations by the L2 learners, there are other important factors such as sociocultural, psycho-social and sociolinguistic dimensions to be considered in the future study. The future study needs to examine the sociolinguistic dimensions related to the collocations because language is used in its social context and collocations are no exception. For such future research, I suggest an approach adopting steps such as: 1) operationalization of the definition of collocations; 2) investigation of the reference corpus in selecting the items for experiments; and 3) analysis of the learner profiles and learning model, while considering language variations to be analyzed, the social context the language is used, and the backgrounds of the participants who use the language. The collected data needs to be analyzed whether the variation of the collocations occurs because of social factors, such as age, gender, status and ethnicity, and/or genre of data.

BIBLIOGRAPHY

Adinolfi, L. (2011) The Teaching and Learning of Lexical Chunks on an Online Second Language Classroom, A Corpus-Based Study. Unpublished Doctoral Thesis, University of Southampton, Faculty of Law, Arts & Social Sciences, School of Education.

Adolhs, S. and Durow (2004) "Social-cultural Integration and the Development of Formulaic Sequences" in Schmitt, N (Ed.) *Formulaic Sequences: Acquisition, Processing and Use*, (pp.107-126). Amsterdam: Johns Benjamins Publishing Company.

Aisenstadt, E. (1979) "Collocability Restrictions in Dictionaries" in R.R.K. Hartmann (Ed.), *Dictionaries and their Users: Papers from the 1978 B.A.A.L. Seminar on Lexicography, University of Exeter.*

Aisenstadt, E. (1981) "Restricted Collocations in English Lexicology and Lexicography". *ITL Review of Applied Linguistics, 53, 53-61.*

Aitchison, J. (1994) *Words in the Mind*, Blackwell Publishers Ltd.

Alexander, J. R. (1984) "Fixed expressions in English: Reference Books and the Teacher". *English Language Teaching Journal*, vol. 38, No. 2, 127-34.

Altenberg, B. (1993) "Recurrent Verb-Complement Constructions in the London-Lund Corpus" in Aarts, J. *et al.* (Eds.) *English Language Corpora: Design, Analysis and Exploitation*, (pp.227-245). Amsterdam: Rodopi.

Altenberg, B. & Granger, S. (2001) "The Grammatical an Lexical Patterning of MAKE in Native and Non-native Student Writing". *Applied Linguistics* 22/2: 173-195.

Bachman, L. F. (1990) *Fundamental Considerations in Language Testing*, OxfordUniversity Press.

Backhouse, A. E. (1981) "Japanese verbs of dress". *Journal of Linguistics* 17: 17-29. Cambridge University Press.

Bahns, J. (1993) "Lexical Collocations: a Contrastive View". *ELT Journal* 47: 56-63.

Bahns, J. & Eldaw, M. (1993) "Should we teach EFL students collocations?" *System*, 21(1), 101-114.

Benson, M. (1985) "Collocations and Idioms", in Ilson, R (Ed.), *Dictionaries, Lexicography and Language Learning*, (pp.61-68). Oxford: Pergamon Press.

Benson, E., Benson, M., & Ilson, R. (1997) *The BBI Dictionary of English Word Combinations*, Amsterdam: John Benjamins Publishing.

Bialystok, E. and Sharwood S. M. (1985) "Interlanguage is not a State of Mind: an Evaluation of the Construct for Second-Language Acquisition", *Applied Linguistics* 6: 101–117.

Biber, D. (2006) *University Language: A Corpus-based Study of Spoken and Written Registers*. Amsterdam: Johns Benjamins Publishing Company.

Biber, D. & Barbieri, F. (2007) "Lexical Bundles in University Spoken and Written Registers". *English for Specific Purposes* 26: 263-286.

Biber, D. et al. (1999) *Longman Grammar of Spoken and Written English*. London and New York: Longman.

Biskup, D. (1992) "L1 Influence on Learners' Renderings of English Collocations: A Polish/German Empirical Study" in Arnaud, P.J.L. and Béjoint, H. (Eds.), *Vocabulary and Applied Linguistics*, (pp.85-93). London: Macmillan.

Bogaards, P. & Laufer, B. (Eds.) (2004) *Vocabulary in a Second Language*, Amsterdam: John Benjamins Publishing Company.

Bolinger, D. (1975) *Aspects of Language*, New York: Harcourt Brace Jovanovich.

Brown, D. F. (1974) "Advanced Vocabulary Teaching: the Problem of Collocation". *RELC Journal* 5 (2), 1-11.

Brown, D. J. (1988) *Understanding Research in Second Language Learning*, Cambridge: Cambridge University Press.

Brown, D. J. & Rodgers, S. T. (2002) *Doing Second Language Research*, Oxford: Oxford University Press.

Brown, K. (2003) *Oxford Collocations Dictionary for students of English*, Oxford: Oxford University Press.

Bybee, J. (2010a) *Language, Usage and Cognition*, Cambridge: Cambridge University Press.

Bybee, J. (2010b) *Phonology and Language Use*, Cambridge: Cambridge University Press.

Cambridge Advanced Learners' Dictionary (2005) Cambridge University Press.

Carter, R. (1998) *Vocabulary*, Routledge.

Carter, R. & McCarthy, M. (1988) *Vocabulary and Language Teaching*, London: Longman.

Chambers, J. K. (2009) *Sociolinguistic Theory*, Wiley-Blackwell.

Chi, M.L.A, et al.(1994) *"Collocational Problems amongst ESL Learners : a Corpus-based Study"* in Flowerdew, L. and Tong, A.K. (Eds): *Entering Text*, (pp.157-65). Hong Kong: University of Science and Technology.

Chomsky, N. (1965) *Aspects of the Theory of Syntax*, The MIP Press.

Coady, J. & Huckin, T. (1997) *Second Language Vocabulary Acquisition*, Cambridge: Cambridge University Press.

Collins Birmingham University International Language Database (1995).

Coleman, L. and Kay, P. (1981) "Prototype Semantics: the English Word 'Lie'". *Language* 57:26-44.

Collier, A. (1993) "Issues of Large-Scale Collocational Analysis" in Aarts, J. *et al.* (eds.) *English Language Corpora: Design, Analysis, and Exploitation*, Amsterdam: Rodopi.

Collins Robert French Dictionary (2005) Collins.

Cook, V. (1999) "Going Beyond the Native Speaker in Language Teaching". *TESOL Quarterly* 33 (2): 185-209.

Cook, V. J. & Newson, M. (2007) *Chomsky's Universal Grammar*, Blackwell Publishing.

Cortes, V. (2004) "Lexical Bundles in Published and Student Disciplinary Writing: Examples from History and Biology". *English for Specific Purposes*, 23, 397-423.

Council of Europe (2001) *Common European Framework of Reference for Languages: Learning, Teaching, Assessment*. Cambridge: Cambridge University Press.

Cowie, A. P. (1981) "The Treatment of Collocations and Idioms in Learners' Dictionaries". *Applied Linguistics*, 2/3, 223-235.

Cowie, A.P. (1988) "Stable and Creative Aspects of Vocabulary Use" in Carter, R. and McCarthy, M. (Eds.) *Vocabulary and Language Teaching*, London: Longman.

Cowie, A.P. (1992) "Multiword lexical units and communicative language teaching" in Arnaud, P. and Bejoint, H. (Eds.) *Vocabulary and Applied linguistics*, London: Macmillan.

Cowie, A.P. (1994) "Phraseology" in Asher, E. (Ed.) *The Encyclopedia of Language and Linguistics* (pp.3168-3171). ELSEVIER.

Cowie, A.P. (Ed.) (1998) *Phraseology: Theory, Analysis and Applications*, Oxford: Oxford University Press.

Croft, W. (2003) "From Idioms to Constructions," in Croft, W. & Cruse, A. (Eds.), *Cognitive Linguistics*, Cambridge: Cambridge University Press.

Cruse, A. (1986) *Lexical Semantics*, Cambridge: Cambridge University Press.

Crystal, D. (1991) *A Dictionary of Linguistics and Phonetics*, Blackwell.

Daulton, F.E. (1998) "Japanese Loanwords Cognates and the Acquisition of English Vocabulary". *The Language Teacher*, 22, 17-25.

De Cock, S. *et al.* (1998) "An Automated   Approach to the Phrasicon of EFL Learners" in Granger, S. (Ed.) *Learner English on Computer*, (pp.67-79). London: Longman.

De Groot, A. (1993) "Word-Type Effects in Bilingual Processing Tasks: Support for a Mixed-Representational System" in Schreuder, R. & Weltens, B. (eds.) *The Bilingual Lexicon, (pp.26-51)*. Amsterdam: Benjamins.

Dewaele, J.M. (2004) "Individual differences in the use of colloquial vocabulary: The Effects of Sociobiographical and Psychological Factors", in Bogaards, P. and Laufer, B. (eds.) *Vocabulary in a Second Language*, (pp.127-154). Amsterdam: John Benjamins Publishing Company.

Durrant, P.(2009) "Investigating the Viability of a Collocation List for Students of English for Academic Purposes". *English for Specific Purposes*, vol.28, No.3, 157-169.

Durrant, P. & Schmitt, N. (2009) "To What Extent Do Native and Non-Native Writers Make Use of Collocations?" *International Review of Applied Linguistics in Language Teaching*, vol.47, No.2, 157-177.

Durrant, P. & Schmitt, N. (2010) "Adult Learners' Retention of Collocations from Exposure". *Second Language Research*, vol.26, No.2. 163-188.

Ellis, C. N. (1997) "Sequencing in SLA: Phonological Memory, Chunking, and Points of Order". *Studies in Second Language Acquisition* 18, 91-126.

Ellis, C. N. (2001) "Memory for Language" in Robinson, P. (Ed.) *Cognition and Second Language Instruction*, (pp.33-68). Cambridge: Cambridge University Press.

Ellis, N. (2002) "Frequency Effects in Language Processing". *Studies in Second Language Acquisition* 24: 143-188.

Ellis, R. (1994) *The Study of Second Language Acquisition*, Oxford: Oxford University Press.

Farghal, M. and Obiedat, H. (1995) "Collocations: a Neglected Variable in EFL". *International Review of Applied Linguistics* 33 :(4), 315-331.

Fernando, C. (1996) *Idioms and Idiomaticity*, Amsterdam: Rodopi.

Field, A. (2009) *Discovering Statistics Using SPSS*, London: SAGE Publications.

Fillmore, W. L. (1976) *The Second Time Around: Cognitive and Social Strategies in Second Language Acquisition*, Doctoral dissertation, Stanford University, 1976.

Firth, J. R. (1957) "A Synopsis of Linguistic Theory 1930-1955". In *Papers in Linguistics 1934-1951* (1957) London: Oxford University Press.

Fontenelle, T. (1998) "Discovering Significant Lexical Functions in Dictionary Entries" in Cowie, P. (ed.) *Phraseology: Theory, Analysis and Applications*, (pp.189-207). Oxford: Oxford University Press.

Foster, P. (2001) "Rules and Routines: A Consideration of their Role in the Task-Based Language Production of Native and Non-Native Speakers" in Bygate, M., Skehan, P. and Swain, M. (Eds.) *Researching Pedagogic Tasks: Second Language Learning, Teaching and Testing*, London: Longman.

Gass, M. S., & Cohen, D.A. & Tarone, E. (1994) *Research Methodology in Second-Language Acquisition*, Hillsdale, N. J.: Lawrence Erlbaum.

Gass, M. S., & Selinker, L. (1993) *Language Transfer in Language Learning*, Rowley, Massachusetts: Newbury House.

Gass, M. S., Selinker, L, & Sorace, A. (1999) *Second Language Learning Data Analysis*, NJ: Lawrence Erlbaum.

Gass, M. S., & Selinker, L. (2001) *Second Language Acquisition*, Lawrence Erlbaum.

Gitsaki, C. (1999) *Second Language Lexical Acquisition: a Study of the Development of Collocational Knowledge*, International Scholars Publications.

Gopnik, A. and Choi, A. (1988) "Three Types of Early Word: the Emergence of Social Words, Names and Cognitive-Relational Words in the One-Word Stage and their Relation to Cognitive Development". *First Language* 8, 49-69.

Gopnik, A. and Choi, A. (1990) "*Do Linguistic Differences Lead to Cognitive Differences? A Cross-Linguistics Study of Semantic and Cognitive Development*". *First Language*, 10, 199-215.

Granger, S. (1990) "Prefabricated Patterns in Advanced EFL Writing: Collocations and Formulae" in Cowie, P. (Ed.) *Phraseology*, Oxford: Oxford University Press.

Granger, S. (1993) "International Corpus in Learner English" in Aarts, J. *et al.* (Eds.) *English Language Corpora: Design, Analysis, and Exploitation* Amsterdam: Rodopi.

Granger, S. (Ed.) (1998) *Learner English on Computer*, Longman.

Granger, S., et al. (Eds.) (2002) *International Corpus of Learner English*, Louvain-la-Neuve: UCL Presses Universitaires.

Greenberg, J. (1974) *Language Typology: A Historical and Analytic Overview.* Berlin: Mouton de Gruyter.

Hakuta, K. (1974) "Prefabricated Patterns and the Emergence of Structure in Second Language Acquisition". *Language Learning* 24, 287-297.

Hakuta, K. (1976) "A Case Study of a Japanese Child Learning English as a Second Language". *Language Learning* 26, 321-351.

Halliday, M.A.K. (1966) "Lexis as a Linguistic Level" in Halliday, M. et al. (Eds.) *In Memory of J.R. Firth*, London: Longman

Halliday, M.A.K. (1993) "Towards a Language-Based Theory of Learning". *Linguistics and Education* 5(2), 93-116.

Halliday, M.A.K., Teubert, W., Yallop, C. and Cermakova, A. (2004) *Lexicology and Corpus Linguistics*, London: Continuum.

Hausmann, F. J. (1989) "Le dictionnaire de collocations." In F. J. Hausmann, H.E. Wiegand & L. Zgusta (Eds.), *Wörterbücher, Dictionaries, Dictionnaire. Ein internationals Handbuch zur Lexikographie* (pp.1010-1019). Berlin: de Gruyter.

Herbst, T. (1996) "What are Collocations: Sandy Beaches or False Teeth?" *English Studies* 4: 379-393.

Hoey, M. (1991) *Patterns of Lexis in Text*, Oxford: Oxford University Press.

Holmes, J. (2008) *An Introduction to Sociolinguistics*, Third Edition, Pearson Education Limited.

Holmes, J. & Ramos, R. (1993) "False Friends and Reckless Guessers: Observing Cognate Recognition Strategies" in Huckin, T., Haynes, M. and Coady, J. (Eds.) *Second Language Reading and Vocabulary*, Norwood, New Jersey: Ablex Publishing Company.

Howarth, P. (1996) *Phraseology in English Academic Writing. Some Implications for Language learning and Dictionary Making.* Niemeyer, Tübingen.

Howarth, P. (1998a) "The Phraseology of Learners' Academic Writing" in Cowie, P. (Ed.). Phraseology: Theory, Analysis and Applications, Oxford: Oxford University Press.

Howarth, P. (1998b) "Phraseology and Second Language Proficiency". *Applied Linguistics* 19(1): 24-44.

Hyland, K. (2008) "As Can be Seen: Lexical Bundles and Disciplinary Variation". *English for Specific Purposes, 27,* (4):4-21.

Hymes, D. (1972) *On Communicative Competence,* Philadelphia, PA: University of Pennsylvania Press.

Irujo, S. (1986) "A Piece of Cake: Learning and Teaching Idioms". *ELT Journal* 40 (3), 236-242.

Irujo, S. (1993) "Steering Clear: Avoidance in the Production of Idioms" *International Review of Applied Linguistics* 31, 3, 205-219.

Jiang, N. & Nekrasova, T. (2007) "The Processing of Formulaic Sequences by Second Language Speakers". *The Modern Language Journal* 91 (3), 433-445.

Jones and Sinclair, J. (1974) "English Lexical Collocations". *Cahiers de lexicologie* 24, 15-61.

Källkvist, M. (1999) *Form-Class and Task-Type Effects in Learner English.* Lund: Lund University Press.

Kellerman, E. (1978) "Giving Learners a Break: Native Language Intuitions as a Source of Predictions about Transferability". *Working Papers on Bilingualism* 15, 59-92.

Kellerman, E. (1979) "Transfer and Non-Transfer: Where are We Now?" *Studies in Second Language Acquisition* 2: 37-57.

Kellerman, E. (1984) "The Empirical Evidence for the Influence of the L1 in Interlanguage" in Davies, A., Criper, C. and Howatt, A.P.R. (Eds.) *Interlanguage,* Edinburgh: Edinburgh University Press.

Kellerman, E. (1985) "If at First You Do Succeed..." In Gass, S. and Madden, C. (Eds.) *Input and Second Language Acquisition* Rowley, MA: Newbury House.

Kennedy, G. (1990) "Collocations: Where Grammar and Vocabulary Teaching Meet" in Anivan, S. (Ed.) *Language Teaching Methodology for the Nineties*, RELC Anthology Series No. 24 (pp.215-229), Singapore: Regional Language Centre.

Kennedy, G. (1998) *An Introduction to Corpus Linguistic*, London: Longman.

Kennedy, G. (2003) "Amplifier Collocations in the British National Corpus: Implications for English Language Teaching". *TESOL Quarterly*, 37, 467-487(2).

Kilgarrif, A. (1997) "Putting Frequencies in the Dictionary". *International Journal of Lexicography*. 10(2), pp. 135–55.

Kjellmer, G. (1982) "Some Problems Relating to the Study of Collocations in the Brown Corpus" in Johansson, S. (Ed.) *Computer Corpora in English Language Research*, Bergen: Norwegian Computing Centre for the Humanities.

Kjellmer, G. (1984) "Some Thoughts on Collocational Distinctiveness" in Aarts, J. and Mijs, W. (Eds.) *Corpus Linguistics: Recent Developments in the Use of Computer Corpora in English Language Research*, Amsterdam: Rodopi.

Kjellmer, G. (1991) "A Mint of Phrases" in Aijmer, K. and Altenberg, B. (Eds.) *English Corpus Linguistics*, London: Longman.

Krashen, S. and Scarcella, R. (1978) "On Routines and Patterns in Language Acquisition and Performance". *Language Learning* 28: 283-300.

Kroll, F. (1993) "Accessing Conceptual Representations for Words in a Second Language" in Schreuder, R. & Wletens,B. (eds.) *The Bilingual Lexicon* (pp.53-82). Amsterdam: Benjamins.

Kuiper, K. (2004) "Formulaic Performance in Conventionalized Varieties of Speech" in Schmitt, N. (Ed.) Formulaic Sequences: *Acquisition, Processing, and Use,* (pp.37-54). Amsterdam: Johns Benjamins Publishing Company.

Larsen-Freeman, D. and M .Long. (1991) *An Introduction to Second Language Acquisition Research*, Addison Wesley Publishing Company.

Laufer, B. (2003) "The Influence of L2 on L1 Collocational Knowledge and on L1 Lexical Diversity in Free Written Expression" in Cook, V. J. (Ed.), *Second Language Acquisition 3: Effects of the Second Language on the First*, Clevedon: Multilingual Matters Limited.

Laufer, B. and Eliasson, S. (1993) "What Causes Avoidance in L2 Learning: L1-L2 Difference, L1-L2 Similarity, or L2 Complexity?" *Studies in Second Language Acquisition* 15:35-48.

Lennon, P. (1996) "Getting 'Easy' Verbs Wrong at the Advanced Level". *International Review of Applied Linguistics* 34, 23-36.

Lewis, M. (2000) *Teaching Collocation*, Hove: Language Teaching Publications.

Lewis, M. (2002) *The Lexical Approach*, Boston: Heinle.

Lewis, M. & Hill, J. (Eds.) (1997) *LTP Dictionary of Selected Collocations*, Hove, England: Language Teaching Publications.

Liu, D. (2010) "Going Beyond Patterns: Involving Cognitive Analysis in the Learning of Collocations". *TESOL Quarterly*, vol.44, No.1, 4-30.

Longman Dictionary of Contemporary English (2003) Longman.

Longman Dictionary of Contemporary English (2009) Longman.

Manning, D.C., & Schutze, H. (2002) *Foundations of Statistical Natural Language Processing*, The MIT Press.

Minkova, D. & Stockwell, R. (2009) *English Words, History and Structure*, Cambridge University Press.

McCarthy, M. (1990) *Vocabulary*, Oxford: Oxford University Press.

McCarthy, M. (1991) *Discourse Analysis for Language Teachers*, Cambridge: Cambridge University Press.

Meara, P. (1993) "The Bilingual Lexicon and the Teaching of Vocabulary" in Schreuder, R. & Wletens,B. (eds.) *The Bilingual Lexicon (pp.279-97)*. Amsterdam: Benjamins.

Mel'cuk, I. (1990) "Collocations and Lexical Functions" in Cowie, P. (Ed.) *Phraseology: Theory, Analysis and Applications*, Oxford: Oxford University Press.

Meyer, C. (2002) *English Corpus Linguistics*, Cambridge: Cambridge University Press.

Miller, G. (1956) "The Magical Number Seven, Plus or Minus Two: Some Limits on Our Capacity for Processing Information". *The Psychological Review*, vol. 63, 81-97.

Miyakoshi, T. (2009) *Investigating ESL Learners' Lexical Collocations: The Acquisition of Verb + Noun Collocations by Japanese Learners of English*, Ph.D. Dissertation, University of Hawai'i at Manoa.

Miyazoe, W. Y. (2002) "Tagengo-supichi Komyuniti Hong Kong ni okeru Nihongo Inta-akushon". *Ja-Net*, No.22, 1.

Moon, R. (1990) "Frequencies and Forms of Phrasal Lexemes in English" in Cowie, P. (Ed.) *Phraseology: Theory, Analysis and Applications*, Oxford: Oxford University Press.

Moon, R. (1992) "Textual Aspects of Fixed Expressions in Learners' Dictionaries" in Arnaud, P. and Béjoint, H. (Eds.). *Vocabulary and Applied Linguistics*, London: Macmillan.

Moon, R. (1997) "Vocabulary Connection: Multi-word Items in English" in Schmitt, N. and McCarthy, M. (Eds.) *Vocabulary: Description, Acquisition and Pedagogy*, (pp.40-63). Cambridge: Cambridge University Press.

Murao, R. (2004) "L1 Influence on Learners' Use of High-frequency Verb+Noun Collocations". *Annual Review of English Language Education in Japan* 14, 1-10.

Nakata, T. (2007) "English Collocation Learning through Meaning-focused and Form-focused Activities: Interactions of Activity Type and L1-L2 Congruence", http://www.paaljapan.org/resources/proceedings/ PAAL11 /pdfs/13.pdf, January 14, 2010.

Nation, P. (1990) *Teaching and Learning Vocabulary*. Boston: Heinle & Heinle.

Nation, P. (2001) *Learning Vocabulary in Another Language*, Cambridge: Cambridge University Press.

Nattinger, J. (1980) "A Lexical Phrase Grammar for ESL". *TESOL Quarterly* 14:337-44.

Nattinger, J. (1988) "Some Current Trends in Vocabulary Teaching" in Carter, R. and McCarthy, M. (Eds.) *Vocabulary and Language Teaching* London: Longman.

Nattinger, J. & DeCarrico, J. (1992) *Lexical Phrases and Language Teaching*, Oxford University Press.

Nesselhauf, N. (2003) "The Use of Collocations by Advanced Learners of English and Some Implications for Teaching". *Applied Linguistics* 24, 223-242.

Nesselhauf, N. (2004) "What are Collocations?" in Allerton, D., Nesselhauf, N. & Skandera, P. (Eds.), *Phraseological Units: Basic Concepts and Their Application* (pp.1-21). Basel: Schwabe.

Nesselhauf, N. (2005) *Collocations in a Learner Corpus*, Amsterdam: Johns Benjamins Publishing Company.

Newell, A. (1990) *Unified Theories of Cognition*, Harvard University Press.

Newman, A. (1988) "The Contrastive Analysis of Hebrew and English Dress and Cooking Collocations: Some Linguistics and Pedagogic Parameters". *Applied Linguistics*, 9 (3), 293-305.

Nist and Olejnik (1995) "The Role of Context and Dictionary Definitions on Varying Levels of Word Knowledge". *Reading Research Quarterly, 30,* 172-193.

Nouveau Petit Royal Dictionnaire Francais Japonais (2007), Tokyo: Obunsha.

Nunan, D. (1992) *Research Methods in Language Learning*, Cambridge: Cambridge University Press.

Odlin, T. (1989) *Language Transfer*, Cambridge: Cambridge University Press.

Oxford Advanced Learners' Dictionary (1990) Oxford University Press.

Oxford Collocations Dictionary for Students of English (2005) Oxford University Press.

Oxford Dictionary of English (2003) Oxford University Press.

Oxford English Dictionary (1989). Oxford University Press.

Palmer, H. E. (1933) *Second Interim Report on English Collocations*, Tokyo: Kaitakusha.

Pawley, A. and Syder, F. H. (1983) "Two Puzzles for Linguistic Theory: Nativelike Selection and Nativelike Fluency" in Richards, J.C. and Schmidt, R.W. (Eds.): *Language and Communication*, (pp.191-226). London: Longman.

Peters, M. A. (1983) *The Units of Language Acquisition*, Cambridge: Cambridge University Press.

Read, J. (2000) *Assessing Vocabulary*, Cambridge: Cambridge University Press.

Read, J. and Nation, P. (2004) "Measurement of Formulaic Sequences" in Schmitt, N. (Ed.), *Formulaic Sequences: Acquisition, Processing and Use*, Amsterdam: Johns Benjamins Publishing Company.

Renouf, A. and Sinclair, J. M. (1991) "Collocational frameworks in English" in K. Aijmer and B. Altenberg (Eds.), *English Corpus Linguistics*. Studies in Honor of Jan Svartcik, London: Londman 128-143.

Richards, J. C. (1976) "The Role of Vocabulary Teaching". *TESOL Quarterly* *10(1)*, 77-89.

Richards, J. C. (1992) *Longman Dictionary of Language Teaching and Applied Linguistics*, Longman.

Richards, J.C. (2006) *Communicative Language Teaching Today*, Cambridge University Press.

Robinson, P. (2001) *Cognition and Second Language Instruction*, Cambridge: Cambridge University Press.

Rosch, E. (1975) "Cognitive Representations of Semantic Categories". *Journal of Experimental Psychology: General, 104*, 192-233.

Saito, H. (1915) *Idiomological English-Japanese Dictionary*. Tokyo: Obunsha.

Schmitt, N. (2002) *An Introduction to Applied Linguistics*, London: Hodder Arnold.

Schmitt, N. & Carter, R. (2004) "Formulaic Sequences in Action: an Introduction" in Schmitt, N. (Ed.), *Formulaic Sequences: Acquisition, Processing and Use*, Amsterdam: John Benjamins Publishing Company.

Schmitt, N. & McCarthy, M. (1997) *Vocabulary: Description, Acquisition and Pedagogy*, Cambridge: Cambridge University Press.

Schreuder, R. & Weltens, B. (1993) *The Bilingual Lexicon*, Amsterdam: John Benjamins Publishing Company.

Scott, M. & Tribble, C. (2006) *Textual Patterns: Key Words and Corpus Analysis in Language Education,*. Amsterdam: Benjamins.

Séguin, H. and Tréville, M.C. (1992) "Les Congénères Interlinguaux : Un Atout pour Accélérer l'Acquisition du Vocabulaire et Faciliter la Compréhension des Textes?" in Courchêne, R. *et al.* (Eds.) *Comprehension Based Second Language Teaching*, Ottawa: University of Ottawa Press.

Seliger, W. H. & Shohamy, E. (1989) *Second Language Research Methods*, Oxford: Oxford University Press.

Selinker, L. (1972) "Interlanguage". *International Review of Applied Linguistics* 10, 209-231.

Shin, D. & Nation, P. (2008) "Beyond Single Words: The Most Frequent Collocations in Spoken English". *ELT Journal* 62(4), 339-348.

Singleton, D. (1999) *Exploring Second Language Mental Lexicon*, Cambridge: Cambridge University Press.

Sinclair, J. M. (1987) "Collocation: a Progress Report" in Steele, R. and Threadgold, T. (Eds.) *Language Topics and International Collection of Papers by Colleagues, Students and Admirers of Professor Michael Halliday to Honour Him on His Retirement*, Amsterdam: John Benjamins Publishing Company.

Sinclair, J. M. (1991) *Corpus, Concordance, Collocation.* Oxford: Oxford University Press.

Sinclair, J. M., Jones, S. & Daley, R. (2004) *English Collocation Studies: The PSTI Report*, London: Continuum.

Siyanova, A. & Schmitt, N. (2008) "L2 Learner Production and Processing of Collocation: A Multi-study Perspective". *The Canadian Modern Language Review* 64(3), 429-458.

Skehan, P. (1998) *A Cognitive Approach to Language Learning,* Oxford: Oxford University Press.

Smith, M. and Kellerman, E. (1986) "Crosslinguistic Influence in Second Language Acquisition: an Introduction" in Smith, S.M. and Kellerman, E. (Eds.). *Crosslinguistic Influence in Second Language Acquisition,* New York: Pergamon.

Stubbs, M. (1995) "Collocations and Cultural Connotations of Common Words". *Linguistics and Education* 7, 379-390.

Stubbs, M. (2001) *Words and Phrases,* Oxford: Blackwell.

Sugiura, M. (2002) "Collocational Knowledge of L2 learners of English: A Case Study of Japanese Learners" in Saito, T., Nakamura, J. and Yamazaki, S. (Eds.): *English Corpus Linguistics in Japan,* (pp.303-323), Amsterdam: Rodopi.

Tannenbaum, R.J. & Wylie, E.C. (2004) *Mapping Test Scores onto the Common European Framework: Setting Standards of Language Proficiency on the Test of English as a Foreign Language (TOEFL), The Test of Spoken English (TSE), The Test of Written English (TWE), and the Test of English for International Communication (TOEIC).* Princeton, NJ: Educational Testing Service.

Tomasello, M. (2003) *Constructing a Language: A Usage-Based Theory of Language Acquisition,* Cambridge: Harvard University Press.

Tomasello, M. & Merriman, E.W. (Eds.) (1995) *Beyond Names for Things* Lawrence Erlbaum.

Tony, M. et al. (2006) *Corpus-Based Language Studies,* New York: Routledge.

Traugott, C. Dasher, R. (2005) *Regularity in Semantic Change,* Cambridge University Press.

Tsunoda, T. (1991) *Sekai no Gengo to Nihongo,* Tokyo: Kuroshio Publishing Company.

Van, R. J. (1990) *French-English Contrastive Lexicology: An Introduction,* Louvain-la-Neuve: Peeters.

Vihman, M.M. (1982) "Formulas in First and Second Language Acquisition" in Obler, L.K. and Menn, Lise (Eds.): *Exceptional Language and Linguistics,* New York: Academic Press.

Walter, E. *et al.* (2005) *Cambridge Advanced Learner's Dictionary,* Cambridge: Cambridge University Press

Wesche, M. & Paribakht, H. (1996) "Assessing Second Language Vocabulary Knowledge: Depth versus Breadth". *The Canadian Modern Language Review 53(1),* 13-40.

Wolter, B. & Gyllstad, H. (2011) "Collocational Links in the Mental Lexicon and the Influence of L1 Intralexical Knowledge". *Applied Linguistics,* 1-21.

Wray, A. (2002) *Formulaic language and the Lexicon,* Cambridge: Cambridge University Press.

Wray, A. and Perkins, M. (2000) "The Functions of Formulaic Language: an Integrated Model". *Language and Communication* 20, 1-28.

Wulff, S. (2008) *Rethinking Idiomaticity: A Usage-Based Approach,* London: Continuum.

Yamashita, J. & Jiang, N. (2010) "L1 Influence on the Acquisition of L2 Collocations: Japanese ESL Users and EFL Learners Acquiring English Collocations". *TESOL Quarterly,* 44, No.4, 647-668.

Yong, W. (1990) "Teaching Collocations for Productive Vocabulary Development". Paper Presented at the Annual Meeting of the TESOL in New York.

Yorio, C.A. (1989) "Conventionalized Language Forms and the Development of Communicative Competence". *TESOL Quarterly,* 14, 433-442.

Zeschel, A. (2008) "Introduction: Usage-based approaches to language processing and representation". *Cognitive Linguistics* 19 (3): 345-355.

ELECTRONIC REFERENCES

International Corpus of Learner English, CD-ROM, Presses Universiaires de Louvain, Louvain.

Kaneko, T. 2000. *Tomoko Kaneko* [Online] Available at http://tomoko-kaneko.com/. [Assessed 03 September 2010].

APPENDICES

Appendix 1

SELECTED COLLOCATIONS BEFORE PILOT STUDY

1)-a: [Verb + Noun] / [+ResComb, +Transp]

1. tell the truth
2. play the violin
3. win the match
4. lose weight
5. read music
6. ask someone a question
7. cross the border
8. flush the toilet
9. attend the meeting
10. draw a line

1)-b: [Verb + Noun] / [-ResComb, -Transp]

11. blow/wipe/pick one's nose
12. answer/pick up the phone
13. offer/provide/give an opportunity
14. throw/shed light
15. break/tell/give the news
16. gain/obtain experience
17. meet/fill/fulfil/answer the needs
18. reach/arrive at/come to a conclusion

2)-a: [Delexicalized Verb + Noun] / [+ResComb, +Transp]

19. keep records
20. do (someone) good
21. have a capacity (for)
22. take a picture
23. keep a secret
24. give an example
25. do (someone) a favour
26. have the (same) effect
27. give (someone) a ring

2)-b: [Delexicalized Verb + Noun] / [-ResComb, -Transp]

28. keep/write a diary
29. make a speech
30. see/make/tell the difference
31. take/make notes
32. have/hold talks
33. make/arrange an appointment
34. receive/obtain an answer
35. have/keep good control
36. take/have a walk
37. have /catch a cold

3)-a: [Adjective + Noun] / [+ResComb, +Transp]

38. bad habit
39. long flight
40. common sense
41. high fever
42. great honour
43. main meal
44. wet season
45. low price
46. next week
47. single room

3)-b: [Adjective + Noun] / [-ResComb, -Transp]

48. poor/ill/bad health
49. thick/heavy fog
50. high/large population
51. deep/long breath
52. poor/bad/low quality
53. high/good standard
54. free/spare/leisure time

4)-a: [Adverb + Adjective] / [+ResComb, +Transp]

    55. deeply hurt

    56. only natural (to do)

    57. extremely serious (about)

    58. highly unlikely

    59. terribly afraid (of)

    60. highly recommended

    61. evenly split/divided

4)-b: [Adverb + Adjective] / [-ResComb, -Transp]

    62. terribly/completely lost

    63. extremely/totally different

    64. readily/widely available

    65. absolutely sure

    66. closely/strongly linked

    67. fully/certainly aware

    68. bitterly/extremely cold

    69. badly/severely affected

    70. highly/extremely competent

    71. deeply/heavily involved

Appendix 2

GAP-FILL QUESTIONS FOR
NATIVE SPEAKERS' PILOT STUDY

Instructions: Find the most appropriate word or words to fill each gap. You can give several answers for each question. Tick(☑) one of the four boxes under each word to indicate how confident you are of your answer:

(1) Instruction: Fill each gap with a **verb** (or **verbs**).

1. You must (   ) the truth to the child.

  1. sure□ 2. fairly sure □ 3. not sure □ 4. guess □

2. He used to (   ) the violin when he was in England.

  1. sure□ 2. fairly sure □ 3. not sure □ 4. guess □

3. France (   ) the game only 5 seconds before the end.

  1. sure□ 2. fairly sure □ 3. not sure □ 4. guess □

4. Girls in their early teens often try to (   ) weight.

  1. sure□ 2. fairly sure □ 3. not sure □ 4. guess □

5. I had to learn to (   ) music before they let me play the piano.

  1. sure□ 2. fairly sure □ 3. not sure □ 4. guess □

6. Patrick saw the chance to (   ) her a question.

  1. sure□ 2. fairly sure □ 3. not sure □ 4. guess □

7. You need your passport to (   ) the border.

    1. sure□   2. fairly sure □   3. not sure □   4. guess □

8. Children, don't forget to (   ) the toilet before you go out.

    1. sure□   2. fairly sure □   3. not sure □   4. guess □

9. All members of the company are invited to (   ) the meeting to

   discuss the issue.

    1. sure□   2. fairly sure □   3. not sure □   4. guess □

10. The teacher told the students to (   ) a line down the middle of the sheet of

   paper.

    1. sure□   2. fairly sure □   3. not sure □   4. guess □

11. She took a handkerchief from her pocket and (   ) her nose.

    [   ] :1. sure□   2. fairly sure □   3. not sure □   4. guess □

    [   ] :1. sure□   2. fairly sure □   3. not sure □   4. guess □

    [   ] : 1. sure□   2. fairly sure □   3. not sure □   4. guess □

    [   ] :1. sure□   2. fairly sure □   3. not sure □   4. guess □

12. When you (   ) the phone, just say "hello" and do not give your

   name and number.

    [   ] :1. sure□   2. fairly sure □   3. not sure □   4. guess □

    [   ] :1. sure□   2. fairly sure □   3. not sure □   4. guess □

    [   ] : 1. sure□   2. fairly sure □   3. not sure □   4. guess □

    [   ] :1. sure□   2. fairly sure □   3. not sure □   4. guess □

13. A growing number of university courses (   ) an opportunity

for a period of study in another country.

[   ] :1. sure□   2. fairly sure □   3. not sure □   4. guess □

[   ] :1. sure□   2. fairly sure □   3. not sure □   4. guess □

[   ] : 1. sure□   2. fairly sure □   3. not sure □   4. guess □

[   ] :1. sure□   2. fairly sure □   3. not sure □   4. guess □

14. Recent research has (   ) light on this problem.

[   ] :1. sure□   2. fairly sure □   3. not sure □   4. guess □

[   ] :1. sure□   2. fairly sure □   3. not sure □   4. guess □

[   ] : 1. sure□   2. fairly sure □   3. not sure □   4. guess □

[   ] :1. sure□   2. fairly sure □   3. not sure □   4. guess □

15. I didn't want to be the one to (   ) the news to him.

[   ] :1. sure□   2. fairly sure □   3. not sure □   4. guess □

[   ] :1. sure□   2. fairly sure □   3. not sure □   4. guess □

[   ] : 1. sure□   2. fairly sure □   3. not sure □   4. guess □

[   ] :1. sure□   2. fairly sure □   3. not sure □   4. guess □

16. She was studying French and went to France to (   )

experience.

[   ] :1. sure□   2. fairly sure □   3. not sure □   4. guess □

[   ] :1. sure□   2. fairly sure □   3. not sure □   4. guess □

[   ] : 1. sure□   2. fairly sure □   3. not sure □   4. guess □

[   ] :1. sure□   2. fairly sure □   3. not sure □   4. guess □

17. This book will (   ) the needs of students.

   [   ] :1. sure□ 2. fairly sure □ 3. not sure □ 4. guess □

   [   ] :1. sure□ 2. fairly sure □ 3. not sure □ 4. guess □

   [   ] : 1. sure□ 2. fairly sure □ 3. not sure □ 4. guess □

   [   ] :1. sure□ 2. fairly sure □ 3. not sure □ 4. guess □

18. Unless we talk about this together, we won't (   ) any conclusions.

   [   ] :1. sure□ 2. fairly sure □ 3. not sure □ 4. guess □

   [   ] :1. sure□ 2. fairly sure □ 3. not sure □ 4. guess □

   [   ] : 1. sure□ 2. fairly sure □ 3. not sure □ 4. guess □

   [   ] :1. sure□ 2. fairly sure □ 3. not sure □ 4. guess □

(2) Instruction: Fill each gap with a **verb** (or **verbs**).

1. Teachers are expected to (   ) records of the work of their students during the semester.

   1. sure□ 2. fairly sure □ 3. not sure □ 4. guess □

2. Some exercise would probably (   ) you good.

   1. sure□ 2. fairly sure □ 3. not sure □ 4. guess □

3. She (   ) a remarkable capacity for learning languages.

1. sure□ 2. fairly sure □ 3. not sure □ 4. guess □

4. Don't give your camera to a stranger and ask him to (   ) a picture of you.

   1. sure□ 2. fairly sure □ 3. not sure □ 4. guess □

5. Can you (   ) a secret?

   1. sure□ 2. fairly sure □ 3. not sure □ 4. guess □

6. I will (   ) you an example.

  1. sure☐   2. fairly sure ☐   3. not sure ☐   4. guess ☐

7. Will you (   ) me a favour?

  1. sure☐   2. fairly sure ☐   3. not sure ☐   4. guess ☐

8. Tea (   ) the same effect as coffee.

  1. sure☐   2. fairly sure ☐   3. not sure ☐   4. guess ☐

9. Please (   ) me a ring in the morning to wake me up.

  1. sure☐   2. fairly sure ☐   3. not sure ☐   4. guess ☐

10. I will (   ) a diary this year.

  [   ] :1. sure☐ 2. fairly sure ☐ 3. not sure ☐ 4. guess ☐

  [   ] :1. sure☐ 2. fairly sure ☐ 3. not sure ☐ 4. guess ☐

  [   ] : 1. sure☐ 2. fairly sure ☐ 3. not sure ☐ 4. guess ☐

  [   ] :1. sure☐ 2. fairly sure ☐ 3. not sure ☐ 4. guess ☐

11. After dinner I'll (   ) a speech to announce our marriage.

  [   ] :1. sure☐ 2. fairly sure ☐ 3. not sure ☐ 4. guess ☐

  [   ] :1. sure☐ 2. fairly sure ☐ 3. not sure ☐ 4. guess ☐

  [   ] : 1. sure☐ 2. fairly sure ☐ 3. not sure ☐ 4. guess ☐

  [   ] :1. sure☐ 2. fairly sure ☐ 3. not sure ☐ 4. guess ☐

12. She cannot (   ) a distinction between Japanese and Chinese.

  [   ] :1. sure☐ 2. fairly sure ☐ 3. not sure ☐ 4. guess ☐

  [   ] :1. sure☐ 2. fairly sure ☐ 3. not sure ☐ 4. guess ☐

  [   ] : 1. sure☐ 2. fairly sure ☐ 3. not sure ☐ 4. guess ☐

  [   ] :1. sure☐ 2. fairly sure ☐ 3. not sure ☐ 4. guess ☐

13. I will (   ) notes, and pass them on to you later.

[   ] :1. sure□   2. fairly sure □   3. not sure □   4. guess □

[   ] :1. sure□   2. fairly sure □   3. not sure □   4. guess □

[   ] : 1. sure□   2. fairly sure □   3. not sure □   4. guess □

[   ] :1. sure□   2. fairly sure □   3. not sure □   4. guess □

14. Prime Minister Tony Blair and President Bush will (   ) talks in New York.

[   ] :1. sure□   2. fairly sure □   3. not sure □   4. guess □

[   ] :1. sure□   2. fairly sure □   3. not sure □   4. guess □

[   ] : 1. sure□   2. fairly sure □   3. not sure □   4. guess □

[   ] :1. sure□   2. fairly sure □   3. not sure □   4. guess □

15. Ask your doctor for any further information or to (   ) an appointment.

[   ] :1. sure□   2. fairly sure □   3. not sure □   4. guess □

[   ] :1. sure□   2. fairly sure □   3. not sure □   4. guess □

[   ] : 1. sure□   2. fairly sure □   3. not sure □   4. guess □

[   ] :1. sure□   2. fairly sure □   3. not sure □   4. guess □

16. Even if you ask him a question, you will not (   ) an answer.

[   ] :1. sure□   2. fairly sure □   3. not sure □   4. guess □

[   ] :1. sure□   2. fairly sure □   3. not sure □   4. guess □

[   ] : 1. sure□   2. fairly sure □   3. not sure □   4. guess □

[   ] :1. sure□   2. fairly sure □   3. not sure □   4. guess

17. The new teacher (   ) good control of his class.

[   ] :1. sure□   2. fairly sure □   3. not sure □   4. guess □

[   ] :1. sure□   2. fairly sure □   3. not sure □   4. guess □

[   ] : 1. sure□   2. fairly sure □   3. not sure □   4. guess □

[   ] :1. sure□   2. fairly sure □   3. not sure □   4. guess □

18. Let's (   ) a walk over the fields.

[   ] :1. sure□   2. fairly sure □   3. not sure □   4. guess □

[   ] :1. sure□   2. fairly sure □   3. not sure □   4. guess □

[   ] : 1. sure□   2. fairly sure □   3. not sure □   4. guess □

[   ] :1. sure□   2. fairly sure □   3. not sure □   4. guess □

19. He was not at school because he (   ) a cold.

[   ] :1. sure□   2. fairly sure □   3. not sure □   4. guess □

[   ] :1. sure□   2. fairly sure □   3. not sure □   4. guess □

[   ] : 1. sure□   2. fairly sure □   3. not sure □   4. guess □

[   ] :1. sure□   2. fairly sure □   3. not sure □   4. guess □

(3) Instruction: Fill each gap with an **adjective** (or **adjectives**).

1. It's a (   ) habit to bite your nails.

    1. sure□   2. fairly sure □   3. not sure □   4. guess □

2. I was very tired after the (   ) flight of 12 hours from Paris to Tokyo.

    1. sure□   2. fairly sure □   3. not sure □   4. guess □

3. Use your (   ) sense, and little can go wrong.

    1. sure□   2. fairly sure □   3. not sure □   4. guess □

4. The symptoms of flu last several days, starting with a (   ) fever of 38 degrees.

    1. sure□   2. fairly sure □   3. not sure □   4. guess □

5. It's a(n) (   ) honour to have him in a little town like this.

   1. sure□   2. fairly sure □   3. not sure □   4. guess □

6. The (   ) meal of the day was chicken followed by something sweet.

   1. sure□   2. fairly sure □   3. not sure □   4. guess □

7. In Japan, June is generally called a (   ) season with heavy rainfall.

   1. sure□   2. fairly sure □   3. not sure □   4. guess □

8. During the sales, they sell expensive clothes at a very (   ) price.

   1. sure□   2. fairly sure □   3. not sure □   4. guess □

9. The host of that program said, "See you (   ) week, same time."

   1. sure□   2. fairly sure □   3. not sure □   4. guess □

10. "Would you like a double room?" "No, I should like a (   ) room, please."

   1. sure□   2. fairly sure □   3. not sure □   4. guess □

11. There is a link between poverty and (   ) health.

   [   ] :1. sure□   2. fairly sure □   3. not sure □   4. guess □

   [   ] :1. sure□   2. fairly sure □   3. not sure □   4. guess □

   [   ] : 1. sure□   2. fairly sure □   3. not sure □   4. guess □

   [   ] :1. sure□   2. fairly sure □   3. not sure □   4. guess □

12. Barry won the ski competition despite the (   ) fog.

   [   ] :1. sure□   2. fairly sure □   3. not sure □   4. guess □

   [   ] :1. sure□   2. fairly sure □   3. not sure □   4. guess □

   [   ] : 1. sure□   2. fairly sure □   3. not sure □   4. guess □

   [   ] :1. sure□   2. fairly sure □   3. not sure □   4. guess □

13. India is not short of resources despite its (   ) population.

[   ] :1. sure□   2. fairly sure □   3. not sure □   4. guess □

[   ] :1. sure□   2. fairly sure □   3. not sure □   4. guess □

[   ] : 1. sure□   2. fairly sure □   3. not sure □   4. guess □

[   ] :1. sure□   2. fairly sure □   3. not sure □   4. guess □

14. When she was nervous, she took a (   ) breath and made herself speak slowly.

[   ] :1. sure□   2. fairly sure □   3. not sure □   4. guess □

[   ] :1. sure□   2. fairly sure □   3. not sure □   4. guess □

[   ] : 1. sure□   2. fairly sure □   3. not sure □   4. guess □

[   ] :1. sure□   2. fairly sure □   3. not sure □   4. guess □

15. Because of the (   ) quality of doors and windows, the car is very cheap.

[   ] :1. sure□   2. fairly sure □   3. not sure □   4. guess □

[   ] :1. sure□   2. fairly sure □   3. not sure □   4. guess □

[   ] : 1. sure□   2. fairly sure □   3. not sure □   4. guess □

[   ] :1. sure□   2. fairly sure □   3. not sure □   4. guess □

16. To pass the exam, a (   ) standard of literacy is required.

[   ] :1. sure□   2. fairly sure □   3. not sure □   4. guess □

[   ] :1. sure□   2. fairly sure □   3. not sure □   4. guess □

[   ] : 1. sure□   2. fairly sure □   3. not sure □   4. guess □

[   ] :1. sure□   2. fairly sure □   3. not sure □   4. guess □

17. What do you do in your (   ) time?

[   ] :1. sure□   2. fairly sure □   3. not sure □   4. guess □

[   ] :1. sure□   2. fairly sure □   3. not sure □   4. guess □

[   ] : 1. sure□   2. fairly sure □   3. not sure □   4. guess □

[   ] :1. sure□   2. fairly sure □   3. not sure □   4. guess □

(4)-1. Instruction: Fill each gap with **an adjective**.

1. She was deeply (   ) that he no longer loved her.
   1. sure□ 2. fairly sure □ 3. not sure □ 4. guess □

2. When you feel sad or unhappy, it is only (   ) to cry.
   1. sure□ 2. fairly sure □ 3. not sure □ 4. guess □

3. He is extremely (   ) about art, but jokes a little about everything else.
   1. sure□ 2. fairly sure □ 3. not sure □ 4. guess □

4. It is highly (   ) that such a strong team will lose the game.
   1. sure□ 2. fairly sure □ 3. not sure □ 4. guess □

5. He was terribly (   ) of being caught by the police.
   1. sure□ 2. fairly sure □ 3. not sure □ 4. guess □

6. It is highly (   ) to wear a suit for a job interview.
   1. sure□ 2. fairly sure □ 3. not sure □ 4. guess □

7. A group of 12 children can be evenly (   ) into two groups of 6.
   1. sure□ 2. fairly sure □ 3. not sure □ 4. guess □

(4)-2. Instruction: Fill each gap with **an adverb**. (Do not use 'very' and 'really'.)

8. I got (   ) lost in the wood and didn't know which way to go.
   [   ] :1. sure□ 2. fairly sure □ 3. not sure □ 4. guess □
   [   ] :1. sure□ 2. fairly sure □ 3. not sure □ 4. guess □

[   ] : 1. sure☐   2. fairly sure ☐   3. not sure ☐   4. guess ☐

[   ] :1. sure☐   2. fairly sure ☐   3. not sure ☐   4. guess ☐

9. The new album starts with a(n)(   ) different version of We Will Rock You.

[   ] :1. sure☐   2. fairly sure ☐   3. not sure ☐   4. guess ☐

[   ] :1. sure☐   2. fairly sure ☐   3. not sure ☐   4. guess ☐

[   ] : 1. sure☐   2. fairly sure ☐   3. not sure ☐   4. guess ☐

[   ] :1. sure☐   2. fairly sure ☐   3. not sure ☐   4. guess ☐

10. Vegetarian meals are (   ) available in this restaurant.

[   ] :1. sure☐   2. fairly sure ☐   3. not sure ☐   4. guess ☐

[   ] :1. sure☐   2. fairly sure ☐   3. not sure ☐   4. guess ☐

[   ] : 1. sure☐   2. fairly sure ☐   3. not sure ☐   4. guess ☐

[   ] :1. sure☐   2. fairly sure ☐   3. not sure ☐   4. guess ☐

11. Are you (   ) sure there's nothing wrong?

[   ] :1. sure☐   2. fairly sure ☐   3. not sure ☐   4. guess ☐

[   ] :1. sure☐   2. fairly sure ☐   3. not sure ☐   4. guess ☐

[   ] : 1. sure☐   2. fairly sure ☐   3. not sure ☐   4. guess ☐

[   ] :1. sure☐   2. fairly sure ☐   3. not sure ☐   4. guess ☐

12. Enthusiasm is (   ) linked with interest.

[   ] :1. sure☐   2. fairly sure ☐   3. not sure ☐   4. guess ☐

[   ] :1. sure☐   2. fairly sure ☐   3. not sure ☐   4. guess ☐

[   ] : 1. sure☐   2. fairly sure ☐   3. not sure ☐   4. guess ☐

[   ] :1. sure☐   2. fairly sure ☐   3. not sure ☐   4. guess ☐

13. We are (   ) aware that he will succeed in the game.

[   ] :1. sure□   2. fairly sure □   3. not sure □   4. guess □

[   ] :1. sure □   2. fairly sure □   3. not sure □   4. guess □

[   ] : 1. sure□   2. fairly sure □   3. not sure □   4. guess □

[   ] :1. sure□   2. fairly sure □   3. not sure □   4. guess □

14. It was a very hard and (   ) cold winter.

[   ] :1. sure□   2. fairly sure □   3. not sure □   4. guess □

[   ] :1. sure□   2. fairly sure □   3. not sure □   4. guess □

[   ] : 1. sure□   2. fairly sure □   3. not sure □   4. guess □

[   ] :1. sure□   2. fairly sure □   3. not sure □   4. guess □

15. Indonesia, India, Sri Lanka and Thailand were all (   ) affected by the tsunami in December 2004.

[   ] :1. sure□   2. fairly sure □   3. not sure □   4. guess □

[   ] :1. sure□   2. fairly sure □   3. not sure □   4. guess □

[   ] : 1. sure□   2. fairly sure □   3. not sure □   4. guess □

[   ] :1. sure□   2. fairly sure □   3. not sure □   4. guess □

16. He is a(n) (   ) competent scientist in the field.

[   ] :1. sure□   2. fairly sure □   3. not sure □   4. guess □

[   ] :1. sure□   2. fairly sure □   3. not sure □   4. guess □

[   ] : 1. sure□   2. fairly sure □   3. not sure □   4. guess □

[   ] :1. sure□   2. fairly sure □   3. not sure □   4. guess □

17. The singers became (   ) involved in songwriting.

[   ] :1. sure□   2. fairly sure □   3. not sure □   4. guess □

[   ] :1. sure□   2. fairly sure □   3. not sure □   4. guess □

[   ] : 1. sure□   2. fairly sure □   3. not sure □   4. guess □

[   ] :1. sure□   2. fairly sure □   3. not sure □   4. guess □

Appendix 3

RESULTS OF PILOT STUDY 1 (1)

Certainty of Answer: A: sure, B: fairly sure, C: not sure, D: guess, N: no-certainty

1)-a:[Verb + Noun] / [+ResComb, +Transp]

Answer \ Student	1	2	3	4	5	6	7	8	9	10	11	12	13	14	Total
1) tell the truth															
speak							B								1
say															
tell	A	A	A	A	B	B	B		A	A	B	A	B	B	13
inform															
2) play the violin															
play	A	A	A	A	A	A	A	A	A	A	B	A	A	B	14
3) win the match															
won		A	B	C	A	B	B	A	A	C	C	B	B		12
lost							B						B		2
drew							B								1
head about	A														1
4) lose weight															
lose		A	A		A		B	A	C	A	C	A			9
loose	A			A		A							B	A	5
5) read music															
read	A	A	A	A	A	B	B	C	B	A	B	A	A	A	14
6) ask someone a question															
ask		A	A	A	A	B	B	A	A	A	B		A		11
answer											B	B			2
(blank)	N														1
7) cross the border															
cross		A	A	A	A	A	A	A	A	A	A			A	11
pass												B			1
ask	A														1
8) flush the toilet															
flush		B	A								A	B			4
use				B				N	C				A		4
go					A		A								2
go to						A				B				A	3
(blank)	N														1
9) attend the meeting															
attend	A	A	B	B	B	A	B	A	A	A	B	A	B	A	14
go to							B								1
10) draw a line															
draw	A	A	A	B	A	A	A	B	A	B	A	B	B	B	14

Results of Pilot Study 1 (2)

Certainty of Answer: A: sure, B: fairly sure, C: not sure, D: guess, N: no-certainty

1)-b:[Verb + Noun] / [-ResComb, -Transp]

Answer \ Student	1	2	3	4	5	6	7	8	9	10	11	12	13	14	Total
11) blow/wipe/pick one's nose															
blew	A	A	A	B	B	B	B	B	N	A	B	N		C	13
wiped	A	A	A	B	B	B			N	A	D		B		10
picked	A										D				2
rubbed			B												1
12) answer/pick up the phone															
answer		A	A	A	A	A	A	B	N	A	B	N	B	B	13
pick up		A	A	A		A	A		N	A	D				8
ring	A														1
dial	A														1
call	A														1
13) offer/provide/give an opportunity															
offer	A		A	A			A		N		C	N		B	8
provide		B	A				A			B	C				5
give			C	B				B							3
have					A	A									2
present						A			N						2
propose						A			N						2
are												B			1
14) throw/shed light															
shed	A	A	A		A	A	A	A	A	A	B	N		B	13
thorwn				B					A				B		3
shown											D				1
15) break/tell/give the news															
break	A	A	A	A	A	A	A	A	N	A	B	N		B	13
tell						A	A						B		3
give										A					1
16) gain/obtain experience															
gain	A	A		A		A	B		N	A		A			8
get				A			B			A	A	B			5
broaden		A											C	C	3
widen		A													1
enhance		A													1
obtain											A				1
consolidate					C										1

17) meet/fill/answer the needs													
meet			A	A				A	C				4
answer	A					C							2
satisfy								B	C				2
fill							N						1
comply with		C											1
provide for		C											1
cater for				C									1
address			A										1
show											N			1
help												B		1
fulfill													C	1
(blank)							N						1
18) reach/draw a conclusion													
reach	A				B		A	A	B		N		B	7
draw	B		A	B	A	C								5
come to			A	A	A	B		A	N	A				7
make					A		N							2
find					A								C	2

RESULTS OF PILOT STUDY 1 (3)

Certainty of Answer: A: sure, B: fairly sure, C: not sure, D: guess, N: no-certainty

2)-a:[Delexicalized Verb + Noun] / [+ResComb, +Transp]

Answer \ Student	1	2	3	4	5	6	7	8	9	10	11	12	13	14	Total
19) keep records															
keep		A	A	A	A		A	A	A	B		B	B		10
maintain	A														1
produce						A									1
make								A				A			2
20) do (someone) good															
do	A	A	A	A	A	A	A	A	A	A	B	A	A	B	14
21) have a capacity (for)															
has	A		A	A	B	A	A	A		A	B	A	A	B	12
shows								B							1
demonstrate		B													1
22) take a picture															
take	A	A	A	A	A	A	A	A	A	A	B	A	A	A	14
23) keep a secret															
keep	A	A	A	A	A	A	A	A	A	A	B	A	A	A	14
24) give an example															
give	A	A	A	C		A	A		A	B	A	A			11
show			A	A	C	A		B					B		6
25) do (someone) a favour															
do	A	A	A	A	A	A	A	A	A	A	A	A	A	A	14
26) have the (same) effect															
has	A	A	A	B	C	A	B	A	A	A	A	A	A	B	14
27) give (someone) a ring															
give	A	A	A	A	A	A	B	A	A	A	B	A	B	D	14

RESULTS OF PILOT STUDY 1 (4)

Certainty of Answer: A: sure, B: fairly sure, C: not sure, D: guess, N: no-certainty

2)-b:[Delexicalized Verb + Noun] / [-ResComb, -Transp]

Answer\Student	1	2	3	4	5	6	7	8	9	10	11	12	13	14	Total
28) keep/write a diary															
keep	A	B	A	A	A	A	A	A	N	A	B		A	A	13
fill in	N														1
write		A		B	B		B		N		D	A			7
carry			A												1
start												A			1
29) give/make a speech															
give	A	B	B	A	A		A	A	B	A	C		B	A	13
make		B	A	B	A				A	A	B	N			8
write						B						B			2
do							C								1
30) see/make/tell the difference															
make	A	B	A	A	A	A	A	A		A	A	N	B	B	13
see						A			A						2
tell									A						1
hear									N						1
31) take/make notes															
take	A	C	A	A		A	A		N	A	B	N	A	A	12
make		C		B	B	A	A	A	N			A			8
write		B			B		A			C					4
keep											C				1
write up			C												1
32) have/hold talks															
have	A			A	B	A	B			B	C		B		8
hold			A						N	A		N		A	5
give		B		D											2
attend								B				B			2
start							B								1
join							B								1
head									N						1
33) make/arrange an appointment															
make	B	A	A	A	A	A		A	A	A	B		B	B	12
arrange			A	A		A	A					A			5
book		A		B			A				D				4

	1	2	3	4	5	6	7	8	9	10	11	12	13	14	Total
organize						A					B				2
reserve								C							1
confirm								C							1
cancel								C							1
get										A					1
34) receive/obtain an answer															
receive				A		A		B		N	D	B	B		7
get	A	A	A					A	A	N	A	B	N		9
obtain							B								1
find			C												1
give					A										1
set					A										1
have			C		B								B		3
gain						A									1
35) have/keep good control															
had	A	B	A	A		B	B	A	N	B	B	N	A		12
took					A	B					C				3
maintained	A		A												2
kept					A			A	D				B		4
gained						B									1
achieved						B									1
36) take/have a walk															
take	A	A	A		A	A	A	B	N	A	C	N	A	B	13
have			B		A			B	C	C					5
go for			A			A		A	C						4
37) have/catch a cold															
had	A	A	A	A	A	A	A	B	B	B	A	B	N	B	14
catch		A										C			2

RESULTS OF PILOT STUDY 1 (5)

Certainty of Answer: A: sure, B: fairly sure, C: not sure, D: guess, N: no-certainty

3)-a:[Adjective+ Noun] / [+ResComb, +Transp]

Answer \ Student	1	2	3	4	5	6	7	8	9	10	11	12	13	14	Total
38) bad habit															
bad	A	A	A	A		A	A	A	A	A	C	A			11
nasty					B								B		2
(blank)														N	1
39) long flight															
long	A	A	A	A	B	A	A	B	B	A	C	B	B	B	14
40) common sense															
common	A			A	A		A	A	A	A	B	N	B	B	14
good		B				B									2
sixth			C												1
41) high fever															
high		B	A	A	A	A	B	A	A	A		A	B	D	12
severe	A														1
(blank)											N				1
42) great honour															
great		A	A	B	B	A	A	C		A		B			10
huge	A					A									2
real								B		C					2
big													B		1
43) main meal															
main	A			B	B		C		B	A	C	A		C	9
best		C													1
last			A												1
favorite						C									1
nice													B		1
(blank)								N							1
44) wet season															
wet	C	A				A	B		B	A	C	A	B		10
rainy			A	C											2
monsoon			A											C	2
summer				C											1
(blank)								N							1
45) low price															
low	B	A		A		A		B		B		A			7
cheap							A	A		A	B				4
reasonable	C			A					A						3

bargain			B									B			2
sale				B		B							B		3
46) next week															
next	A	A	A	B	D	A	A	A	B	A	B	C	B	A	14
47) single room															
single	A	A	A	A	B	A	A	A	A	A	C	A	B	B	14
quadruple	A														1

RESULTS OF PILOT STUDY 1 (6)

Certainty of Answer: A: sure, B: fairly sure, C: not sure, D: guess, N: no-certainty

3)-b:[Adjective + Noun] / [-ResComb, -Transp]

Answer \ Student	1	2	3	4	5	6	7	8	9	10	11	12	13	14	Total
48) poor/ill/bad health															
poor		A	A		A	A	A		A		B	B	B		9
bad		A	A			A	A	A	B	A		B			8
ill			A						A	B					3
good				B											1
mental											D				1
personal							C								1
(blank)	N														1
49) thick/heavy fog															
thick			A	A		A	A		N	A		A		B	8
dense					B				N	A		A	B		5
heavy	A	B	A							A	C				5
bad							C				N				2
low						A									1
incessant									N						1
dreadful									N						1
50) high/large population															
large		A		A	B	A	A	D		A			B		8
high			B							A			B		3
huge	A					A				A					3
dense			A			A					C				3
massive	A	A													2
big					B		A								2
enormous	A								B						2
great							C								1
gigantic	A														1
immense									B						1
considerable									B						1
poor											C				1
51) deep/long breath															
deep	A	A	A	A	A		A	A	A	A	B	B	B	A	13
long						A									1
large						A									1
52) poor/bad/low quality															
poor	A	A	A	A		A	A	B	N		D	N		B	11
bad		A		B			A		N			C			5
low					B				N	B			A		4

233

	1	2	3	4	5	6	7	8	9	10	11	12	13	14	
moderate	B														1
53) high/good standard															
high	A	A	A	B				B							5
good			A		A		B	B		C		A			6
certain		A						B	A					B	4
minimum	A								A						2
sufficient		A													1
decent					A										1
common						C									1
reasonable											N				1
54) free/spare/leisure time															
free	A	A	A	A	A		A	A	A	A		A	A		11
spare		B			A					A	A				4
leisure													B	B	2

RESULTS OF PILOT STUDY 1 (7)

Certainty of Answer: A: sure, B: fairly sure, C: not sure, D: guess, N: no-certainty

4)-a:[Adverb + Adjective] / [+ResComb, +Transp]

Answer \ Student	1	2	3	4	5	6	7	8	9	10	11	12	13	14	Total
55) deeply hurt															
hurt			A	B	B						C	A			5
sad							D	B							2
sure	A		A												2
saddened					A								B		2
affected		B													1
upset						A									1
concerned										C					1
offended														D	1
56) only natural (to do)															
natural	A		A	A				B	A	C	C	B	B		9
normal		A			B		D								3
right				B											1
healthy						A									1
57) extremely serious (about)															
serious	A	A		A	B		B		A	A	C	C	B	B	11
passionate			C												1
funny						B									1
keen								D							1
58) highly unlikely															
unlikely		A	A			A		A	A			C	B	B	8
likely				A	A						C				3
strange	B														1
probable							B								1
unusual										A					1
59) terribly afraid															
afraid	A	B			C	A	B		A	C					7
scared				B				B			D	B	C		5
ashamed			A												1
embarassed														D	1
60) highly recommended															
recommended		A		A			A	C		A	D	C	B		8
used	A														1
important			A												1
commendable					D										1

normal					A										1
acceptable							C								1
advised												D			1
61) evenly split/divided															
split	N		A		B	B	A		A		C	C		B	9
divided		A		A			A	C				B			5

RESULTS OF PILOT STUDY 1 (8)

Certainty of Answer: A: sure, B: fairly sure, C: not sure, D: guess, N: no-certainty

4)-b:[Adverb + Adjective] / [-ResComb, -Transp]

Answer \ Student	1	2	3	4	5	6	7	8	9	10	11	12	13	14	Total
62) completely/terribly lost															
completely	A	C	A	A	A								B		6
terribly											C				1
extremely				A	A								B		3
quite								A				N			2
badly									N						1
hopelessly									N						1
totally										A					1
63) extremely/totally different															
totally		C		B			A		A				B		5
completely			A		A							N			3
extremely						A				D					2
slightly			B								C				2
rather			C												1
dramatically							A								1
new									B						1
interestingly													C		1
(blank)	N														1
64) readily/widely available															
always			A	A	B									A	4
sometimes			A												1
usually				B	A				A						3
normally					A				A						2
often						B									1
readily							A								1
no longer								D							1
only									N						1
now									N						1
greatly										D					1
widely												N			1
never													B		1
(blank)	N														1
65) absolutely sure															
absolutely			A	A					N	A	C		A		6
quite				A			A								2

	1	2	3	4	5	6	7	8	9	10	11	12	13	14	Total
definitely						A					N				2
completely		A													1
(blank)	N			N		N							N		4
66) closely/strongly linked															
closely		A	A					A	D						4
often					A	D	N								3
strongly		C							N						2
highly			B												1
definitely					A										1
always							N				B				2
usually											B				1
(blank)	N														1
67) fully/certainly aware															
fully		A			A	B		A							4
quite			B			N		B							3
extremely			A												1
totally				B											1
openly		C													1
(blank)	N						N			N	N	N			5
68) bitterly/extremely cold															
bitterly		A	A	A			D		C		B	B			8
extremely		A			A										2
long						B									1
particularly	A														1
awfully							A		N						2
69) badly/severely affected															
badly		C			A		N	A				A			5
terribly			A	A											2
deeply		B			A										2
greatly		A	A												2
severely							A								1
seriouly							A								1
strongly								N							1
heavily										B					1
(blank)	N					N		N							3
70) highly/extremely competent															
highly				A				A	N		B				4
extremely		A	A		A	A	A				A	A			7
fully		A													1
fairly							N								1
exceptionally			A												1
truly							N								1
(blank)	N							N							2

71) deeply/heavily involved

deeply			A						N			B	3
heavily					A	A				N		B	4
highly							B						1
extremely											B		1
particularly				B									1
increasingly		B											1
(blank)	N				N	N		N					4

Appendix 4

MULTIPLE CHOICE QUESTIONS TASKS

a) MCQ Tasks for French Learners

University of London Institute in Paris   July 2006

Autorisation pour collecter et utiliser des données

Selon les règlements (pages 9-12) de l'Association britannique pour la linguistique appliquée (BAAL).

Je m'appelle Shino Kurosaki et je suis étudiante en doctorat à l'Université de Londres Institut à Paris. Je fais des recherches sur l'usage des combinaisons lexicales anglaises par les Français et Japonais qui apprennent l'anglais comme langue étrangère.

Pour mes recherches de doctorat, je collecte des données des Français et Japonais qui ont un niveau d'anglais qui correspond à B2 sur l'échelle ALTE.

Mes recherches comportent des tâches où vous devez traduire des mots / expressions de votre langue maternelle vers l'anglais.

Vos réponses écrites resteront évidemment anonymes dans ma thèse et dans toute publication basée sur mes recherches. De plus, en tant que participants volontaires à ma recherche, vous pouvez vous retirer de cette expérience à n'importe quel moment et toutes vos données seront détruites.

Si vous avez des questions concernant mes recherches, prenez contact avec moi (shinokurosaki@m3.gyao.ne.jp)

J'ai reçu et lu un exemplaire des renseignements mentionnés ci-dessus.

Signature: _____

Nom et Prénom: _____   _____

Date: _____

Profil de l'étudiant(e)

1. Quel âge avez-vous ? : (   ) ans

2. Sexe : Masculin / Féminin

3. Combien d'années d'anglais avez-vous faites ? :(   ) ans

4. Avez-vous visité des pays anglophones ? Oui / Non

   Si oui,

   Quel(s) pays avez-vous visité(s) ? _____

   Pendant combien de temps ? (   )

Instruction :

Regardez les phrases et trouvez le mot le plus approprié ou les mots les plus appropriés pour remplir chaque trou. Vous pouvez écrire plusieurs réponses. Entourez la bonne reponse ou les bonnes reponses.

1. You must (   ) the truth to the child.

a. speak   b. say   c. tell   d. inform

2. The teacher told the students to (   ) a line down the middle of the sheet of paper.

a. write   b. design   c. draw   d. paint

3. Because of his efforts, he (   ) the match.

a. gained   b. won   c. beat   d. got

4. Girls in their early teens often try to (   ) weight.

a. reduce   b. lose   c. diminish   d. decrease

5. I had to learn to (   ) music before they let me play the piano.

a. know   b. understand   c. seize   d. read

6. Patrick saw the chance to (   ) her a question.

a. listen to   b. do   c. interrogate   d. ask

7. All members of the company are invited to (   ) the meeting to discuss the issue.

a. attend   b. appear   c. present   d. go to

8. He has been learning to (   ) the violin for five years.

a. perform   b. play   c. execute   d. do

9. You need your passport to (   ) the border.

    a. cross   b. go over   c. go through   d. pass

10. She took a handkerchief from her pocket and (   ) her nose.

    a. blew   b. wiped   c. took   d. bit

11. When you (   ) the phone, say "hello" but do not give your name and number.

    a. respond   b. pick up   c. take   d. answer

12. A growing number of university courses (   ) an opportunity for a period of study in another country.

    a. offer   b. provide   c. have   d. give

13. She was studying French and went to France to (   ) experience.

    a. gain   b. acquire   c. get   d. pile

14. This book will (   ) the needs of students.

    a. meet   b. answer   c. satisfy   d. fill

15. Unless we talk about this together, we won't (   ) any conclusions.

    a. arrive at   b. reach   c. draw   d. come to

16. Teachers are expected to (   ) records of the work done by their students during the semester.

    a. make   b. take   c. note   d. keep

17. Some exercise would probably (   ) you good.

    a. make   b. profit   c. do   d. become

18. Don't give your camera to a stranger and ask him to (   ) a picture of you.

   a. get   b. take   c. have   d. catch

19. Can you (   ) a secret?

   a. hold   b. guard   c. protect   d. keep

20. Will you (   ) me a favour?

   a. make   b. ask   c. give   d. do

21. Tea (   ) the same effect as coffee.

   a. brings   b. does   c. affects   d. has

22. Please (   ) me a ring in the morning to wake me up.

   a. send   b. give   c. ask   d. call

23. I am going to (   ) a diary next year.

   a. keep   b. write   c. note   d. mark

24. After dinner I'll (   ) a speech.

   a. give   b. make   c. pronounce   d. do

25. I will (   ) notes, and pass them on to you later.

   a. take   b. make   c. write   d. put

26. Prime Minister Tony Blair and President Bush will (   ) talks in New York later this year.

   a. have   b. hold   c. do   d. give

27. Phone your doctor to (   ) an appointment.

    a. make   b. arrange   c. take   d. do

28. Even if you ask him a question, you will not (   ) an answer.

    a. get   b. receive   c. find   d. obtain

29. The new teacher (   ) good control of his class.

    a. has   b. keeps   c. takes   d. exercises

30. Let's (   ) a walk over the fields.

    a. have   b. go for   c. do   d. take

31. It's a(n) (   ) habit to bite your nails.

    a. awful   b. nasty   c. wrong   d. bad

32. I was very tired after the (   ) flight of 12 hours from Paris to Tokyo.

    a. short   b. lengthy   c. long   d. distant

33. The symptoms of flu last several days, starting with a (   ) fever of 38 degrees.

    a. severe   b. strong   c. heavy   d. high

34. The (   ) meal of the day was chicken followed by something sweet.

    a. principal   b. main   c. major   d. favourite

35. The host of the TV programme said, "See you (   ) week, same time."

    a. following   b. subsequent   c. coming   d. next

36. "Would you like a double room?" "No, I would like a (   ) room, please."

    a. one   b. single   c. simple   d. only

37. Use your (　　　　　) sense, and little can go wrong.

a. balanced　　　b. good　　　c. ordinary　　　d. common

38. There is a link between poverty and (　　　　　) health.

a. poor　　　b. bad　　　c. inferior　　　d. ill

39. Barry won the ski competition despite the (　　　　　) fog.

a. thick　　　b. dense　　　c. heavy　　　d. deep

40. India is not short of resources despite its (　　　　　) population.

a. high　　　b. many　　　c. dense　　　d. large

41. What do you do in your (　　　　) time?

a. free　　　b. spare　　　c. leisure　　　d. empty

42. To pass the exam, a (　　　　) standard of literacy is required.

a. high　　　b. good　　　c. determined　　　d. certain

43. The government is keeping (　　　　) control over immigration.

a. tight　　　b. severe　　　c. hard　　　d. strict

44. Because of the (　　　) quality of doors and windows, the car is very cheap.

a. poor　　　b. bad　　　c. low　　　d. ill

45. When you feel sad or unhappy, it is only (　　　　) to cry.

a. natural　　　b. normal　　　c. right　　　d. sure

46. He is extremely (　　　) about art, but jokes about everything else.

a. serious　　　b. sincere　　　c. intense　　　d. keen

47. It is highly (   ) that the Japanese football team will beat Brazil.

  a. unlikely   b. unusual   c. strange   d. impossible

48. He was terribly (   ) of being caught by the police.

  a. afraid   b. scared   c. ashamed   d. embarrassed

49. It is highly (   ) to wear a suit for a job interview.

  a. recommended   b. important   c. normal   d. used

50. I got (   ) lost in the wood and didn't know which way to go.

  a. completely   b. extremely   c. perfectly   d. entirely

51. The new CD starts with a(n)(   ) different version of "We Will Rock You".

  a. totally   b. completely   c. extremely   d. entirely

52. We are (   ) aware that he will succeed in the game.

  a. fully   b. quite   c. amply   d. sufficiently

53. Indonesia, India, Sri Lanka and Thailand were all (   ) affected by the tsunami in December 2004.

  a. badly   b. deeply   c. severely   d. greatly

54. He is a(n) (   ) competent scientist in his field.

  a. extremely   b. highly   c. completely   d. fully

55. The singers became (   ) involved in songwriting.

  a. heavily   b. deeply   c. completely   d. profoundly

56. It was a (   ) cold winter.

   a. bitterly   b. extremely   c. terribly   d. violently

Merci beaucoup.

b) MCQ Tasks for Japanese Learners

英語コロケーション問題   July 2006

データの収集と使用に関する承認

この承認は、英国応用言語学会の規則（pp.9-12）に準拠します。
私は、ロンドン大学パリ研究所の博士課程の学生で、黒崎紫乃と申します。現在、英語を第2言語として習得する日本人学習者およびフランス人学習者のコロケーション習得についての研究をしています。博士論文に必要な日本語およびフランス語を母語とする中級英語学習者のデータを現在集めているところです。
このアンケートは、学習者の方々に母語（日本語）から英語への翻訳を行っていただくものです。

ご協力いただいた皆さんの回答は、私の博士論文およびその後このアンケートを使用した論文においては匿名で使用いたします。また、この研究には全くボランティアとして皆さんに協力して頂きますので、いつでもこのアンケートへの回答をお止めになっても構いませんし、またその場合皆さんのデータは全て消去されます。
私の研究について、ご質問等おありの方はいつでもご連絡下さいます様お願いいたします。　（shinokurosaki@m3.gyao.ne.jp）

私は上記の内容を読み、またこれを承認します。

署名：

氏名：

日付：

学習者に関する調査

1. 年齢：（　　　　　　　）歳　　2. 性別：　　男 / 女

3. 学年：（　　　　　　）年

4. 今まで何年間英語を学習してきましたか。　（　　　　　　　）年間

5. (1) これまでに英語圏に滞在したことがありますか。　はい　・
いいえ

　　(2) 上記の (1) で「はい」と答えた人：

　　どの国に滞在しましたか。（　　　　　　　　　　　　）

　　どのくらいの期間滞在しましたか。　（　　　　　　　　　）

6. TOEICのスコア：（　　　　）・TOEFLのスコア：（　　　　）

　英検：　　　（　　　　　　）級

問題：

以下の文をよく読み、（　　　　　）の中にあてはまる適当なものを選びなさい。

答えは１つとは限りませんので、該当すると思うもの全てを○で囲みなさい。

1. You must (　　　　　) the truth to the child.

　a. speak　　b. say　　　c. tell　　　d. inform

2. The teacher told the students to (　　　) a line down the middle of the sheet of paper.

　a. write　　b. design　　c. draw　　　d. paint

3. Because of his efforts, he (　　　) the match.

　a. gained　　b. won　　　c. beat　　　d. got

4. Girls in their early teens often try to (　　　　) weight.

　a. reduce　　b. lose　　　c. diminish　　d. decrease

5. I had to learn to (　　　) music before they let me play the piano.

　a. know　　b. understand　　c. seize　　d. read

6. Patrick saw the chance to (　　　　) her a question.

　a. listen to　　b. do　　　c. interrogate　　d. ask

7. All members of the company are invited to (　　　　) the meeting to discuss the issue.

　a. attend　　b. appear　　c. present　　d. go to

252

8. He has been learning to ( ) the violin for five years.

a. perform   b. play   c. execute   d. do

9. You need your passport to ( ) the border.

a. cross   b. go over   c. go through   d. pass

10. She took a handkerchief from her pocket and ( ) her nose.

a. blew   b. wiped   c. took   d. bit

11. When you ( ) the phone, say "hello" but do not give your name and number.

a. respond   b. pick up   c. take   d. answer

12. A growing number of university courses ( ) an opportunity for a period of study in another country.

a. offer   b. provide   c. have   d. give

13. She was studying French and went to France to ( ) experience.

a. gain   b. acquire   c. get   d. pile

14. This book will ( ) the needs of students.

a. meet   b. answer   c. satisfy   d. fill

15. Unless we talk about this together, we won't ( ) any conclusions.

a. arrive at   b. reach   c. draw   d. come to

16. Teachers are expected to ( ) records of the work done by their students during the semester.

a. make   b. take   c. note   d. keep

17. Some exercise would probably (   ) you good.

  a. make   b. profit   c. do   d. become

18. Don't give your camera to a stranger and ask him to (   ) a picture of you.

  a. get   b. take   c. have   d. catch

19. Can you (   ) a secret?

  a. hold   b. guard   c. protect   d. keep

20. Will you (   ) me a favour?

  a. make   b. ask   c. give   d. do

21. Tea (   ) the same effect as coffee.

  a. brings   b. does   c. affects   d. has

22. Please (   ) me a ring in the morning to wake me up.

  a. send   b. give   c. ask   d. call

23. I am going to (   ) a diary next year.

  a. keep   b. write   c. note   d. mark

24. After dinner I'll (   ) a speech.

  a. give   b. make   c. pronounce   d. do

25. I will (   ) notes, and pass them on to you later.

  a. take   b. make   c. write   d. put

26. Prime Minister Tony Blair and President Bush will ( ) talks in New York later this year.

   a. have   b. hold   c. do   d. give

27. Phone your doctor to ( ) an appointment.

   a. make   b. arrange   c. take   d. do

28. Even if you ask him a question, you will not ( ) an answer.

   a. get   b. receive   c. find   d. obtain

29. The new teacher ( ) good control of his class.

   a. has   b. keeps   c. takes   d. exercises

30. Let's ( ) a walk over the fields.

   a. have   b. go for   c. do   d. take

31. It's a(n) ( ) habit to bite your nails.

   a. awful   b. nasty   c. wrong   d. bad

32. I was very tired after the ( ) flight of 12 hours from Paris to Tokyo.

   a. short   b. lengthy   c. long   d. distant

33. The symptoms of flu last several days, starting with a ( ) fever of 38 degrees.

   a. severe   b. strong   c. heavy   d. high

34. The ( ) meal of the day was chicken followed by something sweet.

   a. principal   b. main   c. major   d. favourite

35. The host of the TV programme said, "See you (   ) week, same time."

  a. following   b. subsequent   c. coming   d. next

36. "Would you like a double room?" "No, I would like a (   ) room, please."

  a. one   b. single   c. simple   d. only

37. Use your (   ) sense, and little can go wrong.

  a. balanced   b. good   c. ordinary   d. common

38. There is a link between poverty and (   ) health.

  a. poor   b. bad   c. inferior   d. ill

39. Barry won the ski competition despite the (   ) fog.

  a. thick   b. dense   c. heavy   d. deep

40. India is not short of resources despite its (   ) population.

  a. high   b. many   c. dense   d. large

41. What do you do in your (   ) time?

  a. free   b. spare   c. leisure   d. empty

42. To pass the exam, a (   ) standard of literacy is required.

  a. high   b. good   c. determined   d. certain

43. The government is keeping (   ) control over immigration.

  a. tight   b. severe   c. hard   d. strict

44. Because of the (   ) quality of doors and windows, the car is very cheap.

  a. poor   b. bad   c. low   d. ill

45. When you feel sad or unhappy, it is only (   ) to cry.

   a. natural   b. normal   c. right   d. sure

46. He is extremely (   ) about art, but jokes about everything else.

   a. serious   b. sincere   c. intense   d. keen

47. It is highly (   ) that the Japanese football team will beat Brazil.

   a. unlikely   b. unusual   c. strange   d. impossible

48. He was terribly (   ) of being caught by the police.

   a. afraid   b. scared   c. ashamed   d. embarrassed

49. It is highly (   ) to wear a suit for a job interview.

   a. recommended   b. important   c. normal   d. used

50. I got (   ) lost in the wood and didn't know which way to go.

   a. completely   b. extremely   c. perfectly   d. entirely

51. The new CD starts with a(n)(   ) different version of "We Will Rock You".

   a. totally   b. completely   c. extremely   d. entirely

52. We are (   ) aware that he will succeed in the game.

   a. fully   b. quite   c. amply   d. sufficiently

53. Indonesia, India, Sri Lanka and Thailand were all (   ) affected by the tsunami in December 2004.

   a. badly   b. deeply   c. severely   d. greatly

54. He is a(n) (   ) competent scientist in his field.

　　a. extremely　　b. highly　　　　c. completely　　　d. fully

55. The singers became (   ) involved in songwriting.

　　a. heavily　　　b. deeply　　　　c. completely　　　d. profoundly

56. It was a (   ) cold winter.

　　a. bitterly　　　b. extremely　　　c. terribly　　　d. violently

ご協力ありがとうございました。

Appendix 5

RESULTS OF MULTIPLE CHOICE
QUESTION TASKS

1)-a:[Verb + Noun] / [+ResComb, +Transp]

No.1	F		J	
tell the truth	raw score	%	raw score	%
tell	30	81.1	28	63.6
speak	1	2.7	4	9.1
say	6	16.2	9	20.5
inform	0	0	3	6.8

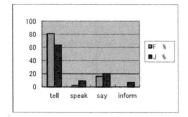

No.2	F		J	
draw a line	raw score	%	raw score	%
draw	25	73.5	24	61.5
paint	0	0	0	0
write	9	26.5	13	33.3
design	0	0	2	5.1

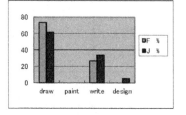

No.3	F		J	
won the match	raw score	%	raw score	%
won	34	94.4	27	71.1
got	2	5.6	7	18.4
gained	0	0	3	7.9
beat	0	0	1	2.6

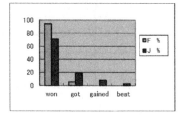

No.4	F		J	
lose weight	raw score	%	raw score	%
lose	30	85.7	26	70.3
reduce	3	8.6	6	16.2
decrease	1	2.9	5	13.5
diminish	1	2.9	0	0

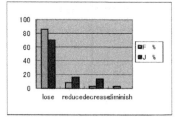

No.5	F		J	
read music	raw score	%	raw score	%
read	27	71.1	11	30.6
seize	2	5.3	8	22.2
understand	5	13.2	11	30.6
know	4	10.5	6	16.7

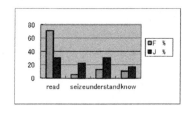

No.6	F		J	
ask (her) a question	raw score	%	raw score	%
ask	31	93.9	25	71.4
listen to	2	6.1	5	14.3
do	0	0	4	11.4
interrogate	0	0	1	2.9

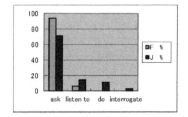

No.7	F		J	
attend the meeting	raw score	%	raw score	%
attend	13	36.1	23	54.8
go to	23	63.9	4	9.5
appear	0	0	1	2.4
present	0	0	14	33.3

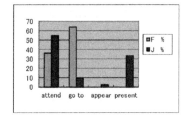

No.8	F		J	
play the violin	raw score	%	raw score	%
play	33	94.3	28	80
perform	2	5.7	4	11.4
do	0	0	2	5.7
execute	0	0	1	2.9

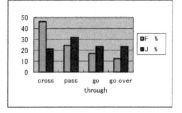

No.9	F		J	
cross the border	raw score	%	raw score	%
cross	19	46.3	10	21.3
pass	10	24.4	15	31.9
go through	7	17.1	11	23.4
go over	5	12.2	11	23.4

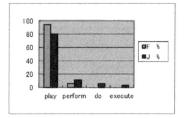

1)-b:[Verb + Noun] / [-ResComb, -Transp]

No.10	F		J	
blew/wiped a nose	raw score	%	raw score	%
blew	18	52.9	14	41.2
wiped	14	41.2	15	44.1
took	2	5.9	3	8.8
bit	0	0	2	5.9

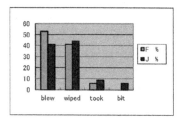

No.11	F		J	
answer/pick up the phone	raw score	%	raw score	%
answer	18	43.9	16	39
pick up	15	36.6	9	30
take	6	14.6	11	26.8
respond	2	4.9	5	12.2

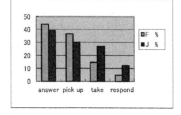

No.12	F		J	
provide/offer/give opportunities	raw score	%	raw score	%
provide	4	7.8	16	41
offer	28	52.9	4	10.3
give	19	37.3	15	38.5
have	1	2	4	10.3

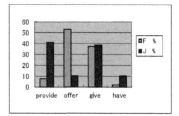

No.13	F		J	
gain/get experiences	raw score	%	raw score	%
gain	4	9.3	20	43.5
acquire	18	41.9	5	10.9
get	20	46.5	21	45.7
pile	1	2.3	0	0

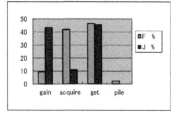

No.14	F		J	
meet/satisfy/answer the needs	raw score	%	raw score	%
meet	4	9.3	6	17.1
satisfy	26	60.5	10	28.6
answer	8	18.6	11	31.4
fill	5	11.6	8	22.9

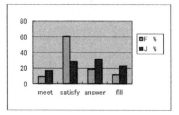

No.15	F		J	
reach/come to/draw any conclusion	raw score	%	raw score	%
reach	10	27.8	21	48.8
come to	15	41.7	18	41.9
arrive at	10	27.8	4	9.3
draw	1	2.8	0	0

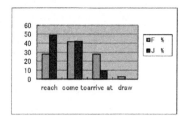

2)-a:[Delexicalized Verb + Noun] / [+ResComb, +Transp]

No.16	F		J	
keep records	raw score	%	raw score	%
keep	14	42.4	14	36.8
make	2	6.1	12	31.6
note	14	42.4	6	15.8
take	3	9.1	6	15.8

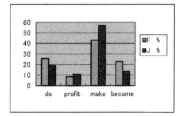

No.17	F		J	
do you good	raw score	%	raw score	%
do	9	25.7	7	18.9
profit	3	8.6	4	10.8
make	15	42.9	21	56.8
become	8	22.9	5	13.5

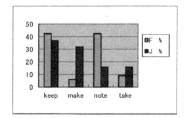

No.18	F		J	
take a picture	raw score	%	raw score	%
take	29	82.9	28	93.3
have	0	0	2	6.7
get	3	8.6	0	0
catch	3	8.6	0	0

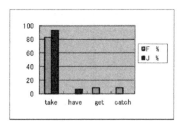

No.19	F		J	
keep a secret	raw score	%	raw score	%
keep	29	80.6	28	80
hold	7	19.4	6	17.1
protect	0	0	1	2.9
guard	0	0	0	0

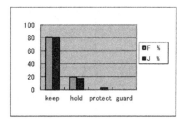

No.20	F		J	
do me a favour	raw score	%	raw score	%
do	10	28.6	11	32.4
give	6	17.1	10	29.4
ask	4	11.4	9	26.5
make	15	42.9	4	11.8

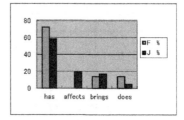

No.21	F		J	
has the (same) effect	raw score	%	raw score	%
has	26	72.2	24	58.5
affects	0	0	8	19.5
brings	5	13.9	7	17.1
does	5	13.9	2	4.9

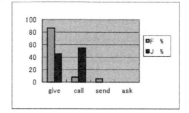

No.22	F		J	
give me a ring	raw score	%	raw score	%
give	32	86.5	14	45.2
call	3	8.1	17	54.8
send	2	5.4	0	0
ask	0	0	0	0

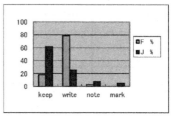

2)-b:[Delexicalized Verb + Noun] / [-ResComb, -Transp]

No.23	F		J	
keep/write a diary	raw score	%	raw score	%
keep	6	18.2	24	61.5
write	26	78.8	10	25.6
note	1	3	3	7.7
mark	0	0	2	5.1

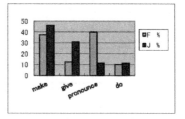

No.24	F		J	
give/make a speech	raw score	%	raw score	%
make	15	37.5	12	46.2
give	5	12.5	8	30.8
pronounce	16	40	3	11.5
do	4	10	3	11.5

No.25	F		J	
take/write notes	raw score	%	raw score	%
take	26	70.3	20	58.8
make	0	0	4	11.8
write	11	29.7	8	23.5
put	0	0	2	5.9

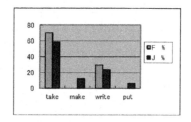

No.26	F		J	
have/hold talks	raw score	%	raw score	%
hold	7	20	8	23.5
have	21	60	12	35.3
give	5	14.3	10	29.4
do	2	5.7	4	11.8

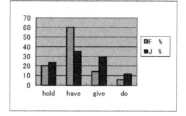

No.27	F		J	
make/arrange/take an appointment	raw score	%	raw score	%
make	15	40.5	29	78.4
arrange	13	35.1	2	5.4
take	8	21.6	4	10.8
do	1	2.7	2	5.4

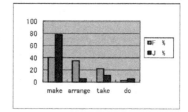

No.28	F		J	
receive/obtain/get an answer	raw score	%	raw score	%
receive	7	15.6	9	23.1
obtain	11	24.4	3	7.7
get	24	53.3	13	33.3
find	3	6.7	4	35.9

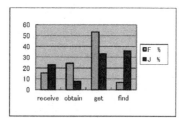

No.29	F		J	
keeps/has good control	raw score	%	raw score	%
keeps	16	41.0	15	41.7
has	22	56.4	9	25
takes	0	0	11	30.6
exercises	1	2.6	1	2.8

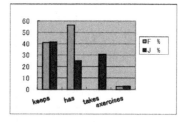

No.30	F		J	
take/go for/have a walk	raw score	%	raw score	%
go for	26	65	20	51.3
take	0	0	17	43.6
have	14	35	2	5.1
do	0	0	0	0

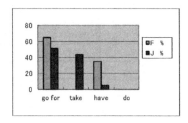

3)-a:[Adjective + Noun] / [+ResComb, +Transp]

No.31	F		J	
bad habit	raw score	%	raw score	%
bad	26	56.5	24	55.8
awful	16	34.8	11	25.6
nasty	3	6.5	4	9.3
wrong	1	2.2	4	9.3

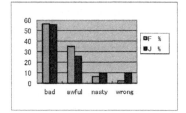

No.32	F		J	
long flight	raw score	%	raw score	%
long	32	94.1	28	82.4
lengthy	2	5.9	1	2.9
distant	0	0	5	14.7
short	0	0	0	0

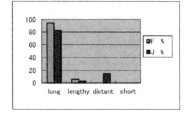

No.33	F		J	
high fever	raw score	%	raw score	%
high	18	43.9	20	62.5
severe	6	14.6	4	12.5
heavy	5	12.2	4	12.5
strong	12	29.3	4	12.5

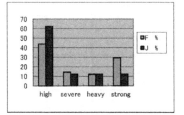

No.34	F		J	
main meal	raw score	%	raw score	%
main	28	75.7	20	66.7
principal	7	18.9	2	6.7
favourite	2	5.4	2	6.7
major	0	0	6	20

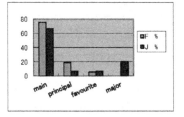

No.35	F		J	
next week	raw score	%	raw score	%
next	33	94.3	29	78.4
following	1	2.9	4	10.8
subsequent	0	0	1	2.7
coming	1	2.9	3	8.1

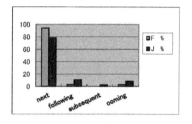

No.36	F		J	
single room	raw score	%	raw score	%
single	33	97.1	29	87.9
one	0	0	2	6.1
only	0	0	1	3
simple	1	2.9	1	3

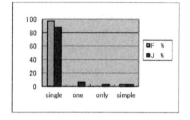

No.37	F		J	
common sense	raw score	%	raw score	%
common	18	51.4	21	65.6
good	17	48.6	6	18.8
balanced	0	0	2	6.3
ordinary	0	0	3	9.4

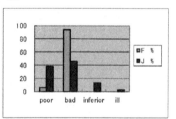

3)-b:[Adjective + Noun] / [-ResComb, -Transp]

No.38	F		J	
poor/bad health	raw score	%	raw score	%
poor	2	6.1	14	37.8
bad	31	93.9	17	45.9
inferior	0	0	5	13.5
ill	0	0	1	2.7

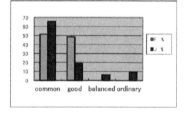

No.39	F		J	
thick/heavy/dense fog	raw score	%	raw score	%
dense	10	28.6	3	8.1
thick	8	22.9	4	10.8
heavy	6	17.1	13	35.1
deep	11	31.4	17	45.9

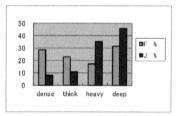

266

No.40	F		J	
large/dense population	raw score	%	raw score	%
large	22	57.9	20	66.7
dense	10	26.3	1	3.3
high	6	15.8	5	16.7
many	0	0	4	13.3

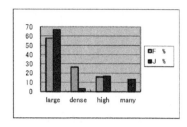

No.41	F		J	
free/spare/leisure time	raw score	%	raw score	%
spare	7	17.5	4	10.3
free	25	62.5	28	71.8
leisure	8	20	6	15.4
empty	0	0	1	2.6

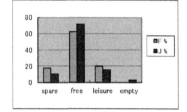

No.42	F		J	
high/good standard	raw score	%	raw score	%
high	18	42.9	17	54.8
good	15	35.7	5	16.1
certain	6	14.3	8	25.8
determined	3	7.1	1	3.1

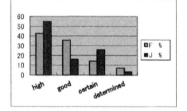

No.43	F		J	
tight/strict control	raw score	%	raw score	%
tight	4	10	4	11.8
strict	23	57.5	14	41.2
hard	4	10	10	29.4
severe	9	22.5	6	17.6

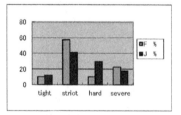

No.44	F		J	
bad/low quality	raw score	%	raw score	%
poor	8	18.6	9	24.3
bad	23	53.5	12	32.4
low	12	27.9	16	43.2
ill	0	0	0	0

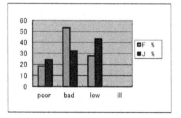

4)-a:[Adverb + Adjective] / [+ResComb, +Transp]

No.45	F		J	
only natural	raw score	%	raw score	%
natural	22	53.7	23	67.6
normal	16	39.0	2	5.9
right	3	7.3	5	14.7
sure	0	0	4	11.8

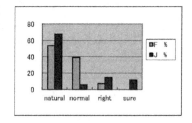

No.46	F		J	
extremely serious	raw score	%	raw score	%
serious	25	71.4	15	50.0
sincere	4	11.4	4	13.3
intense	0	0.0	8	26.7
keen	6	17.1	3	10.0

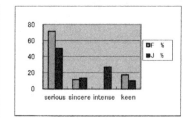

No.47	F		J	
highly unlikely	raw score	%	raw score	%
unlikely	12	30.8	6	17.7
impossible	16	41	21	61.8
unusual	7	17.9	4	11.8
strange	4	10.3	3	8.8

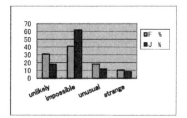

No.48	F		J	
terribly scared	raw score	%	raw score	%
afraid	19	41.3	19	48.7
scared	18	39.1	10	25.6
ashamed	6	13	6	15.4
embarrassed	3	6.5	4	10.3

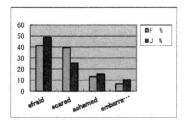

No.49	F		J	
highly recommended	raw score	%	raw score	%
recommended	31	86.3	10	34.5
important	3	8.3	19	44.8
normal	0	0	6	20.7
used	2	5.6	4	10.3

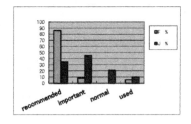

4)-b:[Adverb + Adjective] / [-ResComb, -Transp]

No.50	F		J	
completely/entirely lost	raw score	%	raw score	%
completely	31	88.6	17	47.2
entirely	4	11.4	8	22.2
extremely	0	0	5	13.9
perfectly	0	0	6	16.7

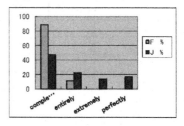

No.51	F		J	
completely/entirely/totally different	raw score	%	raw score	%
completely	10	26.3	12	34.3
entirely	10	26.3	7	20
totally	13	34.2	8	22.9
extremely	5	13.2	8	22.9

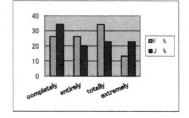

No.52	F		J	
fully/quite aware	raw score	%	raw score	%
fully	17	58.6	5	16.1
quite	11	37.9	15	48.4
sufficiently	1	3.4	6	19.4
amply	0	0	5	16.1

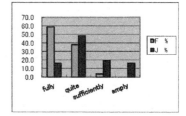

No.53	F		J	
deeply/greatly/badly affected	raw score	%	raw score	%
severely	13	30.2	9	21.4
greatly	8	18.6	11	26.2
badly	4	9.3	11	26.2
deeply	18	41.9	11	26.2

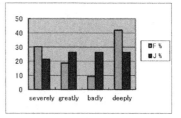

No.54	F		J	
extremely/highly competent	raw score	%	raw score	%
extremely	13	35.1	11	35.5
highly	19	51.4	14	45.2
completely	1	2.7	6	19.4
fully	4	10.8	0	0

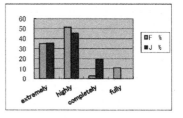

269

No.55	F		J	
deeply/heavily involved	raw score	%	raw score	%
completely	15	46.9	5	15.2
deeply	13	40.6	13	39.4
profoundly	3	9.4	12	36.4
heavily	1	3.1	3	9.1

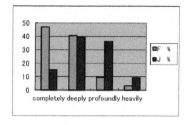

No.56	F		J	
bitterly/extremely/ terribly cold	raw score	%	raw score	%
bitterly	2	5.7	2	5.9
extremely	12	34.3	8	23.5
terribly	21	60	23	67.6
violently	0	0	1	2.9

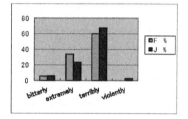

Appendix 6

TRANSLATION TASKS

a) Translation Tasks for French Learners

University of London Institute in Paris   May 2006

Regardez les phrases en français et leur traduction en anglais.
Chaque traduction anglaise comporte un blanc que vous devez remplir.
Ecrivez au moins 2 mots anglais pour remplir chaque blanc.
Plusieurs réponses sont parfois possibles.

Votre langue maternelle : _____ Durée de l'exercise : 25 minutes

1. Tu dois dire la vérité à l'enfant.

You must (   ) to the child.

2. Le professeur de mathématiques demanda aux élèves de tracer une ligne verticale au milieu de la feuille.

The maths teacher told the students to (   ) down the middle of the sheet of paper.

3. Grâce à ses efforts, il remporta le match.

Because of his efforts, he (   ).

4. Les jeunes adolescentes essaient souvent de perdre du poids.

Girls in their early teens often try to (   ).

5. J'ai dû faire du solfège avant qu'on me laisse jouer du piano.

I had to learn to (   ) before they let me play the piano.

6.   Patrick vit l'occasion de lui poser une question.

Patrick saw the chance to (   ).

7.   Tous les membres du personnel sont invités à assister à la réunion pour débattre de la question.

All members of the company are invited to (   ) to discuss the issue.

8.   Il apprend le violon depuis cinq ans.

He has been learning to (   ) for five years.

9.   Il vous faut votre passeport pour passer la frontière.

You need your passport to (   ).

10. Elle a pris un mouchoir dans sa poche et s'est mouchée.

She took a handkerchief from her pocket and (   ).

11. Quand vous répondez au téléphone, dites « bonjour » mais ne donnez ni votre nom ni votre numéro.

When you (   ), say "hello" but do not give your name and number.

12. Un nombre croissant de filières universitaires offre une possibilité de stage dans un pays étranger.

A growing number of university courses (   ) for a period of study in another country.

13. Alors qu'elle étudiait le français, elle vint en France pour acquérir de l'expérience.

She was studying French and went to France to (   ).

14. Ce livre répondra aux besoins des étudiants.

This book will (   ) of students.

15. A moins d'en parler ensemble, nous ne parviendrons à aucune conclusion.

Unless we talk about this together, we won't (   ).

16. On s'attend à ce que les professeurs gardent une trace écrite du travail effectué par leurs étudiants pendant le semestre.

Teachers are expected to (   ) of the work done by their students during the semester.

17. Un peu d'exercice vous ferait probablement du bien.

Some exercise would probably (   ).

18. Ne donnez pas votre appareil photo à un inconnu pour lui demander de vous prendre en photo.

Don't give your camera to a stranger and ask him to (   ) of you.

19. Peux-tu garder un secret ?

Can you (   )?

20. Peux-tu me rendre un service ?

Will you (   )?

21. Le thé a le même effet que le café.

Tea (   ) as coffee.

22. S'il vous plaît, passez-moi un coup de fil demain matin pour me réveiller.

Please (   ) tomorrow morning to wake me up.

23. Je vais tenir un journal l'année prochaine.

I am going to (   ) next year.

24. Après le dîner, je ferai un discours.

After dinner I'll (   ).

25. Je prendrai des notes et te les passerai plus tard.

I will (   ), and pass them on to you later.

26. Le Premier Ministre Blair et le Président Bush s'entiendront à New York plus tard dans l'année.

Prime Minister Blair and President Bush will (   ) in New York later this year.

27. Téléphonez à votre médecin pour prendre un rendez-vous.

Phone your doctor to (   ).

28. Même si vous lui posez une question, vous n'aurez pas de réponse.

Even if you ask her a question, you will not (   ).

29. Le nouveau professeur tient bien sa classe.

The new teacher (   ) of her class.

30. Allons nous promener dans les champs.

Let's (   ) over the fields.

31. Se ronger les ongles est une mauvaise habitude.

It's a (   ) to bite your nails.

32. J'étais très fatigué par le long vol Paris-Tokyo.

I was very tired after the (   ) from Paris to Tokyo.

33. Les symptômes de la grippe durent plusieurs jours et commencent par une forte fièvre de 40 degrés.

The symptoms of flu last several days, starting with a (   ) of 40 degrees.

34. Le repas principal de la journée était du poulet suivi de quelque chose de sucré.

The (   ) of the day was chicken followed by something sweet.

35. Le présentateur de l'émission de télévision dit : « A la semaine prochaine, même heure ».

The host of the TV programme said, "See you (   ), same time."

36. Désirez-vous une chambre double? Non, une chambre simple, s'il vous plaît.

"Would you like a double room?" "No, I'd like a (   ), please."

37. Faites preuve de bon sens, et tout ira bien.

Use your (   ), and little can go wrong.

38. Il y a un lien entre pauvreté et mauvaise santé.

There is a link between poverty and (   ).

39. Barry a gagné la compétition de ski malgré l'épais brouillard.

Barry won the ski competition despite the (   ).

40. L'Inde ne manque pas de ressources malgré son importante population.

India is not short of resources despite its (   ).

41. Que fais-tu pendant ton temps libre ?

What do you do in your (   )?

42. Il faut un bon niveau pour réussir cet examen.

To pass the exam, a (   ) of literacy is required.

43. Le gouvernement maintient un contrôle strict sur l'immigration.

The government is keeping (   ) over immigration.

44. A cause de la faible qualité de ses roues et de ses pneus, cette voiture n'est pas chère.

Because of the (   ) of its wheels and tyres, the car is very cheap.

45. Quand vous vous sentez triste ou malheureux, il est tout à fait normal de pleurer.

When you feel sad or unhappy, it is (   ) to cry.

46. Il est très sérieux quant à l'art mais plaisante sur tout le reste.

He is (   ) about art, but jokes about everything else.

47. Il est très peu probable que l'équipe de football japonaise batte le Brésil.

It is (   ) that the Japanese football team will beat Brazil.

48. Il avait terriblement peur de se faire prendre par la police.

He was (   ) of being caught by the police.

49. Il est fortement recommandé de porter un costume pour un entretien d'embauche.

It is (   ) to wear a suit for a job interview.

50. Je me suis complètement perdu dans les bois et ne savais plus quel chemin prendre.

I got (   ) in the wood and didn't know which way to go.

51. Le nouveau CD commence avec une version entièrement différente de 'We will rock you'.

The new CD starts with a(n) (   ) version of "We will rock you".

52. Nous sommes parfaitement conscients du fait qu'il va gagner la partie.

We are (   ) that he will succeed in the game.

53. L'Indonésie, l'Inde, le Sri Lanka et la Thaïlande ont tous été gravement touchés par le tsunami en décembre 2004.

Indonesia, India, Sri Lanka and Thailand were all (   ) by the tsunami in December 2004.

54. C'est un scientifique hautement compétent dans son domaine.

He is a (   ) scientist in his field.

55. Les chanteurs se sont sérieusement impliqués dans l'écriture des chansons.

The singers became (   ) in song writing.

56. C'était un hiver au froid vif.

It was a (   ) winter.

Merci beaucoup.

Thank you very much.

b) Translation Tasks for Japanese Learners

University of London Institute in Paris   May 2006

日本語の意味に合うように、（　　　）の中に適切な語句を入れてください。

ひとつの（　　　）につき少なくとも2語入れてください。ひとつの（　　　）につき、複数の答えを入れても良いです。

1.　子供には真実を言わなくてはいけない。

You must (　　　　　　　) to the child.

2.　数学の先生は生徒たちに用紙の中央に縦に一本線を引くように言った。

The maths teacher told the students to (　　　　　　　　) down the middle of the

sheet of paper.

3.　努力したおかげで、彼は試合で優勝した。

Because of his efforts, he (　　　　　　　).

4.　十代前半の女の子たちはしばしば減量しようとする。

Girls in their early teens often try to (　　　　　　).

5.　彼らが私にピアノを弾かせる前に、私は楽譜の読み方を学ばなければならなかった。

I had to learn to (　　　　　　) before they let me play the piano.

6.　パトリックは彼女に質問するなら今だと思った。

Patrick saw the chance to (　　　　　　).

7. 全社員がその問題を議論するための会議に出席するよう要請されている。

All members of the company are invited to (　　　　　　　　) to discuss the issue.

8. 彼は、バイオリンを5年間習い続けている。

He has been learning to (　　　　　　) for five years.

9. 国境を越えるにはパスポートが必要だ。

You need your passport to (　　　　　).

10. 彼女はポケットからハンカチを取り出し、鼻をかんだ。

She took a handkerchief from her pocket and (　　　　　).

11.　電話に出るときは、「もしもし」と言うようにして、名前や番号は言ってはいけない。

When you (　　　　　), say "hello" but do not give your name and number.

12.　以前にも増して多くの大学のコースが、一定期間別の国で勉強する機会を提供している。

A growing number of university courses (　　　　　　　) for a period of study in another country.

13.　彼女はフランス語を勉強中で、経験を積むためにフランスに行った。

She was studying French and went to France to (　　　　　　).

14. この本は、学生の必要性に応えるでしょう。

This book will (　　　　　　) of students.

15. このことについて一緒に話し合わなければ、どんな結論も引き出せないだろう。

Unless we talk about this together, we won't (   ).

16. 学期中、教師は生徒の学習の記録をつけるよう求められている。

Teachers are expected to (   ) of the work done by their students during the semester.

17. 少し運動するとたぶん効果があるだろう。

Some exercise would probably (   ).

18. 知らない人に自分のカメラを渡して、写真をとって欲しいと頼んだりしてはいけない。

Don't give your camera to a stranger and ask him to (   ) of you.

19. 秘密を守ることができますか。

Can you (   )?

20. ちょっとお願いを聞いてもらえますか。

Will you (   )?

21. 紅茶にはコーヒーと同じ効果がある。

Tea (   ) as coffee.

22. 明日の朝、私に電話をかけて起こしてください。

Please (   ) tomorrow morning to wake me up.

23. 来年私は日記をつけようと思う。

I am going to (   ) next year.

24. 夕食の後、私はスピーチをする。

After dinner I'll (   ).

25. 私はノートを取って、それを後であなたに渡しましょう。

I will (   ), and pass them on to you later.

26. ブレア首相とブッシュ大統領は、ニューヨークで今年後半に会談の予定である。

Prime Minister Blair and President Bush will (   ) in New York later

this year.

27. 予約を取るために医者に電話をしなさい。

Phone your doctor to (   ).

28. 彼女に質問しても、返事はもらえないでしょう。

Even if you ask her a question, you will not (   ).

29. 新しい先生は自分の担任のクラスをよく管理している。

The new teacher (   ) of her class.

30. 野原を散歩しましょう。

Let's (   ) over the fields.

31. 爪をかむのは悪い習慣だ。

It's a (   ) to bite your nails.

32. パリから東京までの長い飛行の後で、私はとても疲れた。

I was very tired after the (   ) from Paris to Tokyo.

33. インフルエンザの兆候は数日間続くが、始めは４０度の高熱で始まる。

The symptoms of flu last several days, starting with a (　　　　　) of 40 degrees.

34. その日の主な料理は鶏肉で、続いて甘いものが出ました。

The (　　　　　　　) of the day was chicken followed by something sweet.

35. テレビ番組の司会者は、「来週、同じ時間にお会いしましょう」と言った。

The host of the TV programme said, "See you (　　　　　), same time."

36. 「ダブルベッドの部屋がよろしいですか。」「いいえ、シングルベッドの部屋をお願いします。」

"Would you like a double room?" "No, I'd like a (　　　　　), please."

37. 常識を働かせなさい、そうすればあまり悪いようにはならないでしょう。

Use your (　　　　　　　　), and little can go wrong.

38. 貧乏と不健康との間には関連性がある。

There is a link between poverty and (　　　　　).

39. バリーは、濃い霧にもかかわらずスキー競技で優勝した。

Barry won the ski competition despite the (　　　　　).

40. インドは、多くの人口にも関わらず資源は不足していない。

India is not short of resources despite its (　　　　　).

41. 暇なときには何をしますか。

What do you do in your (　　　　　　　)?

42. 試験に合格するには、優れた読み書き能力が求められている。

To pass the exam, a ( ) of literacy is required.

43. 政府は、移民に対して厳しい制限を設けている。

The government is keeping ( ) over immigration.

44. 車輪とタイヤの悪い品質のために、その自動車はとても安い。

Because of the ( ) of its wheels and tyres, the car is very cheap.

45. 悲しいときや不幸なときに泣くのは全く自然なことです。

When you feel sad or unhappy, it is ( ) to cry.

46. 彼は芸術には非常に真剣だが、それ以外の全てに対しては少し冗談を言う。

He is ( ) about art, but jokes a little about everything else.

47. 日本のサッカーチームがブラジルに勝つことはまずありそうにない。

It is ( ) that the Japanese football team will beat Brazil.

48. 彼は警察につかまることをひどく恐れていた。

He was ( ) of being caught by the police.

49. 就職の面接には、スーツを着ることが大いに勧められる。

It is ( ) to wear a suit for a job interview.

50. 私は森の中で完全に迷い、どちらに行ったらよいか分からなかった。

I got ( ) in the wood and didn't know which way to go.

51. 新しいCDは、"We will rock you"（という曲）の全く違うバージョンから始まる。

The new CD starts with a(n) (   ) version of "We will rock you".

52. 彼がその試合で成功するだろうということは、私たちにはよく分かっている。

We are (   ) that he will succeed in the game.

53. インドネシア、インド、スリランカ、タイはいずれも２００４年12月の津波で深刻な被害を受けた。

Indonesia, India, Sri Lanka and Thailand were all (   ) by the tsunami in December 2004.

54. 彼はその分野で極めて有能な科学者である。

He is a (   ) scientist in his field.

55. 歌手たちは、作詞に深く関わるようになった。

The singers became (   ) in song writing.

56. その冬は、ひどく寒かった。

It was a (   ) winter.

ご協力どうもありがとうございました。

Appendix 7

RESULTS OF TRANSLATION TASKS (1)

1)-a:[Verb + Noun] / [+ResComb, +Transp]

*:F: French learners, J: Japanese learners

( ) : Types of mistakes listed below the table, *Italic*: L1 Likely errors

No.	F/J *	Target/Acceptable Collocation	Raw Score	%	Infelicitous Collocation	Raw Score	%	Non-target/Wrong Collocation	Raw Score	%
1	F	tell the truth	20	83.3				*say the truth* (b)	2	8.0
								say true (a, b, c)	1	4.2
								say the right (a, b)	1	4.2
	J	tell the truth	23	60.5				*say the truth* (a)	12	31.6
								give a truth (a)	1	2.6
								speak true (a, b)	1	2.6
								talk a truth (a)	1	2.6
2	F	draw a line	4	25.0	draw a *vertical* line (e)	9	52.9	*trace a vertical ligne* (a, d)	2	12.5
								design a *vertical* line (a, d)	1	6.3
	J	draw a line	6	31.6				*write a line* (a)	10	52.6
								write the line (a, c)	1	5.3
								put a line (a)	2	10.5
3	F	won the match	13	68.4				won the party (b)	1	5.3
		won the game	3	15.8				won the play (b)	1	5.3
								succeed in *the match* (e, f)	1	5.3
	J	won the game	25	75.8	become champion (c)	1	3.0	won the first place (b)	1	3.0
		became a champion	1	3.0				got the game (a, b)	1	3.0
		won the first prize	2	6.1				won the victory (b)	1	3.0
								won all games (b)	1	3.0
4	F	lose weight	12	80.0	lose some weight (c)	2	8.0	take weight (a)	1	6.7
	J	lose weight	3	9.7	*lose their weight* (c)	6	19.4	*reduce their weight* (a, d)	9	29.0
								decrease their weight (d)	4	12.9

								weight down (e)	2	6.5
								diet on (e)	2	6.5
								get down the weight (a, c)	2	6.5
								put down their weight (a, c)	2	6.5
								decline their weight (a, c)	1	3.2
5	F	read music	1	12.5				read music notes (b)	3	37.5
								do solfege (e)	2	25.0
								play solfege (e)	1	12.5
								write music (a)	1	12.5
	J	read music	0	0.0	read scores (b)	6	37.5	read music papers (b)	3	18.8
					read notes (b)	1	6.3	read the code (b)	2	12.5
								understand text (e)	2	12.5
								see music papers (a, b)	1	6.3
								read the tune (b)	1	6.3
6	F	ask him a question	19	82.6	ask him something (b)	1	4.3	put him a question (a)	1	4.3
					ask a question (d)	1	4.3			
					ask him for question (c, f)	1	4.3			
	J	ask her a question	5	18.5	ask a question to her (e, f)	1	3.7	question (c, d)	1	3.7
					ask her (c, e, d)	13	48.1	say the question (a)	1	3.7
					question to her (a, b, d)	4	14.8	tell the question (a)	1	3.7
								give a question to her (a)	1	3.7
7	F	attend the meeting	5	26.3				assist to/at the meeting (a, f)	8	42.1
		come to the meeting	4	21.1				get the meeting (a)	1	5.3
		be present at the meeting	1	5.3						
	J	attend the meeting	17	73.9	attend to the meeting (f)	3	13.0	join the meeting (a)	1	4.3
		take part in the meeting	1	4.3				come to discussion (b, c)	1	4.3

8	F	play violin	20	87.0				violin (d)	2	8.7
								make violin (a)	1	4.3
	J	play the violin	29	96.7	study violin (a)	1	3.3				
9	F	cross the border	5	26.3				pass the border (a)	9	47.4
								go through the fronteer (a, b)	2	10.5
								go out the fronteer (a, b)	1	5.3
								pass the limit (a, b)	1	5.3
								cross the limit (b)	1	5.3
	J	cross the border	1	3.0	across the border (d)	2	6.1	pass the border (a)	1	3.0
		go over the border	1	3.0				go abroad (e)	11	33.3
								exceed the border (a)	1	3.0
								go beyond countries (e, h)	1	3.0
								beyond the border (d)	1	3.0
								jump border (a, c)	1	3.0
								go to other country (e)	1	3.0
								go over the lines (e)	1	3.0
								go thrgouth countries (e)	1	3.0

<Types of Mistakes>

a   wrong choice of verb

b   wrong choice of noun

c   missing/adding determiners (article)

d   wrong structure

e   different expression

f   preposition

g   number

RESULTS OF TRANSLATION TASKS (2)

1)-b:[Verb + Noun] / [-ResComb, -Transp]

*:F: French learners, J: Japanese learners

( ) : Types of mistakes listed below the table, *Italic*: L1 Likely errors

No.	F/J*	Target/Acceptable Collocation	Raw Score	%	Infelicitous Collocation	Raw Score	%	Non-target/Wrong Collocation	Raw Score	%
10	F	blew her nose	4	44.4				sneezed herself (e)	4	44.4
		wiped her nose	1	11.1						
	J	blew her nose	1	12.5				cleaned her nose (a)	3	37.5
								sniffed her nose (a)	1	12.5
								sneezed her nose (a)	1	12.5
								take nose (a, c)	1	12.5
								take a nose water (a, b)	1	12.5
11	F	answer the phone	12	52.2	*answer to the phone* (f)	5	21.7	have a call (a,)	1	4.3
		pick up the phone	2	8.7	take a call (a, c)	1	4.3	hold on phone (a, c)	1	4.3
								get the phone (c)	1	4.3
	J	answer the phone	7	25.9	answer a phone (c)	1	3.7	catch the phone (a)	5	18.5
		get a call	2	7.4	answer phone (c)	1	3.7	take a phone (a, c)	7	25.9
		receive a phone call	2	7.4				*catch a call (a)*	2	7.4
12	F	offer the posibility	6	40.0	*offer opportunity* (c)	2	13.3	*offer internships (b, c,g)*	1	6.7
		give an opportunity	1	6.7				give a possibility (b, c)	2	13.3
		offer a chance	2	13.3				propose training courses (a, b)	1	6.7
	J	offer the opportunity	4	22.2	*provide the chances* (c, e, h)	4	22.2	give chances (c, g)	6	33.3
		give an opportunity	2	11.1				supply chances (a, c, g)	1	5.6
		offer a chance	1	5.6						
13	F	get experiences	6	30.0				acquire experience (a, g)	5	25.0
								improve experience (a, g)	2	10.0

								achieve her experience (a, c, g)	1	5.0
								endorse experience (a, g)	1	5.0
								have experiences (a)	5	25.0
	J	gain experiences	2	10.0				have experiences (a)	5	25.0
		get experiences	7	35.0				*accumulate experience* (a, h)	1	5.0
								make an experience (a, c, h)	1	5.0
								gather experiences (a)	1	5.0
								take experiences (a)	1	5.0
								grow her skills (e)	1	5.0
								brush up her skill (e)	1	5.0
14	F	fulfill the needs	1	5.9	*answer to the needs* (f)	8	47.1	fit the needs (a)	2	11.8
		answer the needs	5	29.4				fill the needs (a)	1	5.9
	J	meet the needs	5	21.7	meet needs (c)	2	8.7	fill the needs (a)	1	4.3
		answer the needs	2	8.7	fulfil needs (c)	1	4.3	make the needs (a)	1	4.3
		match the needs	2	8.7	meet to needs (c)	1	4.3	require the needs (a)	1	4.3
					answer to needs	1	4.3	pay the necessity (a, b)	1	4.3
								take necessity (a, b, c)	1	4.3
								do the necessary (e)	1	4.3
								answer the necessary (b)	1	4.3
								support to needs (a, c, f)	1	4.3
								suite the requirement (a, b)	1	4.3
15	F	reach any conclusion	2	10.5	get to a conclusion (a, c)	2	10.5	found any conclusion (a)	6	31.6
		come to any conclusion	1	5.3				have a conclusion (a, c)	5	26.3
								arrive to a conclusion (f, c)	2	10.5
								get any conclusion (a)	1	5.3

289

J	reach any conclusion	1	5.0	get any conclusion (a)	6	30.0	get any results (a, b)	3	15.0
				come to conclusion (c)	1	5.0	get any answer (a, b)	1	5.0
							reach the consequence (b)	1	5.0
							reach any result (b)	1	5.0
							decide conclusion (a, c)	2	10.0
							lead any conclusion (a)	1	5.0
							lead the answer (e)	1	5.0
							have any answer (a, b)	1	5.0
							have any conclusion (a, b, e)	1	5.0

<Types of Mistakes>

a   wrong choice of verb

b   wrong choice of noun

c   missing/adding determiners (article)

d   wrong structure

e   different expression

f   preposition

g   number

RESULTS OF TRANSLATION TASKS (3)

2)-a:[Delexicalized Verb + Noun] / [+ResComb, +Transp]

*:F: French learners, J: Japanese learners

( ) : Types of mistakes listed below the table, *Italic*: L1 Likely errors

No.	F/J*	Target/Acceptable Collocation	Raw Score	%	Infelicitous Collocation	Raw Score	%	Non-target/Wrong Collocation	Raw Score	%
16	F	keep records	0	0.0	keep a note (a, b)	3	17.6	*keep a written proof* (a, b)	12	70.6
								keep a copie (a, b)	2	11.8
	J	keep records	1	9.1				*write the records* (a)	2	18.2
								write a record (a, b)	1	9.1
								take records (a)	1	9.1
								take a records (a, c)	2	18.2
								make records (a)	3	27.3
								leave records (a)	1	9.1
17	F	do you good	0	0.0	do you some good (d)	1	6.7	make you feel better (e)	6	40.0
		be good for you	6	40.0				help you (e)	1	6.7
								fits you better (e)	1	6.7
	J	do you good	1	6.7	do good (d, e)	2	13.3	*make an effect* (e)	4	26.7
		be good for you	1	6.7				*give you a good effect* (e)	3	20.0
								take an effect (e)	1	6.7
								have an effect (e)	1	6.7
								make you good (a)	1	6.7
								provide the effect (e)	1	6.7
18	F	take a picture/pictures	18	78.3				make a photo (a)	1	4.3
		take a photo	2	8.7				keep a picture (a)	1	4.3
								picture photo (a, c)	1	4.3
	J	take a picture	24	72.7	take photo (c)	1	3.0	take a snap (b)	1	3.0
		take pictures	2	6.1	take picture (h)	1	3.0	photo you (e)	1	3.0
		take a photo	3	9.1						

19	F	keep a secret	24	96.0				take a secret (a)	1	4.0
	J	keep a secret	26	72.2	*keep the secret (c)*	3	8.3	keep it secret (e)	2	5.6
					keep secret (c)	4	11.1			
					keep my secret (c)	1	2.8			
20	F	do me a favour	3	12.5				help me (e)	9	37.5
								give me a help (e)	2	8.3
								give me a favour (a)	3	12.5
								give me a service (a, b)	2	8.3
								render me a service (a, b)	1	4.2
								make me a favour (a)	1	4.2
								do something for me (e)	1	4.2
								give me a hand (e)	1	4.2
								do me a device (b)	1	4.2
	J	do me a favour	5	21.7				*ask me a favour (a)*	9	39.1
								give me a favour (a)	1	4.3
								take my favor (a, c)	1	4.3
								accept my require (e)	1	4.3
								hear my wish (e)	1	4.3
								help me (e)	5	21.7
21	F	has the same effect	16	88.9				has same impact (b, c)	1	5.6
								is the same effect (a)	1	5.6
	J	has the same effect	2	8.7	*has a same effect (c)*	5	21.7	do good (e)	1	4.3
					has the effect (e)	1	4.3	has the effect as well (e)	3	13.0
					has same effect (c)	4	17.4	is same effect (a, c)	1	4.3
								is as effective (e)	1	4.3
								have an effect (e)	4	17.4
								works good (e)	1	4.3
22	F	give me a ring	2	9.1				take me a call (a)	1	4.5
		give me a call	5	22.7						

	call me	8	36.4							
	phone me	6	27.3							
J	call me	27	87.1							
	phone me	1	3.2							
	give me a call	1	3.2							
	ring me	2	6.5							

<Types of Mistakes>

a   wrong choice of verb

b   wrong choice of noun

c   missing/adding determiners (article)

d   wrong structure

e   different expression

f   preposition

g   number

RESULTS OF TRANSLATION TASKS (4)

2)-b:[Delexicalized Verb + Noun] / [-ResComb, -Transp]

*:F: French learners, J: Japanese learners

( ) : Types of mistakes listed below the table, *Italic*: L1 Likely errors

No.	F/J*	Target/Acceptable Collocation	Raw Score	%	Infelicitous Collocation	Raw Score	%	Non-target/Wrong Collocation	Raw Score	%
23	F	keep a diary	4	20.0				write a paper (b)	2	10.0
		write a diary	4	20.0				*hold a newspaper* (a, b)	1	5.0
								manage a *newspaper* (a, b)	1	5.0
								create a *newspaper* (a, b)	1	5.0
								work for a *newspaper* (a, b, f)	2	10.0
								lead a *newspaper* (a, b)	2	10.0
								hold diary (a)	1	5.0
								hold on a diary (a, f)	1	5.0
								write a boardpaper (b)	1	5.0
	J	keep a diary	7	24.1	*write diary* (c)	1	3.4	make a diary (a)	2	6.9
		write a diary	16	55.2	write down a diary (f)	1	3.4	take a diary (a)	2	6.9
24	F	make a speech	10	45.5				*do a speech* (a)	5	22.7
		give a speech	2	9.1				have a speech (a)	2	9.1
								give a talk (b)	1	4.5
								do a talk (a, b)	1	4.5
								do a discussion (a, b)	1	4.5
	J	make a speech	9	29.0	make speech (c)	1	3.2	have a speech (a)	10	32.3
		give a speech	1	3.2				take a speech (a)	2	6.5
								do speech (a, c)	1	3.2
								get a speech (a)	1	3.2
								talk speech (a, c)	1	3.2
								speak a speech (a)	2	6.5
25	F	take notes	23	74.2	take some notes (c, h)	5	16.1	write notes down (e)	1	3.2

		write notes	1	3.2	write some notes (c, h)	1	3.2			
	J	take notes	1	4.3	*take a note* (c, h)	6	26.1	*take notebook* (b)	3	13.0
		make notes	1	4.3	*take the note* (c, h)	2	8.7	write the notebook (b,c)	3	13.0
					write down notes (c)	4	17.4	note it down (e)	2	8.7
								make my note (c, g)	1	4.3
26	F	have a meeting	1	5.3				meet (e)	10	52.6
		have a discussion	1	5.3				*speak together* (e)	2	10.5
								talk together (e)	2	10.5
								have an argument (b)	1	5.3
								get together (e)	1	5.3
								meet each other (e)	1	5.3
	J	have a meeting	6	31.6				take a discussion (a, b)	3	15.8
		hold a meeting	2	10.5				*open the conference* (a, b, c)	1	5.3
		have a discussion	1	5.3				get meeting (a, c)	1	5.3
								meet each other (e)	2	10.5
								make a discussion (a, b)	1	5.3
								make a meeting (a)	2	10.5
27	F	have an appointment	7	31.8				take an appointment (a)	5	22.7
		make an appointment	2	9.1				take a date (b)	3	13.6
		get an appointment	1	4.5				get a meeting (b)	1	4.5
								have a meeting (b)	1	4.5
								ask for an appointment (a, f)	1	4.5
								get a date (b)	1	4.5
	J	make an appointment	7	28.0				*take an appointment* (a)	5	20.0
		get an appointment	3	12.0				*take a reservation* (a, b)	3	12.0
		have an appointment	1	4.0				reserve for an appointment (a, f)	2	8.0
		book an appointment	1	4.0				make a book (b)	1	4.0
								take a book (a, b)	2	8.0

28	F	have an answer	4	23.5	have the answer(c)	4	23.5	obtain an answer (a)	1	5.9
		get an answer	8	47.1						
	J	get an answer	7	35.0	get her answer (c)	4	20.0	get her responses (a, b, c, h)	1	5.0
		get a reply	1	5.0	receive her answer (c)	3	15.0	accept her answer (a, c)	1	5.0
		receive an answer	1	5.0	get the answer (c)	1	5.0	have her response (a, b,c)	1	5.0
29	F	keep good control	0	0.0				hold well (e)	2	25.0
								take good care (e)	2	25.0
								is the master (e)	1	12.5
								is a good manager (e)	1	12.5
								has a good control (c)	1	12.5
								manages (e)	1	12.5
	J	keep good control	0	0.0				take care (c, e)	2	20.0
								is good at managing	1	10.0
								control well (e)	2	20.0
								is a good manager (e)	1	10.0
								do manage (e)	1	10.0
								is in charge (e)	1	10.0
								keep good condition (e)	1	10.0
								has good command (c)	1	10.0
30	F	have a walk	10	52.6	go to walk (c, f)	1	5.3	go walking (b, f)	4	21.1
		go for a walk	1	5.3				go outside (e)	2	10.5
								walk away (e)	1	5.3
	J	take a walk	14	48.3	go on walk (f)	1	3.4	walk around (e)	3	10.3
		go for a walk	8	27.6	take walking (b, c)	1	3.4	walk out (e)	2	6.9

<Types of Mistakes>

a	wrong choice of verb
b	wrong choice of noun
c	missing/adding determiners (article)
d	wrong structure
e	different expression
f	preposition
g	number

RESULTS OF TRANSLATION TASKS (5)

3)-a:[Adjective + Noun] / [+ResComb, +Transp]

*:F: French learners, J: Japanese learners

( ) : Types of mistakes listed below the table, *Italic*: L1 Likely errors

No.	F/J *	Target/Acceptable Collocation			Infelicitous Collocation			Non-target/Wrong Collocation		
			Raw Score	%		Raw Score	%		Raw Score	%
31	F	bad habit	19	76.0	badly habit (d)	1	4.0	*wrong habit* (a)	1	4.0
								bad custom (b)	1	4.0
								bad use (b)	1	4.0
								bad rule (b)	1	4.0
								bad things (b)	1	4.0
	J	bad habit	11	40.7				*bad custom* (b)	9	33.3
								bad behaviour (b)	1	3.7
								bad manner (b)	4	14.8
								bad routine (b)	1	3.7
								bad use (b)	1	3.7
32	F	long flight	13	50.0	*long fly* (b)	5	19.2	flight (a)	5	19.2
					long flying (b)	1	3.8	large flight (a)	1	3.8
								oversea flight (a)	1	3.8
	J	long flight	29	80.6	*long flying* (b)	2	5.6	long trip (b)	1	2.8
					long fly (b)	1	2.8	long tarveling (b)	1	2.8
								air travel (e)	1	2.8
								long travel	1	2.8
33	F	high fever	2	11.8				*strong fever* (a)	9	52.9
		high temperature	3	17.6				huge fever (a)	2	11.8
								strong temperature (a)	1	5.9
	J	high fever	10	40.0				*high heat* (b)	3	12.0
		high temperature	8	32.0				bad fever (a)	2	8.0
								hot heat (a, b)	1	4.0
								serious fever (a, b)	1	4.0
34	F	main meal	9	39.1				*principal meal* (a)	6	26.1
		main dish	1	4.3				main lunch (b)	2	8.7
								main course (b)	2	8.7
								big lunch (a, b)	1	4.3
								best meal (a)	1	4.3
								first plate (a, b)	1	4.3
	J	main meal	1	2.8				main dinner (b)	1	2.8
		main dish	31	86.1				*main cooking* (b)	3	8.3

35	F	next week	28	96.6				next time (b)	1	3.4
	J	next week	36	97.3				next time (b)	1	2.7
36	F	single room	14	56.0				*simple room* (a)	4	16.0
		single one	4	16.0				*simple* one (a)	2	8.0
								one room (a)	1	4.0
	J	single room	25	65.8				single bedroom (b)	1	2.6
		single one	12	31.6						
37	F	common sense	4	23.5				*good sense* (a)	5	29.4
								good mind (a, b)	2	11.8
								good feelings (a, b)	2	11.8
								rational raison (a, b)	1	5.9
								good knowledge (a, b)	1	5.9
								logical thinking (a, b)	1	5.9
								logical sense (a)	1	5.9
	J	common sense	14	70.0				normal knowledge (a, b)	1	5.0
								common knowledge (b)	2	10.0
								general knowledge (a, b)	1	5.0
								common image (b)	1	5.0
								normalization e)	1	5.0

<Types of Mistakes>

a	wrong choice of verb
b	wrong choice of noun
c	missing/adding determiners (article)
d	wrong structure
e	different expression
f	preposition
g	number

RESULTS OF TRANSLATION TASKS (6)

3)-b:[Adjective + Noun] / [-ResComb, -Transp]

*:F: French learners, J: Japanese learners

( ) : Types of mistakes listed below the table, *Italic*: L1 Likely errors

No.	F/J*	Target/Acceptable Collocation			Infelicitous Collocation			Non-target/Wrong Collocation		
			Raw Score	%		Raw Score	%		Raw Score	%
38	F	bad health	20	83.3	bad healthy (b)	3	12.5			
		health problems	1	4.2						
	J	bad health	11	47.8				*unhealthy* (e)	4	17.4
		poor health	3	13.0				not healthy (e)	2	8.7
								unhealthy living (a, b)	3	13.0
39	F	heavy fog	3	23.1				big fog (a)	2	15.4
		thick fog	2	15.4				large fog (a)	2	15.4
		deep fog	1	7.7				important fog (a)	2	15.4
								huge mist (a, b)	1	7.7
	J	heavy fog	3	13.6	heavy mist (b)	3	13.6	*deep mist* (b)	6	27.3
		deep fog	2	9.1				deep smog (b)	1	4.5
		dense fog	2	9.1				hard fog (a)	1	4.5
		thick fog	1	4.5				strong fog (a, b)	1	4.5
								heavy smog (b)	2	9.1
40	F	large population	3	15.0				*important population* (a)	7	35.0
		huge population	2	10.0				numerous population (a)	2	10.0
		big population	3	15.0				mass population (a)	1	5.0
								heavy population (a)	1	5.0
								dense population (a)	1	5.0
	J	large population	15	48.4				much population (a)	3	9.7
		huge population	2	6.5				*many population* (a)	2	6.5
		big population	2	6.5				*a lot of population* (a)	2	6.5
								great number of population (a)	5	16.1

41	F	free time	20	71.4						
		spare time	7	25.0						
		leisure time	1	3.6						
	J	free time	29	90.6				empty time (a)	1	3.1
		leisure time	1	3.1				useless time (a)	1	
42	F	high standard	0	0.0				good level (b)	24	82.8
								high level (b)	4	13.8
								upper level (a, b)	1	3.4
	J	high standard	0	0.0				good ability (b)	9	40.9
								great ability (a, b)	6	27.3
								great potential (a, b)	1	4.5
								great capacity (a, b)	1	4.5
								excellent talent (a, b)	1	4.5
								great skill (a, b)	1	4.5
								high ability (b)	2	9.1
								great technique (a, b)	1	4.5
43	F	strict control	19	82.6				tough check (a, b)	1	4.3
		tight control	1	4.3				hard control (a)	1	4.3
								strict check (b)	1	4.3
	J							hard limit (a, b)	2	9.5
								strict limit (b)	8	38.1
								severe limit (a, b)	3	14.3
								strict limitation (b)	3	14.3
								strict rule (b)	2	9.5
								heavy limit (a, b)	1	4.8
								exact limit (a, b)	1	4.8
								hard law (a, b)	1	4.8
44	F	low quality	8	30.8				weak quality (a)	4	15.4
		poor quality	5	19.2				cheap quality (a)	2	7.7
		bad quality	5	19.2				little quality (a)	2	7.7
	J	bad quality	14	53.8	bad qualities (b)	2	7.7	bad condition (b)	3	11.5
		low quality	6	23.1						
		poor quality	1	3.8						

<Types of Mistakes>

a	wrong choice of verb
b	wrong choice of noun
c	missing/adding determiners (article)
d	wrong structure
e	different expression
f	preposition
g	number

RESULTS OF TRANSLATION TASKS (7)

4)-a:[Adverb + Adjective] / [+ResComb, +Transp]

*:F: French learners, J: Japanese learners

( ) : Types of mistakes listed below the table, *Italic*: L1 Likely errors

No.	F/J *	Target/Acceptable Collocation			Infelicitous Collocation			Non-target/Wrong Collocation		
			Raw Score	%		Raw Score	%		Raw Score	%
45	F	only natural	0	0.0				*totally normal* (a, b)	6	42.9
								perfectly normal (a, b)	2	14.3
								really normal (a,b)	2	14.3
								completely normal (a, b)	1	7.1
								simply normal (a, b)	1	7.1
								entirely normal (a, b)	1	7.1
								absolutely usual (a, b)	1	7.1
	J	only natural	0	0.0				very natural (a)	9	47.4
								quite natural (a)	5	26.3
								completely natural (a)	2	10.5
								much natural (a)	1	5.3
								entirely natural (a)	1	5.3
								a natural thing (e)	1	5.3
46	F	extremely serious	0	0.0				very serious (a)	20	83.3
								really serious (a)	2	8.3
								terribly serious (a)	1	4.2
								so serious (a)	1	4.2
	J	extremely serious	0	0.0				very serious (a)	16	84.2
								much serious (a)	1	5.3
								very hard (a, b)	1	5.3
								very crazy (a, b)	1	5.3
47	F	highly unlikely	0	0.0				very unprobable (a, b)	2	28.6
								not possible (e)	3	42.9
								very impossible (a, b)	1	14.3
								not probable (e)	1	14.3
	J	highly unlikely	0	0.0				very impossible (a, b)	1	14.3
								almost impossible (a, b)	2	28.6
								impossible (a, b)	2	28.6
								not possible (e)	2	28.6
48	F	terribly afraid	7	30.4				very scared (a, b)	3	13.0

		awfully afraid	1	4.3				terribly scared (b)	3	13.0
								tatally scared (a, b)	1	4.3
								terribly terrified (b)	2	8.7
								extremely afraid (a)	1	4.3
								absolutely horrified (a, b)	1	4.3
								completely frightened (a, b)	1	4.3
								entirely freightened (a, b)	1	4.3
								strongly afraid (a)	1	4.3
								very afraid (a)	1	4.3
	J	terribly afraid	2	9.5				very afraid (a)	11	52.4
								very scared (a, b)	2	9.5
								greatly scared (a, b)	1	4.8
								highly afraid (a)	1	4.8
								badly frightened (a, b)	1	4.8
								so afraid (a, b)	1	4.8
49	F	highly recommended	2	10.5	strongly recommended (a)	10	52.6	really recommended (a)	4	21.1
								usually recommended (a)	1	5.3
								srongly recommended (a, b)	1	5.3
								truly recommended (a)	1	5.3
	J	highly recommended	0	0.0	strongly recommended (a)	1	7.7	much recommended (a)	2	15.4
								very recommended (a)	1	7.7
								very encouraged (a, b)	1	7.7
								very good (a, b)	2	15.4
								often recommended (a)	1	7.7
								quite recommended (a)	2	15.4
								so recommended (a)	2	15.4
								generally recommended (a)	1	7.7

\<Types of Mistakes\>

- a   wrong choice of verb
- b   wrong choice of noun
- c   missing/adding determiners (article)
- d   wrong structure
- e   different expression
- f   preposition
- g   number

RESULTS OF TRANSLATION TASKS (8)

4)-b:[Adverb + Adjective] / [-ResComb, -Transp]

*:F: French learners, J: Japanese learners

( ) : Types of mistakes listed below the table, *Italic*: L1 Likely errors

No.	F/J *	Target/Acceptable Collocation			Infelicitous Collocation			Non-target/Wrong Collocation		
			Raw Score	%		Raw Score	%		Raw Score	%
50	F	completely lost	12	50.0				*entirely lost* (a)	2	8.3
		totally lost	9	37.5				absolutely lost (a)	1	4.2
	J	lost completely	5	20.8				*lost perfectly* (a)	5	20.8
								lost badly (a)	1	4.2
								lost entirely (a)	1	4.2
								lost myself (a)	3	12.5
								lost absolutely (a)	1	4.2
								lost the way (e)	5	20.8
								lost my way (e)	3	12.5
51	F	totally different	7	36.8				completely new (b)	3	15.8
		completely different	2	10.5				entirely new (b)	2	10.5
		entirely different	2	10.5				totally new (b)	2	10.5
								fully new (a, b)	1	5.3
	J	quite different	8	47.1				very different (a)	4	23.5
		completely different	3	17.6				*absolutely different* (a)	1	5.9
								much different (a)	1	5.9
52	F	perfectly aware	5	23.8				*perfectly conscious* (b)	7	33.3
								totally aware (a)	3	14.3
								totally *conscient* (a, b)	2	9.5
								entirely aware (a)	1	4.8
								totally *conscientious* (a, b)	1	4.8
								completely aware (a)	1	4.8
								totally sure (a, b)	1	4.8
	J	perfectly aware	0	0.0				much sure (a, b)	1	16.7
								very sure (a, b)	3	50.0

					highly sure (a, b)	1	16.7
					fairly sure (a, b)	1	16.7
53	F	badly damaged	1	6.7	heavily damaged (a)	1	6.7
		seriously damaged	1	6.7	profoundly *touched* (a, b)	1	6.7
					deeply *touched* (a, b)	1	6.7
					grievely *touched* (a, b)	1	6.7
					badly hurt (b)	2	13.3
					deeply damaged (a)	1	6.7
					badly hit (b)	1	6.7
					badly striken (b)	1	6.7
					strongly *touched* (a, b)	2	13.3
					seriously hurt (a, b)	1	6.7
					badly *touched* (b)	1	6.7
	J	badly damaged	1	6.3	*damaged heavily* (a)	1	6.3
		damaged seriously	9	56.3	suffered seriously (a, b)	1	6.3
					hurted seriously (b)	1	6.3
					sufferred serious damage (e)	1	6.3
					badly sufferred (a, b)	1	6.3
					very damaged (a)	1	6.3
54	F	highly competent	5	29.4	very competent (a)	6	35.3
					very skilled (a, b)	2	11.8
					highly skilled (b)	1	5.9
					very qualified (a, b)	1	5.9
					very talented (a, b)	1	5.9
					highly recognized (b)	1	5.9
	J	highly competent	0	0.0	very efficient (a, b)	1	11.1
					very professional (a, b)	1	11.1
					ultimately special (a, b)	1	11.1
					very intelligent (a, b)	3	33.3
					extremely special (a, b)	1	11.1
					supremely good (a, b)	1	11.1
					especially good (a, b)	1	11.1
55	F	deeply involved	0	0.0	*seriously* implied (a, b)	6	42.9
					seriously involved (a)	3	21.4
					deeply implied (b)	2	14.3

								seriously engaged (a, b)	1	7.1
								seriously committed (a, b)	1	7.1
								deeply committed (b)	1	7.1
	J	deeply involved	2	33.3				deeply related (b)	2	33.3
								deeply concerned (b)	1	16.7
								have a deep relation (e)	1	16.7
56	F	bitterly cold	0	0.0				very cold (a)	10	83.3
								chilly and cold (e)	1	8.3
								dry and cold (e)	1	8.3
	J	bitterly cold	0	0.0	terrible cold (a)	4	17.4	very cold (a)	14	60.9
		terribly cold	1	4.3	bad cold (a)	2	8.7	so cold (a)	1	4.3
								too cold (a)	1	4.3

<Types of Mistakes>

- a   wrong choice of verb
- b   wrong choice of noun
- c   missing/adding determiners (article)
- d   wrong structure
- e   different expression
- f   preposition
- g   number

CPSIA information can be obtained
at www.ICGtesting.com
Printed in the USA
BVOW06s1252100117

473100BV00012B/77/P